THE CATHEDRALS' CRUSADE

THE CATHEDRALS' CRUSADE

The Rise of the Gothic Style in France

by

Ian Dunlop

HAMISH HAMILTON LONDON

First published in Great Britain 1982
by Hamish Hamilton Ltd
Garden House 57-59 Long Acre London WC2E 9JZ

Published in the United States of America by
Taplinger Publishing Co. Inc.

British Library Cataloguing in Publication Data

Dunlop, Ian
    The cathedrals' crusade.
    1. Cathedrals — France — History
    I. Title
    944'.021   DC20
    ISBN 0-241-10689-3

Photoset in Great Britain by
Rowland Phototypesetting Ltd, Bury St Edmunds, Suffolk
and printed by St Edmundsbury Press, Bury St Edmunds, Suffolk

to
DEIRDRE
with all my love

CONTENTS

LIST OF ILLUSTRATIONS

LIST OF DRAWINGS IN TEXT

(*All of the above, except where otherwise stated,
are from Viollet-le-Duc.*)

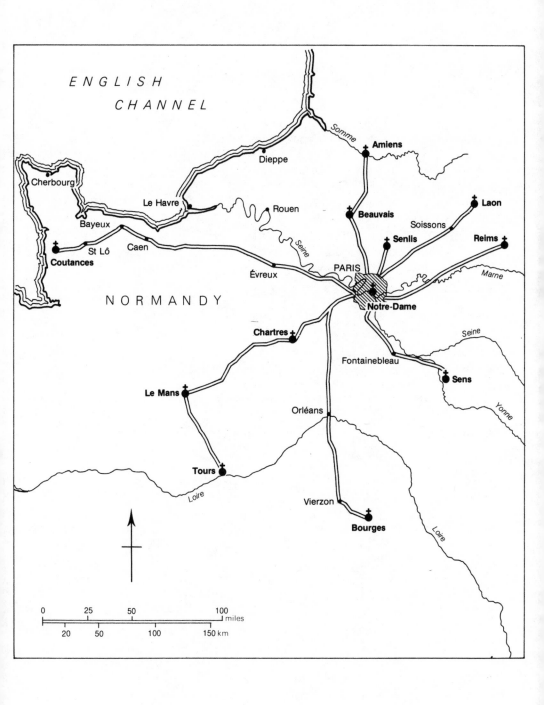

ENGLISH
CHANNEL

Cherbourg

Le Havre
Dieppe
Bayeux
Rouen
St Lô
Caen
Coutances
Évreux
Somme
Amiens
Beauvais
Laon
Soissons
Senlis
Reims
PARIS
Seine
Marne
Notre-Dame
NORMANDY
Chartres
Fontainebleau
Seine
Sens
Le Mans
Orléans
Yonne
Tours
Vierzon
Loire
Bourges
Loire

0   25   50   100 miles
20   50   100   150 km

Acknowledgements

I would like to express my gratitude to Mr Richard Auty, British Council Representative and Cultural Attaché to the British Embassy in Paris, and to his staff, for all their help and useful introductions: to Monsieur Bertrand Monnet, Architecte en Chef des Monuments Historiques, Monsieur A. Gigot, Architecte en Chef des Monuments Historiques and Monsieur Bernard Vitry, Inspecteur Général des Monuments Historiques for privileged access to the cathedrals; to the Bishop of Coutances for his help and hospitality; to Madame Suzanne Martinet at the Library of Laon, Monsieur Guy de Tourtier, Président des Amis de la Cathédrale d'Amiens; Madame Jacques Allain, Président de la Société France-Grande Bretagne at Bourges and to Madame Lotte of the Centre de Documentation sur les Monuments Historiques.

I would like to thank Mr & Mrs Philip Hawkes, the princesse Thérèse de Caraman-Chimay, the marquise de Brissac and the marquise de Contades for their help and hospitality; Madame Simonet for her unfailing hospitality at Compiègne and the princesse Maria-Pia d'Orléans-Bragance, comtesse de Nicolay, for her charming hospitality at Le Lude.

I would like to thank Monsieur Vincent for the aerial photographs of Chartres and Reims; Miss Jane Erith for typing the manuscript.

Translations
I have retained a number of quotations in the original French for the benefit of those readers who can appreciate the language. I have usually selected these to give authenticity to a quotation or where the original French loses something in the translation. I have, however, appended a footnote translation to most of the longer quotations.

Ian Dunlop
The Close, Salisbury.

'Pour avoir le droit de porter un jugement sur les artistes du moyen age, il faut commencer par comprendre ce qu'ils ont voulu faire.'

Emile Mâle.

'The Cathedral is an embarrassment to Reason, which fears, on entering it, having to admit the existence of the Sacred. Such a sentiment would explain how this architecture – both rational and French – has been so long ignored by French rationalists, who refuse to ask the question *Why* in order the better to date and describe in answer to the question *How*; it is just like describing a man in terms of his clothes, his muscles and his skeleton and refusing to see what animates him, what gives him his life and the light in his eye.'

François Cali.

Introduction

'Let us build so great a Church to the glory of God that those who come after us will think us mad even to have attempted it.' Such was the resolution passed on 8 July 1401, by the Chapter of Seville Cathedral. It could have come just as aptly from the Chapter of Beauvais a century and three quarters earlier; they seemed determined to outdo all records. At Sens, the first of the great Gothic cathedrals, the architect had been content with a vault just over eighty feet high. The quest for height may be taken as starting with Notre-Dame in 1163 with a vault of 108 feet. Thirty years later Chartres surpassed this by some thirteen feet, only to be overtaken by Bourges and Reims which rose to 123 and 124 feet nine inches respectively. In 1220 Amiens added another fourteen feet to the existing record with a height of 138 feet ten inches. Finally in 1225 the builders of Beauvais attained the almost unbelievable altitude of 157 feet six inches – just about twice the height of Salisbury Cathedral.

The great vaults of Beauvais stood for twelve years and then the south-west corner collapsed. It was not until 1337 that the choir was rebuilt and only in the sixteenth century were the transepts added. They were made to carry a spire as tall as that of Salisbury but springing from a building already one hundred feet higher. Four years after its completion the spire also fell and the builders, at last discouraged, contented themselves with the truncated edifice which we see today. Beauvais is not what it was intended to be. Nevertheless, to stand in the centre of the crossing and to crane one's neck to look into the vertiginous recesses of its vaults is to have an architectural experience of the most exciting nature.

On all sides the accent of the architecture is strongly vertical. It does not appear as the downward thrust of perilously balanced weights, but as upward movement, like the jet of some mighty fountain. The clustered columns shoot straight into the air for a hundred and thirty feet before they splay out into the slender ribs of the delicate sexpartite vault. The narrow arches of the great arcade are so tall that the façades of the aisles behind them are of three storeys, with their own arcade, their own triforium and their own clerestory – enough to constitute in themselves a lofty church. Above them the theme is taken up again. The slender colonnettes which subdivide the arcading of the triforium rise without interruption to become the centre mullions between the slim lancets of the clerestory, continuing up until they lose themselves in the fretted tracery of the topmost arch. The vertical shafts always pass in front of the horizontal divisions so that their lines are unbroken and the eye is guided upward and ever further upward with the mounting crescendo of a musical sequence. The 'Faith Theme' in Parsifal is the musical counterpart of the architecture of Beauvais. *'Dans le mouvement unanime et altier de toutes ces pierres vers le ciel,'* wrote the comte de Montalembert, *'n'y a-t-il pas une sorte d'abdication de la servitude matérielle et un élancement de l'âme affranchie vers son Créateur?'* *

Another distinguished visitor was Auguste Rodin. 'Confronted with the Cathedral,' he wrote, 'the first impression is of utter astonishment. The mind strains itself to comprehend the Past and to penetrate it with new insights.'

It is impossible not to ask oneself a thousand questions. What was the motive behind so fantastic a project? What sublime notions of religion, and what secular undercurrents of royal prestige and civic pride are here expressed? What was the connection between the architecture and the thought forms of contemporary Scholasticism? What liturgical use was envisaged for the vast theatre which a cathedral offered? And how was it paid for? How were the workmen organised, the stones quarried and the materials transported?

It is to try and answer such questions that this book is primarily designed. The answers may be sought in a general study of the great campaign of cathedral building christened by Jean Gimpel *'la Croisade des Cathédrales'*. It can be taken as starting in about 1130 with the building of Sens and as ending with the collapse of the vaults of Beauvais in 1284. All the great Gothic cathedrals of the north of France were put up during this period.

Viollet-le-Duc saw the collapse of Beauvais as the turning-point in the development of the Gothic. 'From this moment imagination begins to give place to calculation and the constructions of the end of the thirteenth century are the expression of an art that has reached its maturity, based on experience and calculation, which has nothing more to discover.' The late twelfth and early thirteenth centuries constituted the Golden Age of the French Gothic.

---

* 'In the movement, unanimous and lofty, of all these stones towards the heavens, is there not a sort of renouncing of subjection to the material and a flight of the liberated soul towards its Maker?'

CHAPTER ONE

Suger of Saint-Denis

'The French Cathedral,' wrote Viollet-le-Duc, 'was born with the monarchical power.' A glance at a map of the early Gothic cathedrals will show that the great ones were all built on land subject to the King of France, or only built after the land had been annexed.

The obvious link between the Gothic style and the Capetian dynasty was the Abbey of Saint-Denis at the gates of Paris. It so happened that at the beginning of the twelfth century Saint-Denis was in the hands of a truly remarkable man, the Abbot Suger. Himself a pupil at the abbey school, he had there become the life-long friend of the future Louis VI. The son of a peasant, he rose to be Regent of France. It was in his capacity for administration that his real strength lay; his biographer describes him as being 'capable of governing the Universe'. Under his rule the estates of the monastery was restored 'from sterility to fecundity'. Equipment was improved, ruinous buildings were repaired and predatory lords brought under discipline, with the result that agriculture prospered, populations increased and some of their newfound wealth began to flow into the coffers of Saint-Denis. When Suger came to his great task of re-building the abbey church he had already to hand the financial resources indispensable for a quick and comprehensive campaign. The choir and apse were completed in the short space of three and a quarter years.

The time was exactly ripe for the birth of the Gothic style. All things seemed to work together ot make France the cultural centre of Europe, the Capetian dynasty the centre of vitality in France and the Abbey of Saint-Denis the spiritual powerhouse of the Capetian dynasty.

The twelfth century was an age worthy of the name Renaissance. 'The intellect of Europe,' wrote H. A. L. Fisher, 'was on the march.' The focal point of Christendom, however, was not Rome but Paris. In the early twelfth century the popularity of the University of Paris was largely due to the renown of Abelard. 'Rome,' wrote Foulques de Deuil to the great Doctor, 'showed, by sending you her scholars, that your wisdom prevailed over hers. Neither distance nor lofty mountains, neither depth of valleys nor paths bristling with dangers and infested by brigands, prevented them from hastening to you. The throng of young Englishmen feared neither the sea crossing nor its terrible tempests. Scorning all danger they ran to you.' As Odo de Châteauroux observed, 'France is the oven where the intellectual bread of humanity is cooked.'

It is difficult to accept the similarities between medieval thought and medieval architecture as simple coincidence. The rise of Scholasticism and the rise of the Gothic style were co-terminous both in time and place: the twelfth and early thirteenth centuries and the cathedral cities within about a hundred miles of Paris. Nor does the coincidence end here, for the great builders of the Cathedrals' Crusade were not infrequently the great scholars of their age: Geoffroy de Lèves, Gauthier de Mortagne, Maurice de Sully—all had been the heads of their cathedral schools before they became bishops, and as bishops they became builders.

The significant movement of the twelfth century was, in fact, the movement away from the monastic schools and towards the cathedral schools. It brought the two forces of scholastic learning and building technique together. Their marriage was immediately blessed with issue.

Roger Lloyd, in his beautiful portrait of Peter Abelard, offers an excellent introduction to the understanding of Scholasticism. 'In the year that Peter Abelard was born, 1079, the curtain was slowly rising upon the most vivid and, in a sense, the most satisfactory century of Christian history. The Golden Middle Age was at hand.' As always in a time of renaissance there was an Old Order to be overthrown. The eleventh century had been the great age of the monasteries and the Romanesque style was theirs – strong and austere, but also dark and numinous. Their vast buildings speak to us of the Mystery of Faith, not of the Light of Reason.

In the eleventh century no one really doubted the primacy of Faith over Reason – a primacy distilled by Anselm of Bec into his famous aphorism *Credo ut intellegam* – 'I believe in order that I may understand'. But in the following century these words were to be, in effect, inverted by Abelard: 'I understand in order that I may believe'.

By the middle of the twelfth century the schools were largely free from monkish restraints. The monastery schools had given place to the cathedral schools and in Paris the cathedral school was already giving place to the University. The star of Reason was beginning to rise.

'All roads once led to Rome,' continues Roger Lloyd, 'so in the Paris of the twelfth century, all academic discussions led sooner or later to the problem of problems, the question of Nominalism and Realism. Is "Humanity" a mere *name* given for the sake of convenience to denote the totality of human beings? Or is "Humanity" a *real* essence having an objective existence of its own? The Realist, leaning on Plato, would say that "Humanity" was a *real* substance, identical in every man and woman; the Nominalist denied that "Humanity" was any more than the *name* given to the general mass of men and women to distinguish them from the general mass of dogs or fish.'

This philosopher's question had its bearing on representational art, for a sculptor may be seeking to represent an idealised Humanity or to portray an individual. The contrast between the noble, stylised figures on the west front of Chartres – what Emile Mâle has called a *'figure idéale, exprimant un type plutôt qu'un individu'* – and the smiling, village maiden-type Madonnas of the late thirteenth century illustrates the movement from Realism to Nominalism. It has been pointed out by Erwin Panofsky that the advent of naturalistic flora at Reims and Amiens coincides with the rediscovery of Nature that came with a renewed interest in Aristotle. 'A plant was thought to exist as a plant, not as the copy of the idea of a plant.'

But the real trouble lay in the bearing of this question upon the doctrine of the Trinity. The Realist could easily find that he was skating on the thin ice of heresy. It was this that proved the downfall of Abelard, and it was at Sens, before a council dominated by St Bernard, that Abelard's writings were condemned.

The connection between the philosophy of the age and its architecture, however, was already apparent at Saint-Denis. The name of Saint-Denis derives from Dionysius to whom legend attributed the conversion of Fance. He was mistakenly identified with Dionysius the Areopagite who was wrongly supposed to be the author of a treatise called *The Heavenly Hierarchies*. He had been consecrated by pious imagination to the See of Athens. It was, as Lord Clark has said, 'a typical medieval muddle', but the mistaken authorship is important, for it made it possible to attribute these neo-Platonic writings to the saint mentioned in St Luke as a companion of St Paul. It mattered much to the medieval mind that its theory of aesthetics should derive from such a source. Odo, Suger's successor at Saint-Denis, could claim that 'Dionysius is believed to hold the first rank after the Apostles'. The belief, rather than the truth of its assertions, was what mattered.

As the result of this belief Louis the Pious obtained a copy of *The Heavenly Hierarchies* from the Byzantine Emperor, Michael the Stammerer, and added it to the treasured possessions of Saint-Denis. It came to the notice of Suger because Abelard had made inconvenient investigations into the authenticity of the treatise, an intrusion for which he received a severe whipping. These writings gave Suger the philosophical basis which he required. At the very moment when the prestige of the monarchy and the wealth of the Abbey made a reconstruction of the royal Sanctuary both desirable and possible, a document was placed in is hands which provided the intellectual basis necessary for a new departure.

Of all the theories in *The Heavenly Hierarchies*, two are of particular relevance to our theme. One was that the human mind can only attain to spiritual things by means of earthly things, which thus became the stepping stones to Heaven; the other is that Light is the divine quality in material things which, by illuminating the intellect, enables it to use those stepping stones.

Suger's new preoccupation with the principles of Dionysius led him into one of the great controversies of the age. There are two strands in the Christian faith, one warmly humanist, the other austerely ascetic, which have co-existed throughout the centuries in more or less uneasy tension. At the moment when the Gothic style was ready to be born these two extremes were championed by two of the greatest men of their age – Suger of Saint-Denis and Bernard of Clairvaux. The two have been called 'the ill-assorted godparents of the Gothic style'.

For St Bernard the world and all its attributes were dangers to be shunned. Even food and sleep were regarded as necessary evils to be reduced to a minimum – a minimum which he himself observed with fastings and vigils 'ultra possibilitatem humanam'.

For Suger, thanks to Dionysius, the world was a series of stepping stones to Heaven. It offered to man his only materials for the outward expression of his faith, the only imagery in terms of which the Kingdom of God could be represented. He made the entrance to his Abbey Church through doors of gilded bronze on which were in-scribed the words: 'The dull mind rises to truth through that which is material.' But Suger was in all things temperate. 'Devoutly festive, festively devout', he astonished his biographer by his failure to put on weight after his appointment to the abbacy. Fasting had its place in his regimen, but so had feasting and one of his first acts as Abbot was to revive the custom whereby, in honour of Charles the Bald, the monks of Saint-Denis enjoyed once a mouth 'an exceptionally good dinner'. Whereas St Bernard decreed that 'silence and perpetual remoteness from all secular turmoil' should be the rule in order to 'compel the mind to meditate on celestial things', Suger lived in a whirlwind of administration, rising to be Regent of France – an office which one can hardly imagine being discharged in silence.

Starting from such diametrically opposite positions, the two Abbots were in predictably opposing camps in their approach to worship. To St Bernard it was axiomatic that 'no secular person has access to the House of God . . . the curious are not admitted to the sacred objects'. To Suger it was essential that they were. Their contrary attitudes were naturally reflected in the architecture and the paraphernalia of worship of Clairvaux and Saint-Denis.' The buildings of St Bernard were deliberately devoid of ornament. Sculpture, mural painting and stained glass were expressly forbidden; vestments of fustian, candlesticks of iron and crucifixes of wood were obligatory; only the chalices were allowed the luxury of silver. St Bernard, in his own words, 'deemed as dung whatever shines with beauty, enchants the ear, delights through fragrance, flatters the taste or pleases the touch'. To him the senses were carnal affections to be denied, distrusted and if possible allowed to atrophy.

To Suger the opposite was true. Every enrichment of art, every enchantment of music, every emotion that could be aroused by colour, harmony and light, was pressed into the service of devotion. While he agreed with Bernard that 'a saintly mind, a pure heart and a faithful intention ought to suffice for the purpose', he asserted that 'we must do homage also through the outward ornaments of the sacred vessels'. And by sacred vessels he did not intend to exclude the very structure of the Church which was the House of God.

St Bernard made the famous accusation: 'The Church clothes her stones with gold but lets her sons go naked'. Suger, while not insensitive to the needs of the poor, was determined to clothe at least the altars, retables and reliquaries of Saint-Denis with gold and precious stones. He managed to convince himself that an unexpected present of very magnificent jewels, 'such as it would be rare to find even in the house of a King', came as the result of the direct intervention of St Rustique and St Eleuthère whose shrine in the Abbey Church required adornment. It was, he explained to Bernard, 'as if the Holy Martyrs had wished to convey to us by their own words: "whether you wish it or not, only the best is good enough for us." ' Suger was intoxicated by the effect of all his gold and precious stones and tried to record his own impressions of their lustre:

> Resplendit en splendeur ce que l'on unit splendidement,
> Et l'oeuvre magnifique qu'inonde une lumière nouvelle resplendit.

'Flooded with a new light' – in these words Suger lays down his own specification for the new architectural style that he was to play so large a part in creating.

*

But light was not the only quality which determined the form of the new-born style. The scholars of the Middle Ages – and notably those

5

of the School of Chartres – were, in Otto von Simson's words, 'obsessed with mathematics, especially geometry'. They naturally saw a metaphysical significance in figures. The square, resulting from the multiplication of a figure by itself, expressed the relationship of God the Father with God the Son. The equilateral triangle extended this to include the Holy Spirit and symbolised the Trinity. Viollet-le-Duc observed that the vaults of Reims could all be inscribed within an equilateral triangle. It has been said, and not without a measure of truth, that under Thierry's influence, the School of Chartres attempted to change theology into geometry.

Mathematics also provided the link, dear to Augustine, between music and architecture. The scholars of Chartres may have regarded the Creation as a Symphony, but they thought of the Creator not as a musician but as an architect. It is not uncommon in medieval illumination to find God the Father represented as the 'elegans architectus' holding a large pair of compasses. Harmonic proportion represented the very principle behind the creation of the Universe and was therefore regarded as the secret both of the beauty and of the stability of a building.

Owing to the Dionysian theory of light, the role which had been assigned under the Romanesque architects to paintings on the wall was now transferred to the stained glass windows. There is, however, something misleading about the very word 'window'; it suggests an aperture in a wall. In the fully developed Gothic style the walls themselves were replaced by screens of coloured glass. There can be no doubt that the demands of the glaziers had a controlling influence on the creation of the Gothic style. Not very much is known of the art before its appearance at Saint-Denis, but it is clear that Suger was able to call upon experts who knew exactly what they were doing. It would have been typical of him to have seen the hitherto unrealised potential of their work and to have brought into the front rank an art which had so far been groping for its destiny.

At about this time, Roger of Helmershausen, writing under the name of Theophilus, produced a *Treatise of Divers Arts* in which each country was described as having its own proper and special contribution to make. His list culminates with the phrase: 'all that France loves in precious variety of windows'. It is clear that France already led the field in this particular art.

Ottin, one of the first historians of stained glass in France, states that Suger 'obtained sapphires in great abundance, which he pulverised and melted into the glass to give it its azure colour'. If Suger really did grind down sapphires, he deluded himself as to the result. The colouring matter in a sapphire is negligible. Blue glass is obtained from the use of oxide of cobalt, which could be imported from

Bohemia; the addition of a little manganese produced a lovely, slightly violet azure. Red was made from oxidised copper, which resulted in an almost opaque scarlet. To overcome this opacity it had to be applied in a thin layer upon white glass – a process known as 'flashing'. Green came from bioxide of copper: yellow from mixing manganese with ferrous oxide.

All this the French glaziers of the early twelfth century knew. They also understood the relative radiancy of translucent colours, of which blue has the most powerful brilliance. It is noticeable at Chartres that blue predominates in the north windows through which the sun never shines. This blue was the foundation of the style started at Saint-Denis and developed at Chartres; it is rightly known as *bleu de Chartres*. Paul Claudel has described this blue as *'l'obscurité devenue visible'*. More analytic in his approach, Viollet-le-Duc wrote, à propos the glass of Chartres: 'after studying our best French windows, one might maintain, as their secret of harmony, that the first condition for an artist in glass is to know how to manage blue'. This is certainly borne out by the windows that have survived from that great age of glass-making. 'If there is only one red, two yellows, two or three greens at the most,' continues Viollet-le-Duc, 'there are infinite shades of blue, and these blues are placed with a very delicate observation of the effects they would produce on other tones and other tones on them.'

The juxtaposition of blue and red results in a radiation of blue over the red which turns it to violet. By surrounding the blue with black paint, so as to increase the insulation already provided by the leads, this radiation can be reduced and the red allowed to shine forth in its purity. Similarly a white or pale green band can be contained by painting, often in the form of a pattern or of a blacking out that leaves only a string of 'pearls'. The roundel of the Annunciation at Saint-Denis, which shows Suger prostrate at the feet of the Virgin, is surrounded by just such a ring of pearls. 'These elementary principles,' wrote Viollet-le-Duc, 'were put into practice by the glass painters of the twelfth century with such a sureness and experience of touch that we needs must credit these artists with a long continuity of observation.'

Suger was not only fascinated by colour and light; he was also deeply concerned with the iconography of his windows, which is complex and richly symbolic. It was he who stated the principle of the 'Poor Man's Bible', claiming that 'the pictures in the windows are there for the sole purpose of showing simple people, who cannot read the Holy Scriptures, what they must believe' – a statement which provokes the reflection that the simple people of his day must have been endowed with abnormally keen eyesight. A pair of binoc-

7

ulars is usually required for deciphering the subject matter of the windows.

The colours used in the twelfth century were mostly rich and therefore of a limited translucence. In order to let through sufficient light the windows needed to be as large as possible. This need provided the motive for that quest for height which typifies the first expansive period of Gothic – *the Croisade des Cathédrales*. It demanded the concentration of all the weight upon the pillars which upheld the vault, in order to leave the entire wall space available to the glazier. Thus the skeletonic system was evolved. The structure was conceived as a series of stone canopies carried on columns and stabilised by flying buttresses.

There remains one other aspect of the cathedral to be accounted for: the surface area which it covered which normally attained to four or five thousand square metres. Many cathedrals could have accommodated the entire populations of their city and still had room.

There were, of course, the great occasions of the Church's year when the cathedral would lay on some liturgical drama which attracted large numbers of the populace. It must be remembered that congregations were not provided with chairs in the Middle Ages. A stone bench, running along the inside of the outer wall, might have offered seating to the elderly and the infirm, but most of the people remained upon their feet. It is less fatiguing to walk about than to stand still, so the Church wisely provided plenty of processions. Different portions of the liturgy were performed in different parts of the cathedral, whose straight aisles and curling ambulatories facilitated the orderly conduct of the procession. 'Les Cathédrales,' wrote Félix Clément, *'étaient les vastes scènes où se déroulait le drame'*. An immense throng formed the audience – but an audience which was involved, with its own part to play in the performance. Clément was studying manuscripts of the thirteenth century which he claims to have been 'the most illustrious of all, both with regard to liturgy and art'.

After the fourteenth century a period of general decline succeeded to the great days of the Cathedrals' Crusade, and it was this period which the critics of the Renaissance had in mind when stigmatising the Middle Ages as 'Gothic'. Boileau, in his *Art Poétique*, dismissed with contempt the performances of the *'troupe grossière . . . sottement zélée'* who played religious drama. Félix Clément, taking us back to the Golden Middle Age, restates the truth. 'With what delicacy these 'barbarians' interpreted the impenetrable mysteries of our Faith; with what gentleness and charm they conveyed them into the hearts of the people by means of their minds, their ears and their eyes!'

But it is in the cult of the relic that we find the principal occasion for the vast crowds which flooded into these sanctuaries on the special festivals that piety demanded. With the shrines of Dionysius, Eleutherus and Rusticus, together with one of the Nails and the Crown of Thorns, the Abbey Church of Saint-Denis was an important centre for relic worship.

With the ever-growing throng of pilgrims – whose number was considerably increased by the establishment of the great Fair called the Lendit – Suger records how the crowds in the church became so dense that 'not one among the thousands of people could move a foot, so tightly were they packed together; they had to remain immobile, frozen like marble statues'. What was meant to be a religious procession became a hurly-burly; men were screaming; women fainted and had to be passed out over the heads of the crowd; the monks themselves were sometimes obliged to escape with their precious relics through one of the windows.

It was in the first place to provide more ample accommodation for these vast crowds and to permit easier circulation within the church that the reconstruction of Saint-Denis was planned, but Suger admitted that it had been a boyhood ambition of his to provide the Abbey with a worthier place of worship. The granting of the Lendit to the jurisdiction of the Abbey both necessitated and made possible the rebuilding. The Fair produced the crowds and the crowds produced the money. More than half the cost of the reconstruction was financed by these means. In 1137 the work started with the building of a narthex at the west end of the nave.

We must remember that this was the very beginning of the great architectural tradition of the Ile de France. Suger had no local style and little local expertise on which to base his new creation. We must remember, too, that the position of architect, as we now understand the term, had no place in the medieval scheme. A patron such as Suger would have provided the controlling ideas himself. He required, as Pierre du Colombier has put it, 'not the ability to execute the building himself, but rather the knowledge of what was technically possible, the execution of which might then be delegated to others'.

In the new west front there was, for the first time, a focus of interest on the three portals that gave access to the nave and its two aisles. A comparison between the façade of Saint-Denis and that of its most obvious prototype, St Etienne de Caen, makes this at once apparent. Suger's building is Norman in inspiration, but whereas at St Etienne the façade is dominated by the towers, Suger's west front makes sense without them. In fact, once it was complete up to the battlements behind which the towers were to rise, Suger broke off to turn his attention to the choir and apse.

The façade, with its three great portals surrounded by sculptured figures and surmounted for the first time by a rose window, is the Gateway of Heaven – the archetype of all the Gothic portals that were to come. It remains true to its Norman ancestry in the retention of the rounded arch. The sculpture, little of which remains intact, reveals Suger's debt to Burgundy. The central tympanum, which is the most complete survival, can be compared with that of the great Cluniac monastery of Beaulieu. The huge figure of the seated Christ dominates both in the same way. But whereas at Beaulieu he is surrounded by a chaotic turmoil of saintly figures, lost souls and chimerical monsters, at Saint-Denis all is order and decorum. The writhing figures of the damned are contained within the archivolt on the right-hand side and contrast with the peaceful figures of angels on the left, where the souls of the righteous – represented as children – are in the hands of God. Beneath the tympanum the historical imagination should place the gilded doors on which Suger had caused explanatory verses to be inscribed. These were to enable the 'dull mind' to rise by reason of their scintillating light to the true vision of Christ who had said 'I am the door'.

In 1140, when the façade without the towers had been completed, work ceased abruptly and the scene of activity shifted to the choir and apse. It is reasonable to suppose that by now Suger had acquired enough experience of building and had at his disposition a master mason of sufficient expertise to have conceived the new possibilities which the cross-ribbed vault opened up, for an edifice in which light was to be the all-controlling medium.

For his new departure Suger had at hand for a model the important church of St Martin-des-Champs in Paris. Here, in tentative experimental form, was a double ambulatory describing two concentric arcs round the apse from which the bays of the outer ring bulged into segmental projections large enough to contain an altar, but entirely glazed. The dispositions, however, were so irregular and the supporting piers so massive that not much of the light admitted by these windows ever penetrated into the choir. A comparison of the ground plan of St Martin with that of Saint-Denis shows their relationship to be, in Otto von Simson's words, 'like that between a first awkward sketch and a consummate, definitive rendering of the same theme'. At Saint-Denis all the piers are aligned on axes radiating out from the centre point of the apse. They are also far more slender in design. The result is that the light from the chapel windows floods unimpeded into the choir.

From a constructional point of view there was almost nothing new at Saint-Denis. All the component parts were already in current use; the cross-ribbed vault was well known in Normandy, the pointed arch had become established in Burgundy. But neither Normans nor Burgundians had seen – perhaps because they were not looking for them – the new possibilities of luminosity already within their reach. The typical Norman apse was still roofed with a *cul-de-four* or half-dome which made clerestory windows impossible. The architecture was still heavy and the building dark.

One particular circumstance assisted Suger: the discovery near Pontoise of a quarry that yielded an abundant supply of the most excellent limestone. Norman vaulting was usually of rubble. The beautiful, strong and eminently workable stone of the Ile de France enabled the vaults to be constructed of the finest ashlar; they could be half the thickness, and therefore half the weight, of their Norman counterparts.

The original ambulatories of Saint-Denis still exist and show us the style of Suger and his master mason in all its purety. The upper parts of the choir, however, were entirely rebuilt by Pierre de Montreuil in the thirteenth century and we have practically no evidence of their original appearance.

On 11 July 1144, the new choir was consecrated with great solemnity. All the notables of France, lay and ecclesiastical, had been invited and it was the occasion of the reconciliation between the King and his most formidable opponent, Thibault the Great, Count of Champagne and of Chartres. Suger's consummate and peace-loving diplomacy had helped to bring this about and Thibault had in fact been one of the most generous contributors to the fabric fund.

The ceremony, which was of the utmost magnificence and faultless in its stage-management, had a significance far deeper than the mere dedication of a new religious edifice to God. In the background was the tradition, implicitly believed by all good Frenchmen, that the first sanctuary of Saint-Denis had been consecrated by Jesus Christ in person accompanied by the celestial hierarchy of saints and angels. This was deliberately reflected in Suger's ceremonial. The visiting bishops were arranged in hemicycles of nine, corresponding to the nine tiers of angels described by Dionysius. The order of service unmistakably implied that just as St Denis stood supreme among patron saints, so the King of France stood supreme among the feudal lords. In the ceremonial Louis VII appeared as the direct representative of Christ. Suger had not hesitated to suggest that the King of France 'bears in his person the living image of Christ'. He was the Lord's Anointed, the *Christus Domini*. Thus the worldly rule of the King was made the reflection of the divine rule of Christ, the earthly hierarchy the image of the Heavenly Host.

From this ceremony the new Gothic architecture acquired a considerable political importance. 'Precisely because it evoked the mystical archetype of the political order of the French monarchy,' wrote Otto von Simson, 'the style of Saint-Denis was adopted for all the Cathedrals of France and became the monumental expression of the Capetian idea of Kingship.' The political significance of the cathedral is defined by Viollet-le-Duc; *'L'unité monarchique et religieuse, l'alliance de ces deux pouvoirs pour constituer une nationalité, font surgir les Cathédrales du nord de la France'.**

Like the château, the monastery, with its far-flung estates and its jealously-guarded feudal rights, had provided an obstacle to both royal and episcopal authority. It often enjoyed the direct protection of the Pope. The rise of an urban, as opposed to an agrarian civilisation presented to kings and bishops alike the opportunity to develop a power which eluded the feudal system. The granting of a charter to a city was often the signal for the rebuilding of the cathedral, which thus became the focal point of civic aspiration, the symbol both of the liberation from feudal oppression and of a sense of loyalty to the nation which alone could account for the outburst of enthusiasm which carried the building programme through. The cathedral, says Viollet-le-Duc, was the first building *'vraiment populaire'* erected by a people liberated from the domination of the feudal castle. To a lesser degree it was also a challenge to the supremacy of the great abbeys.

It was, nevertheless, within the precincts of an abbey that the movement started. The consecration of Saint-Denis was Suger's high moment of glory. The final scene was enacted before the most distinguished audience that France could provide. Among their ranks were men who were to play an important role in the development and propagation of the new style.

* 'The unity of the Crown and the Church, the alliance of these two powers to form a nationality, gave rise to the Cathedrals of northern France.'

CHAPTER TWO

Sens

Among the bishops who played the most creative roles in the development of the Gothic cathedral, there was one who was not present at the consecration of St Denis – Henri le Sanglier, Archbishop of Sens. He had died in the previous year. Had he survived long enough to have seen Suger's completed choir, he would no doubt have taken a quite particular interest, for he was already engaged in building a Gothic cathedral of his own.

It was entirely appropriate that the first cathedral to be rebuilt in the Gothic style should have been the great metropolitan Church of Sens. For just as Canterbury had become, for remote historical reasons, the seat of England's southern primacy, so Sens was the Archbishopric which numbered both Paris and Chartres among its suffragans. The new Cathedral was almost certainly begun earlier than the choir of St Denis. We know from the chronicle of Geoffroy de Courlon that there was a fire at Sens in 1128. He also states that 'Henry began to renovate the great church'. This suggests a possible date of about 1130, in which case Henry's building would have been independent, so far as the basic plan is concerned, of the discoveries of Suger. To some extent it is the exception to the general principles and implications of the last chapter. It was built very much under the influence of St Bernard and thus constitutes a rival as much as a parallel development to St Denis.

There was, however, another side to St Bernard than the rigid asceticism revealed in his controversy with Suger. Bernard may have attacked the grotesque aspect of Romanesque art: 'What business has there that ridiculous monstrosity, that amazing misshapen shapeliness and shapely misshapenness? Those unclean monkeys? those fierce lions? Those monstrous centaurs? those semi-human beings?' He denounced the great Abbey Church of Cluny for its 'immense' height, its 'immoderate' length and its 'supervacuous' width. But here he was criticising specifically the church of a religious order. Christianity in the Middle Ages was based on a double standard – the 'religious' and the 'secular'. For secular churches – and this included most cathedrals – Bernard was less insistent on aesthetic austerity; 'since the devotion of the carnal

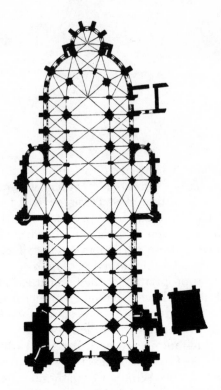

Ground Plan of Sens as originally built

populace cannot be incited by spiritual ornaments it is necessary to employ material ones'. His permission was grudging, but it was granted. The Cathedral of Sens has a moderation and a restraint about it which probably owes much to the influence of St Bernard.

It is clear that from the very start it was intended to cover the nave and choir with a sexpartite vault. The proof of this is that, at the bases of the great piers, the columns destined to receive the transverse ribs are set obliquely in anticipation. We must remember that this was the first building of anything like its size to be entirely covered with a cross-ribbed vault. It was something of a pioneer enterprise and the architect has proceeded with understandable caution. The nave is wide – fifteen metres from pillar to pillar – so that the area to be roofed is considerable. It would have been foolhardy at this early stage of Gothic construction to attempt any great height. The vault ribs meet their keystones at just over eighty feet above floor level.

The proportions dictated by this combination of width and height may have occasioned a further distinctive feature – the omission of tribunes. These great vaulted galleries which formed the first storey of the façade of so many early Gothic churches served as dual

14

purpose; they offered extra accommodation for any overflow of the congregation and they provided abutment to the stone vaults. In St Etienne de Caen – one of the obvious forerunners of the Gothic style – the tribunes were surmounted by the clerestory only, giving a three-storied façade. In most of the early Gothic cathedrals, such as Noyon and Laon, the tribunes were surmounted by a triforium *and* clerestory, thus making a four-storied façade. At Sens there is a three-storied façade, but it is composed of the great arcade, the triforium and the clerestory, an arrangement which was to become the classic formula for the great cathedrals from Chartres onwards. The triforium being smaller than the tribunes, this arrangement created proportions which are far more satisfying than those of St Etienne de Caen and confer a great dignity and serenity upon the structure.

The dignity and the serenity are preserved from monotony by the strong rhythm imposed by a sexpartite vault. Here again, Sens might be compared with the nave of St Etienne de Caen, which is also covered with a sexpartite vault. At first sight St Etienne appears to offer a straight succession of identical piers. Between the heavy arches of the main arcade a semicircular colonnette rises without interruption to the vault spring. A closer inspection reveals that each alternate colonnette is set against a flat pilaster which breaks a few inches forward from the wall. These are the colonnettes which receive the triple thrust of the main cross-rib and the two transverse ribs. The simple colonnettes with which they alternate receive only the thrust of the single intermediary rib. There is a rythm, but it is barely perceptible.

At Sens the alternation between these two sorts of piers, known as *pile forte* and *pile faible*, is dramatically pronounced. The number of vault shafts collected on the capitals of the *pile forte* has been increased by two. This is due to the inclusion of wall ribs which frame the aperture of the clerestory windows, and entails a *pile forte* which collects a group of five colonnettes. Each of the capitals of these colonnettes is turned at the appropriate angle to receive its load of thrust, and this disposition is repeated in the bases, thus proving that the vault system was intended from the very start. Between the two *piles fortes* the bay is divided into two by the *pile faible*, which takes the form of coupled columns of almost Corinthian proportions and capitals. From their square abacus rises a single, slender colonnette to receive the thrust of the intermediary cross-rib. As the original Cathedral had no transepts, this noble rhythm was continued without interruption from the west end to the apse.

In the early fourteenth century, under the episcopate of Etienne Bécard, the choir was separated from the nave by the construction of a stone screen or *jubé* and the grand perspective from west to east was lost for the next four hundred years. In not originally having a *jubé*, Sens was in line with St Denis. Suger had abolished the choir screen 'in order that the beauty and magnificence of the church should not be obscured by such a barrier'. This primitive plan, which was realised, with the exception of the west front, by 1164, was for a single vessel. What appear on the ground plan to be transepts were in fact mere continuations of each aisle by a further bay, half the height of the nave, each of which bulged out towards the east in an apsidal chapel vaulted archaically in a half-dome or *cul-de-four*.

Although the Gothic 'skeleton' is here for the first time apparent, the original windows were small – so small that in the thirteenth century it was found necessary to enlarge them. The architect of Sens was not inspired with that passion for luminosity which motivated Suger. In the bay between the towers, to the north of the organ loft, can be seen the original vaulting and the smaller, round arched windows – which are here blind – which show how the Catherdral was originally lit and how it would have appeared in its pristine state. By comparing this with the first bay of the nave we can see immediately how the windows were enlarged by adjusting the vault to what is aptly named a 'ploughshare'. The extent to which the clerestory windows were increased is nowhere more evident than in the three eastern lights of the apse. Here a kink in the containing wall rib shows very clearly the spring of the original arch.

It does not take much mental adjustment to imagine Sens as it was originally conceived. The Cathedral possessed that austere grandeur which, in a man, so often accompanies asceticism. In this it reflected the character of the man under whose influence it was built – St Bernard of Clairvaux. Sens may therefore be contrasted with St Denis in the same way that we have seen Suger to have been opposed to St Bernard. The beauty of Sens is based upon a severely intellectual theory of proportion.

St Bernard was first and foremost a disciple of St Augustine and as such deeply interested in the connection between musical harmony, visual proportion and ultimate Truth. His almost iconoclastic attitude to the embellishments of a religious edifice was confined to the visual arts. It seems to be historically true that, except with the extreme puritan, iconoclasm is not extended to music. The English Reformation, busy breaking statues and smashing windows, was a period of great productivity in sacred music; denuded churches and desecrated cathedrals resounded to the complex harmonies of Tallis and Byrd. The reason for this can be traced back to Augustine. It is significant that music and architecture were the only two art forms that appear to have interested him. Alone among the fine arts, music found its way into the syllabus of the cathedral schools.

The distinctive fact about music is that harmony is a matter of objective truth. The human ear is so constituted as to register the octave, even in the absence of any aesthetic taste. Augustine was deeply impressed by the observation that the harmonic intervals can be represented as intervals of length along the string of a musical instrument. From here it is an easy step to the theory that these intervals of length constitute harmonic proportions which are as pleasing to the eye as their equivalents in sound are pleasing to the ear. This theory is stated most clearly in the work of Augustine's pupil Boethius, *de Musica*, but he puts it the other way round. 'The ear is affected by sounds in exactly the same way as the eye is by optical impressions.'

It had already been suggested by Plato in the *Timaeus* that this harmony lay at the very root of the Creation. So, to Augustine, beauty was a quality that derived from metaphysical reality. Audible and visible harmonies were intimations of a fundamental harmony between the Creator and his Creation; the enjoyment that our senses derive from such harmonies, says Otto von Simson, 'is our intuitive response to the ultimate reality that may defy human reason, but to which our entire nature is mysteriously attuned'. The Platonists of Chartres believed that the structural coherence of the Universe was the result of the perfect proportions on which it was constructed. From this derived their belief that the principles of sound construction coincided with the formula for perfect beauty.

It was probably Abelard who first pointed out that the biblical account of the building of Solomon's temple is chiefly concerned with a recital of its dimensions and that these dimensions largely correspond with the harmonic proportions of the Platonic school. In the liturgy for the dedication of a new church one of the lessons prescribed was the account of the building of the Temple.

Another lesson was the lovely passage in Revelation, chapter 21, about the vision of the Celestial City, the New Jerusalem, 'coming down from God out of Heaven, prepared as a bride for her husband'. When the medieval illuminator tried to depict this vision of the dwelling place of God, he could find no more appropriate an image than that of a Gothic sanctuary. 'If the architect designed his sanctuary according to the laws of harmonious proportion,' writes Otto von Simson, 'he did not only imitate the order of the visible world, but conveyed an intimation of the perfection of the world to come.'

This was the aesthetic theory embraced by St Bernard. A building was no longer conceived as a canvas to be covered with mural paintings or a frame to be filled with sculptured figures. Its beauty was regarded as belonging to the very bones of its construction. The

17

skeletonic system of Gothic architecture proclaims that a beautiful building is a building which is structurally sound; it would be structurally sound if it were firmly based on the musical proportions that owed their authenticity to Divine precedent. The builders of Sens would have agreed with the saying of Friedrich von Schelling that 'architecture is frozen music'.

The application of this system to the new Cathedral at Sens was extremely simple. The Square bays of the nave and choir are divided into two by the middle rib of the sexpartite vault. Thus they are twice the width of the bays in the aisles, giving in each case the ratio 1:2 which is the octave. Owing to the adoption of a three-storey façade, Otto von Simson has pointed out: 'It is possible to give the same proportion to the relative heights of nave and aisles. The elevation of the nave to the spring of the vaults, however, is subdivided at the level of the arcade imposts into two equal parts: the octave ratio 1:2 permeates the whole edifice.'

There are, of course, other contributing factors to the success of the design of Sens. It is an extremely beautiful stone, which gives to the interior the freshness of a structure that has only just been built. St Augustine's theory of proportion may or may not be true. What is true is that it is a very refreshing experience to visit a building constructed according to these principles. The simplicity, purity and logic of Sens creat a satisfying sensation that everything is just right.

Bernard's influence on Sens was exerted through his friendship with the Archbishop, Henri le Sanglier, who was enthroned in 1122. His early behaviour, which earned the nickname 'the Boar', brought down upon him the rebuke of St Bernard. The rebuke was accepted and the reformed Archbishop became the lifelong friend of his former critic. Bernard's treatise 'On the Conduct and Office of a Bishop' was composed at the request of Henri le Sanglier, who submitted to the ascetic requirements contained in it. One of these requirements was 'moderation in building'.

The alliance between Bernard and the Archbishop was no doubt one of the reasons why Sens was a dangerous place for Abelard, yet it was here, on 2 June 1140, that he confronted the Synod of Sens. Bernard, in the usual vituperative language of medieval controversy, had inveighed against Abelard: 'Scrutiniser of Majesty and fabricator of Heresy, he deems himself able by human reason to comprehend God altogether.' Bernard was content to see in a glass darkly what Abelard hoped to see face to face. 'Thus the human intellect usurps everything to itself, leaving nothing to Faith; it wants to go too high in enquiries which go beyond its power.'

It is possible to argue that the faith of Abelard was stronger than that of Bernard. Abelard was prepared to stake all on the statement 'I am the Truth'; to believe therefore that in seeking the Truth in intellectual honesty he must be seeking Jesus Christ. This was the secret of Abelard's appeal to students. As Morison writes in his *Life and Times of St Bernard*; 'They said that the pronouncing of words that the intellect could not follow was useless, nor was it possible for anything to be believed unless it were first understood. It was ridiculous for a man to preach to others that which neither he himself nor they could intellectually grasp.'

Abelard's achievement is probably best summed up in Gordon Leff's phrase: 'He prised theology away from Authority and exposed it to the scrutiny of human reason'. To this Authority was bound to object, and those who confronted Abelard at Sens constituted the most formidable block of opposition by which a man can be faced – those who feel threatened in their most fundamental presuppositions. Abelard dodged the issue and appealed to the higher court of Rome.

Such was the intellectual climate in which the new Cathedral of Sens was to grow. François Cali has related this intellectual position to the architecture itself. 'St Bernard,' he writes, 'condemns the intellectuals of Paris, the book-learning and the logic of Abelard. They remain still, and wish to remain still, in Plato's Cavern – in St Augustine's Crypt. Outside, Aristotle is crying "Come and see the world as it really is in the natural light of your reason". They mistrust him and detect in him the accent of Islam. This mistrust exists also in their architecture, where they possess the method of the ribbed vault and the pointed arch, which make possible the alignment of the keystones and the reduction of the thrust – but they do not take the advantage of this that they were logically able to take.' There is a powerful restraint about Sens that gives the impression of holding something back.

Henri le Sanglier was succeeded by Hughes de Toucy. We learn from the chroniclers that he 'bestowed much work' upon the Cathedral. In 1163 he was able to receive Pope Alexander III 'with a great concourse of Bishops and Cardinals of the Holy Roman Church' in the Cathedral. On 19 April 1164, Alexander consecrated an altar 'in ecclesia nova'. This certainly suggests that the main structure of the choir and nave was in all important respects complete, except for the west front. On 6 April 1165, the Pope solicited the generosity of the faithful for the completion of the great task.

The west portal – one of the first of its sort – was very badly mutilated by the Revolution. But it had already suffered serious damage in 1268, when the south tower collapsed, and the present tympanum dates only from that period. It can be fairly confidently stated, however, that the subject of the original tympanum must have been the Last Judgment. On the uprights to either side of the main doorway the figures of the Wise and Foolish Virgins are still identifiable and in the two roundels to right and left of the main archway are represented the open and closed doors which point the moral of the parable and connect it with the theme of the Last Judgment. It is quite clear that the panels with the wise and foolish virgins have been added to the ensemble, and the graceful flow of their draperies, with its suggestion of underlying anatomy, also speaks of a later date.

All the statue columns have gone, but the beautiful figure of St Stephen in the long, simple dalmatic of a Deacon and holding the Gospel which it was the Deacon's function to read at Mass, has miraculously survived. On 7 November 1793, when the *enragés* were smashing the statues, they decided to cap St Stephen with the *bonnet rouge* and to inscribe his Gospel with the words: *'Livre de la Loi'*. With these certificates of civism he escaped destruction. The elegance of the figure of St Stephen, which seems to mark the moment of transition between the statue columns of Chartres and the early masterpieces of Reims, was presumably shared by the figures of the Twelve Apostles which have all disappeared. Their loss is irreparable.

Beneath their empty niches the bases are carved with two tiers of figures which were spared by the hammers of the Revolutionaries. The lower register is devoted to the Mirror of Nature, with figures taken from the Bestiaries of the period. Most of the animals are real and recognisable; some are purely fabulous, such as the Sciapod – supposed to represent the mysteries of the Orient – whose typical position was to lie on his back and shelter from the sun beneath his one, enormous foot. Above these are the liberal arts and on the right the labours of the months. Enough remains of the original carvings to attest their excellent quality.

Inside the Cathedral, the stained glass seems to have fared rather better than the statuary. There are some fine survivals from the late twelfth century in the choir ambulatory. *'Le climat qu'elles créent par le jeu de leurs coloris,'* writes Bishop René Fourrey, *'a quelquechose d'enchanteur. C'est un étalage de pierres précieuses. On songe aux murs de saphirs, de rubis, de topazes, d'éméraudes de la Jérusalem Céléste.'**

They seem to form a group with certain windows at Canterbury and Chartres. It is suggested by Chartraire that the same team of

---

* 'The atmosphere which they create by the interplay of their colouring has something magical about it. It is a display of precious stones. It calls to mind the walls of sapphires, of rubies, of topaz and emerald of the Celestial Jerusalem.'

glaziers may have travelled from Canterbury to Sens and from Sens to Chartres. One of these windows, the first in the north ambulatory, is dedicated to St Thomas of Canterbury. He was well known at Sens, having spent four years of his exile at the Abbey of Ste Colombe. Shortly after his canonisation this window was set up to commemorate him.

It is therefore not altogether surprising that the immediate impact of Sens was not upon any cathedral in France, but upon Canterbury. The story is told in the tract written by the monk Gervase: *De Combustione et reparatione Cantuariensis Ecclesiae.* It is a remarkable eye-witness account of an all too familiar event.

'In the year of grace one thousand, one hundred and seventy-four, by the just but inscrutable judgment of God, the Church of Christ at Canterbury was consumed by fire, in the fortieth year from its dedication, that glorious choir, to wit, which had been so magnificently completed by the care and industry of Prior Conrad.

'Now the manner of the burning and repair was as follows: In the aforesaid year, on the nones of September, at about the ninth hour and during an extraordinary violent south wind, a fire broke out before the gates of the church, and outside the walls of the monastery, by which three cottages were half destroyed. From thence, while the citizens were assembling and subduing the fire, cinders and sparks carried aloft by the high wind were deposited upon the church, and being driven by the fury of the wind between the joints of the lead, remained there among the half rotten planks, and shortly glowing with increasing heat, set fire to the dry woodwork of the rafters, from these the fire was communicated to the larger beams and their braces, no one yet perceiving or helping. For the well-painted ceiling below, and the sheet lead covering above concealed between them the fire that had arisen within.

'Meantime, the three cottages, whence the mischief had arisen, being destroyed, and the popular excitement having subsided, everybody went home again, while the neglected church was consuming with fire all unknown to them. But beams and braces burning, the flames rose to the slopes of the roof, and the sheets of lead yielded to the increasing heat and began to melt. Thus the raging wind finding a freer entrance increased the fury of the fire, and the flames beginning to show themselves, a cry arose in the churchyard, "See, see! the church is on fire!" ' At this dramatic juncture the monk Gervase slips into the historic present; 'Then the people and the monks assemble in haste, they draw water, they brandish their hatchets, they run up the stairs full of eagerness to save the church, already, alas, beyond their help. But when they reach the roof and perceive the black smoke and scorching flames that pervade it throughout, they abandon the attempt in despair, and thinking only of their own safety make all haste to descend.

'And now that the fire had loosened the beams from the pegs that bound them together, the half burnt timbers fell into the choir below on the seats of the monks; the seats consisting of a great mass of woodwork caught fire, and then the mischief grew worse and worse. And it was marvellous, though sad, to behold how that glorious choir itself fed and assisted the fire that was destroying it. For the flames multiplied by the mass of timber and extending upwards full fifteen cubits, scorched and burnt the walls, and more especially injured the columns of the church.'

Thus was the church of Prior Conrad, 'hitherto delightful as a paradise of pictures', reduced in a few hours to 'a despicable heap of ashes'. It was a stunning blow to the community. 'The people were astonished that Almighty God should suffer such things, and mad-dened with an excess of grief and perplexity, they tore their hair and beat the walls and pavements of the church with their heads and hands, blaspheming the Lord and His Saints, the Patrons of the church . . . their wailings were as the Lamentations of Jeremiah.'

For five years they continued to worship in the ruins of the nave. Then they summoned 'artificers' from England and France to advise them on the possibility of restoration. It is just worth pausing over this word 'artificer'. In at least one hymn of the period the term 'artifex in opera' is used of God in His Creation. In using the word, Gervase was assigning the creative role to the man so designated.

Amongst those who came was William of Sens, 'a man active and ready and as a workman most skilful both in wood and stone. Him therefore they retained, on account of his lively genius and good reputation, and dismissed the others. And to him, and to the pro-vidence of God, was the execution of the work committed.' William first addressed himself to the procuring of stone from Caen and to this end 'he constructed ingenious machines for loading and unloading ships and for drawing cement and stone. He delivered moulds [in Latin 'formas'; the technical term would be 'templates'] for shap-ing the stones to the sculptors who were assembled, and diligently prepared other things of the same kind.'

It is not clear whether William of Sens sent the molds to Caen or merely supplied them to the workmen. The practice of having the stones cut, or at least rough-hewn, at the quarries was one of the biggest economies devised by the medieval builder. Pierre du Colombier provides some interesting information on the subject. At Troyes, towards the end of the thirteenth century, the workmen went from the *chantier* to the quarries and dressed the stones themselves. In other places the quarries seem to have been ready to cut the stone to prescribed dimensions. This naturally diminished the weight, and therefore the cost, of the stone to be transported. Occasionally accounts have survived. We can follow a load of stone from Caen to Norwich in 1289. Its price at the quarry was £1:6:8. Freight to Yarmouth put this up by £2:10:8. It then had to be unloaded, transferred to a barge and taken up the river Yare to Norwich. By the time it was delivered it had cost £4:8:8. River transport often involved a series of tolls from the riparian authority. One of the ways in which a landlord could contribute to the building of a cathedral was to grant immunity from these tolls.

Having obtained his stone, William of Sens proceeded with great expedition to erect his choir. Beginning on 5 September – the feast of St Bertin – 1175. By the following summer three pairs of pillars had been erected together with the outer walls 'upon which he framed seemly arches and a vault, that is, three *claves* on either side'. This suggests a double bay of sexpartite vaulting with the vaults up on the side aisles. In the following year he raised 'the principal pillars' of the crossing 'which he decorated with marble columns placed around them'. This work, together with the transepts and their curious arrangement of a double triforium, occupied him up to the beginning of the fourth year. In the summer of 1178 he put up five more bays east of the crossing, with their arches and vaults, and had 'completed on both sides the triforia and upper windows'. In the fifth year he was just setting about 'turning the great vault' when the scaffolding gave way beneath him and he fell some fifty feet to the ground. For some time he continued to direct operations from his sick bed – 'and thus was completed the *ciborium* between the four principal pillars'. The word *ciborium* was at that date used of the canopy over the altar, but it is here applied to the canopy of stone formed by each bay of the vaulting.

The architecture of Canterbury does not afford an overall likeness to that of Sens, but round the hemicycle the coupled columns of almost Corinthian proportions bear a distinct resemblance to the *piles faibles* of their prototype.

The monk Gervase was more impressed by the excellence of the carving and the richness of the decoration than by any advance of technique imported from France. In the old church, he recalls, 'the arches and everything else were plain, or sculptured with an axe, not with a chisel. But here, almost throughout, is appropriate sculpture.'

Gervase's account provides a sudden flood of light into the world of the medieval cathedral. For the first time we have a detailed eye-witness account of the building of a choir and of that all-too-common occurrence, the destruction of the previous edifice by fire.

On 23 June 1184, another fire devastated the city of Sens and left its traces upon the walls of the ambulatory of the Cathedral. It may have been the damage occasioned by this fire that necessitated the repairs in the course of which flying buttresses were added at about the end of the twelfth century. In 1230 the clerestory windows were enlarged and the vaults adjusted accordingly.

Thus, with a few minor modifications, the Cathedral of Sens was completed, except for its towers, according to the original inspiration of the Master Builder. It represents the dawn of the new style. It was destined also to represent its sunset.

Marius Vachon, in his study of the architects of the Chambiges family, has drawn attention to the great revival of Gothic architecture at the end of the fifteenth and beginning of the sixteenth centuries – *'une période de renouveau de l'architecture ogival, qui, à l'heure de son déclin, semble, comme le soleil, jeter le même éclat et rayonner aussi brillamment qu'à son aurore.'** Cathedrals, whose completion had been interrupted by a century of warfare, were again *en chantier*. Their spires were erected, their façades, especially those of the transepts, were completed and their dilapidations were restored. *'Le style flamboyant semble l'image de la flamme nouvelle du génie des vieux maîtres-maçons,'*† Camille Enlart has listed 647 buildings thus brought to their perfection, among them the 'Tour de Beurre' at Rouen, the porch at Albi, the 'Tour Nouvelle' at Bourges. But the most distinguished of all were the works of Martin Chambiges at Sens, Senlis and Beauvais.

At the end of the fifteenth century the Archbishopric of Sens was held by Tristan de Salazar, who combined in his person the qualities of a great Churchman and of a distinguished patron of the arts. In 1489 the coffers of the Cathedral contained 1500 livres. It was decided to invite Martin Chambiges to draw up *'le devys de la croisée'* – the design for the transept. The new undertaking received royal support. In March 1496, Charles VIII passed through Sens and made a ten-year grant to the Cathedral of 100 livres a year from the salt tax. His successor Louis XII followed this up in 1501 with 400 livres a year from the *taille*.

What Chambiges had done to deserve so important an order is not known but his designs were approved and he began his construction *'du côté du palais archiépiscopal'* to the south. Machinery was immediately ordered including *'cinges'* and *'écrevisses'* for the hoisting and carriage of heavy loads. Members of the Chapter

* 'a period of renewal of Gothic architecture which, at the hour of its declining, seems, like the sun, to emit the same radiance and to shine with the same brilliance as it its rising.'
† 'The Flamboyant style seems to reflect the new flame of genius of the old master masons.'

dispatched to the quarries of Ivry and St Leu d'Esserent to order stone. On 8 November 1490, Chambiges was ready to start. He had with him only eight *maçons tailleurs de pierre*.

Fortunately the Chapter accounts for the period have survived and we can learn some fascinating details of the progress of the work. In 1491 the Chapter made a contract with Pierre Gramain, *'tailleur d'ymages'* from Auxerre. He received twenty-one livres for eight statues. It is clear that the elaborate façades of niches both here and at Beauvais were originally peopled with statues.

In 1497 Chambiges went to another job in Paris, leaving Hughes Cuvelier *'maître de l'oeuvre'* in charge. But he continued his oversight – *'à cause qu'il est maître de l'entreprise et conducteur d'icelle croysée'*.

In 1496 the south portal was nearing completion, for it was possible to dispense with the "gruat" – presumably some sort of a crane. On 8 July in the following year the expenditure of five francs is recorded for a ceremony which always marked the completion of any particular feature – the *"vin d'honneur"* for the workmen – *'pour leur vin du jour que le bouton et l'ymage de Notre-Dame furent mise sur le pignon de la croisée'.** Another curious recompense is recorded in one *écu* expended on a pair of shoes for Martin Chambiges 'in respect of the services which he rendered to the Canons in Paris to obtain stone'. The quarries of Notre-Dame-des-Champs had in fact provided some of the stone for the transepts.

In 1501 work began on the north transept. Hughes Cuvelier directed the operation, but Chambiges continued to make visits *'pour mieux dresser et mener à perfection l'édifice'*. In October 1506 he was treated to a dinner at the Hostellerie de Jean Jouand at a cost of twenty-one sous. The menu included an omelette of twenty-four eggs, fifty gudgeons from the Yonne, a roast gigot – which only accounted for five sous – honey, cheese and fifteen litres of wine which cost eight sous.

The statuary of the north porch was more lavish than that of the south, presumably because it was for public use. The south porch, opening into the courtyard of the episcopal palace, was private to the Bishop. Accordingly in April 1503 Pierre Gramain signed a contract for twenty-six 'ymaiges' for the architraves of the 'according to the plan' (*devis*) provided by Canon Hodoard'. In this we see the clergy still dictating the iconography to the artist. At the same time André Lecoq received an order for six large statues for the portal and for two more specified as Augustine and Abraham. In 1516 the carpenter was paid for dismantling the scaffolding. The work of Martin Chambiges was complete. Twenty-two thousand

---

* 'for their wine on the day that the finial and the statue of Our Lady were set up on the gable of the transept.'

livres had been expended – 9,710 on the south transept and 12,290 on the north.

At about the same time, Tristan de Salazar erected the monument to his parents which stands against the second *pile forte* on the north side of the nave. It is, in miniature, an exquisite example of the style in which the Cathedral was completed. In the minute intricacy of their interlacing architecture and in the chiselled precision of their execution the three canopies represent Flamboyant decoration in its perfection. Here we can see in stone what the stalls of Amiens so miraculously provide in wood – the last realisation of the dream that found its first flowering at St Denis and here in Sens Cathedral.

CHAPTER THREE

Chartres (1)

Of all the dignitaries who had attended the Consecration of St Denis, the most significant, from the point of view of the Cathedrals' Crusade, was Geoffroy de Lèves, Bishop of Chartres. It was he who had been responsible for introducing Henri le Sanglier to St Bernard, with important results for the architecture of Sens. It was he who had brought about the rapprochement between St Bernard and Louis VI. A statesman of the first quality, he was also a considerable scholar and under him the School of Chartres attained its apogee – 'the finest age of the School of Chartres,' wrote Clerval; 'the most productive of writings, the richest in famous Masters.'

The names of Gilbert de la Porée, Guillaume de Conches, Thierry, Bernard de Chartres and John of Salisbury will for ever be associated with this brilliant renaissance. Under them the School of Chartres became one of the main seats of learning where Plato and Aristotle, Priscian and Cicero, Ptolemy and Pythagoras were studied as well as Holy Scripture.

Geoffroy de Lèves was a personal friend of Suger's and well acquainted with what he was doing with his Abbey Church. No one, in fact, was in a better position to appreciate the efficacy of the new style, for he had had a unique experience at St Denis. When the main skeleton of Suger's choir had been erected and the wooden centring of the arches removed, the structure was subjected to the most exacting of tests. A terrible storm arose – 'such a force of opposing winds buffetted against the aforesaid arches . . . that they threatened destructive collapse at any moment, trembling miserably and as it were swaying back and forth. The Bishop [of Chartres, who was celebrating Mass at the time] became greatly alarmed by this vibration of the arches and the roofing, but the tempest was unable to dislocate these isolated, recently built arches wavering up aloft'. The first essay in Gothic construction had triumphed.

It would have been unthinkable for Geoffroy de Lèves not to have built something important that would express his views on harmony and proportion and light in the newly discovered idiom of Gothic architecture.

He had already as his Cathedral the imposing Romanesque edifice

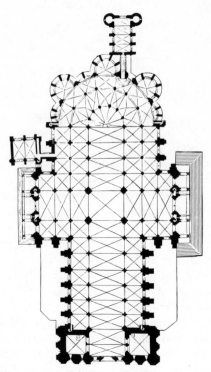

Ground Plan of Chartres

begun in 1020 under Robert the Pious with the financial assistance of Canute. It was essentially the creation of Bishop Fulbert, but was only dedicated under his successor Thierry in 1037. It was by this time the centre, for France if not for Europe, of the increasingly popular cult of the Virgin Mary. In 878 Charles the Bald had presented Chartres with one of the most breathtaking of all relics – the chemise allegedly worn by the Virgin on the occasion of the Annunciation. In due course Chartres came to be regarded as her chosen residence on earth; no pains could be spared to provide a worthy palace for such a Queen. The cult of the relic and the cult of the Virgin Mary are the basic facts on which an understanding of Chartres Cathedral must be founded.

As so often happened in the history of cathedrals, it was a fire which gave Geoffroy de Lèves his opportunity. The extent of the damage is unknown, but in 1134 he began a square bell-tower some distance from the west front of Fulbert's building and exactly in line with the north aisle. Donations mentioned in the Obituary between 1134 and 1142 refer to 'turris' in the singular. The existence of windows on all four faces of this tower prove that it was once free-standing.

28

In 1145 the plural 'turres' occurs for the first time. Significantly this was the year following the dedication of St Denis. It was at this time, too, that we first hear of that remarkable upsurge of faith described by Robert de Torrigni and Abbot Haimon. Men and women, high and low, young and old, harnessed themselves to carts which brought the stones from the quarries of Berchères or delivered the provisions for the sustenance of the workmen. These convoys were conducted with a reverent and almost liturgical discipline, either in silence or to the accompaniment of psalmody. Unable to complete their arduous journey in a single day, they would camp out for the night and the great plain of La Beauce would twinkle with the constellation of their many fires.

It is clear that by now Geoffroy de Lèves was engaged on something far more important and inspiring than the mere erection of a new belfry. That could hardly have caught the popular imagination in so sensational a manner. We know that a second tower, symmetrical with the north belfry and on an alignment with the south aisle, was under construction. The most obvious explanation of this second tower is that Geoffroy had already decided to extend Fulbert's nave so as to join the towers and thus to form a new west front and narthex – and in so doing he would have been following closely the example of Suger at St Denis.

The west front was at first set back between the two towers. In about 1150 it was decided to advance this front so as to make it flush with the western faces of the towers. The whole decorative scheme was enlarged in the process. Unfortunately a minor inaccuracy in the alignment of the towers led to difficulties in the re-erection of the triple portal. The central line of the nave, when extended, passed slightly to the south of centre between the towers. In order to make the middle archway coincide with the axis, the archway to the south of it had to be made narrower. A scrutiny of the depiction of the Nativity in the lower lintel will show that the recumbent figure of the Virgin, which is clearly meant to be central, is well to the right of centre, and that the right hand shepherd has been sawn in half.

Because of the somewhat tentative process by which the façade evolved, the three portals of Chartres all open into the nave and are therefore closely grouped together. At St Denis and most of its derivative cathedrals the three doors correspond with the ends of the nave and the aisles respectively and are consequently set farther apart. At Chartres the three archways form a single decorative whole and present a single unified theme.

The theme chosen was the ultimate unity of all knowledge. To appreciate Chartres we must recapture some of that spirit of intellectual excitement which pervaded the era – the feeling which was to find its highest expression in the *Summa* of St Thomas Aquinas, that all knowledge, spiritual, philosophical and scientific, could be held together in one mighty synthesis with Theology, the Queen of Sciences, the keystone of the arch.

It was no less than this that Geoffroy de Lèves chose as the subject for the sculptural decoration of the west portal which has come to be known as the *Portail Royal*. To the right, the south doorway or *Portail de la Vierge*, represents the first coming of Christ. He is seen in the place of honour, the tympanum, seated on his mother's knees. The Virgin thus made her first appearance at a level hitherto reserved for Deity.

To the left, the north doorway depicts the Ascension of Christ into Heaven. In the central tympanum He is seen coming again to judge the world – a picture taken from the Apocalypse. In each group He is supported by His precursors in the Old Testament, represented as statue-columns, and surrounded in the triple archivolts by symbolic scenes of human life.

This humanity is shown in terms of Man's labour; in the north doorway the labours of the body – the ceaseless, seasonal struggle with Nature, over which preside the signs of the Zodiac; in the south doorway are the labours of the mind, represented by the Seven Liberal Arts together with some of their more distinguished exponents. While these figures of the *Portail Royal* were being carved, the Chancellor, Thierry de Chartres, was writing his great treatise on the Seven Liberal Arts. These were Grammar, Rhetoric, and Dialectic (the Trivium) and Arithmetic, Geometry, Astronomy and Music (the Quadrivium). *'Les sciences humaines,'* wrote Emile Mâle, *'qui rendent hommage à Notre-Dame dans l'École, lui firent cortège à la façade de la Cathédrale.'**

The Seven Liberal Arts had been transmitted from Antiquity to the Middle Ages by a series of authors of whom Augustine and Boethius are the best known. Far more important from the point of view of medieval art was the work of an African of the fifth century, Martianus Capella. In a highly fanciful piece of writing, the *Marriage of Mercury and Philology*, he introduces the seven arts as the bridesmaids. It looks like the sort of gimmick to which a preacher might resort who had despaired of being able to hold the attention of his audience by more conventional means. His appeal was not to the intellect but to the visual imagination, for not only were the arts personified, but they were laden with symbolic attributes. Thus Grammar carries an ivory casket which contains not only the obvious

---

* 'The Humanities, which did homage to Our Lady in the School of Chartres, provided her escort on the façade of the Cathedral'.

instruments of writing, but a birch, a file marked out by golden rings into eight sections, representing the eight parts into which a discourse was traditionally divided, and a scalpel, signifying the loosening of the tongue for speech achieved by those who had mastered the subject.

This symbolism captivated, and indeed dominated the medieval mind from Gregory of Tours to Botticelli. It appears again and again in the writing of scholars. Being in a vividly pictorial form, it was easily translated into the sculptures and stained glass windows of the great cathedrals. Chartres was the stronghold of classical thought. From Fulbert, known to his pupils as 'that venerable Socrates', to Bernard de Chartres and John of Salisbury, they all fought to preserve the place of the Classics in the mind of the Church. It was Bernard who made the great statement about the Philosophers of Antiquity: 'if we can see further than they could, it is not because of the strength of our own vision, it is because we are raised up by them and borne at a prodigious height. We are dwarfs mounted upon the shoulders of giants'.

There was a most attractive broadmindedness about the School of Chartres. 'Quite the most beautiful sign of the power of the true Christian Catholic Faith,' wrote Ruskin, 'is this continual acknowledgement of the brotherhood – nay, more, the fatherhood of the older nations who had not seen Christ, but had been filled with the Spirit of God and obeyed, according to their knowledge, the unwritten Law.'

What more natural, therefore, than that the Seven Liberal Arts and the greatest names associated with them should adorn the archivolts round the figure of the Virgin and Child in the right hand porch of the *Portail Royal*? In the central architrave Music hammers out a chime upon a peal of bells, while Grammar presides grimly with book and birch over two cowering pupils. In the outer register Aristotle bends in frowning concentration over a little writing table, Euclid traces a geometrical figure upon a desk also balanced on his knees; Priscian, Pythagoras, Ptolemy and Cicero complete the scene.

On the left hand side, two signs of the Zodiac – Gemini and Pisces – have overflowed from the *Portail de l'Ascension*. This, the north doorway, presents the theme of the labours of the body. If the scholar could gaze with intellectual satisfaction upon the symbolism of the *Portail de la Vierge*, no less could the agricultural labourer see his routine chores ennobled by their inclusion in the *Portail de L'Ascension*.

Probably no age has had a deeper sense of the dignity and spiritual value of work than the age of the Cathedrals' Crusade. By his work – either by the labours of the intellect or by the labours of the body – man was able to contribute to his own salvation. Ignorance and bodily need were held to be the results of the Fall of Man. *'Ipsa restitutio sive restoratio,'* wrote Vincent de Beauvais, *'per doctrinam efficitur'* – Man can compass his re-instatement or restoration by means of knowledge.

As for the dignity of agriculture and commerce, the carvings of the north porch and the forty-two windows representing the artisans of Chartres may speak for themselves. As Emil Mâle insists: 'It was not in those days considered that there was any impropriety in placing pictures of everyday life alongside the heroic scenes of the lives of the Saints. Work was shown thus with its own dignity and its own sanctity'.

To the agricultural worker himself the message was of necessity somewhat simpler. The scything of a meadow, the pruning of a vinestock or the threshing of a load of corn were all somehow something to do with Jesus Christ who had drawn so much of his religious teaching from homely scenes – a sower sowing his seed, a shepherd tending his flocks or a woman sweeping a room. And as Christ's humanity is here seen raised in glory, so the daily round and common task were correspondingly transfigured. Scholar and peasant alike could stand before the portals of Chartres and see that he had his place in the Temple of God. The months of the year, represented by their appropriate activities on the farm, are depicted with a directness and naïvety suited to the subjects. 'In these little scenes Man plays his eternal role,' writes Emil Mâle. 'No doubt it was the peasant of France that the artist intended to represent, but it is also Man throughout the ages, bent towards the earth, the immortal Adam.'

These two lateral doorways express a view of the relationship between God and Man. The tympanum of the central door is rather more narrowly theological in its imagery. It represents the words in the Creed: 'He shall come again in glory'. Christ is surrounded in the archivolts by figures of Angels and of the twenty-four Elders mentioned in the Apocalypse, of whom only twenty have found a place. The stone of which these figures are carved is capable of receiving the most delicate chiselling, but it has not always resisted the erosion of the elements. Fortunately the figures nearest to the spectators are the best preserved. The Elders are represented as the members of an orchestra, and like the members of an orchestra, their eyes are fixed on their conductor. The artist has created a wonderful impression of concerted concentration which is of the essence of worship. Of these figures Emile Mâle had written: 'Perhaps the twelfth century produced no work of greater perfection.'

Such are the broad outlines of the scheme. A secondary theme is provided by the capitals above the statue-columns which form a continuous frieze of sculpture depicting incidents in the life of Christ. A few of the subjects are from the Apocryphal Gospels and are not easily recognised, but most of the familiar scenes are there. It is strange, however, that in all this there should be no direct reference to the crucifixion.

Beneath these highly decorated archivolts and capitals are the statue-columns for which the west front of Chartres is above all famous. Several sculptors collaborated in their creation. The two kings on the left of the *Portail de l'Ascension* are by the same hand. The folds of the draperies are entirely stylised, often forming a series of concentric rings, reminiscent of the figures in the tympanum at Vézelay. The artist seems to have gone from Chartres to Notre-Dame d'Etampes, where the figures of David and Solomon are in exactly the same style.

The statue-columns in the central bay come from another hand and have a pre-eminence entirely their own. There is no canopy overhead to break the upward movement; their feet rest upon the slightest of supports; their elongated figures and closely pinioned arms accentuate their structural allegiance. They are as much columns as statues.

It is supremely in the female figures that the artist has shown his genius: taller and more attenuated than the men, their pendant sleeves and plaited tresses reaching almost to the ground, these noble ladies epitomise the cult of chivalry. With their high necklines revealing only the face and their delicately fluted draperies betraying no trace of underlying anatomy, they are almost sexless. Thus did medieval man exalt his liege lady to the status of a goddess; thus did the Catholic faith exalt the virginity of the Mother of God.

As late as the nineteenth century vestiges of paint and gold leaf could still be discerned on these statues. The historical imagination should see the *Portail Royal* brightly coloured and richly gilded. Today not only the original colouring but often the original surface of the stone has weathered away and the figures are being replaced by facsimiles. This operation is only possible because a hundred years ago mouldings were made from which the accuracy of these copies can be assured. In the interests of this accuracy they retain certain mutilations. If a figure was headless when the moulding was made, it remains headless in the copy. It is, nevertheless, something of a miracle that the *Portail Royal* has survived so nearly intact.

This new formula for the western entrance to a church was immediately copied, not only in the façades of cathedrals, but in parish churches, some of which were quite small – at Etampes, at St Ayoul de Provins, at St Quentin-lès-Beauvais, Donnemarie-en-Montois all of which have suffered terribly from time and vandals. But by a happy chance one of the most charming is one of the most perfectly preserved – the little Church of St Loup-de-Naud in the region of Provins. It is a *Portail Royal* in miniature; there was only room for three statue-columns on either side and for only eight of the Apostles in the lintel – aesthetic considerations always outweighing statistical accuracy in the medieval mind. But it has an artistic excellence which is quite astonishing to find in so small a village. The link with Chartres may, in this case, be dynastic. In 1170 St Loup-de-Naud received a generous donation from Henri le Libéral, comte de Champagne, whose brother was the comte de Chartres.

It was not only as an ensemble of sculpture that Geoffroy de Lèves's new west end to his Cathedral was important: its windows were to house some of the best stained glass ever made. It was Abbot Suger who first really grasped the opportunity offered by the glaziers of France, and in the three west windows of Chartres – those immediately above the *Portail Royal* – we can see what Suger's glass was really like, for these were made by the same workshop and represented the same subjects. In particular, the right hand light, the Tree of Jesse, shows what the mutilated remnant at St Denis must have looked like in its perfection. It has been called by Emile Mâle 'the most beautiful window ever made'.

In the first window of the south choir aisle, as one enters it from the transept, is another remnant of the twelfth-century glass. It occupies the top three squares of the left hand light and can be identified easily by the pale sapphire blue which predominates. It represents a large Virgin and Child who has for centuries been known as *Notre-Dame de la belle verrière*.

The happy survival of these three windows – for twelfth-century windows are scarce – is one of the many miracles of Chartres.

CHAPTER FOUR

Senlis

About the time that Geoffroy de Lèves was engaged in the construction of the west front of Chartres, together with the sculptural ensemble of the *Portail Royal*, Bishop Thibault of Senlis began the rebuilding of his own Cathedral Church.

Senlis was the smallest diocese in the whole of France, having only seventy-three parishes. It was the smallest cathedral foundation. Its earliest statutes, drawn up shortly after its consecration in 1191, provide only for a dean, a chantre, a sous-chantre, one archdeacon and twenty-six canons; it was a fairly skeleton staff for a medieval cathedral and it is hardly surprising that it should have been one of the smallest of cathedral towns. It is also one of the most beautiful. As early as the fourteenth century it attracted a lyrical description from Jean de Jandum which deserves to be quoted in full.

> The town rises from the middle of a forest whose tall trees are set far enough apart to let the sunlight through, so that beneath them one can gather strawberries, blackberries and hazel nuts: beautiful orchards, laden with delicious fruit, meadows enamelled with flowers where the water flows from a crystal source, separate the houses from the forest: the wines are delicious, the fish abundant. The houses are built not of plaster, as in Paris, but of stone – a hard, resistant stone: the cellars are deep and cool: the town is paved, clean and free from mud, and aired by gentle breezes. There is only one complaint: the frogs, which make such a noise that they impede the slumbers of the honest men who inhabit the banks of the Nonette.

In a country where frogs were by no means rare, Senlis seems to have suffered from a superfluity of the creatures. Gerard de Nerval recounts the tradition that St Rieul, the patron saint of the town, found himself unable to preach against their united chorus and had to resort to miraculous powers to reduce them to silence.

Senlis has a history as long as the Christian era and it suffered the vicissitudes common to most European cities during the first millenium. These vicissitudes followed a pattern which has been traced by Henri Pirenne in his study of *Villes et Institutions Urbaines*.

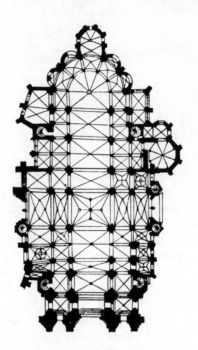

Ground Plan of Senlis

As in Rome itself, the Church usually became the heir to the civic structures that Rome had built. It was often the only claimant left. The barbarian invasions had deprived the cities of their municipal organisation and the fall of the Mediterranean countries to Islam, putting a virtual end to trade and commerce, and robbing them of their bourgeois populations. The city only survived into the Carolingian era as a fortress – a place of resort in time of danger. Its essential inhabitants were the military – and of course the ecclesiastical – personnel. This decline in the political importance of the towns did much to enhance the power and prestige of the Bishop. The secular lords lived almost without exception in country *palatia* or châteaux set in the centre of a domain which was largely self-supporting. The spiritual lords were left to dominate the towns.

Then in the tenth and eleventh centuries, led by the cities of Venice and Amalfi, the civilisation of northern Europe began to rediscover its commercial life. By this time, however, the Church had established itself in an almost impregnable position and it tended to be hostile to commercial enterprise. '*Le marchant*,' it was said, *ne peut que difficilement plaire à Dieu.*'* The Church's teaching on usury was likely to give him a guilty conscience: consciences that were

* 'The merchant can only with difficulty please God.'

36

guilty could be eased by the benefaction of some ecclesiastical endeavour. In a city this was often the building or rebuilding of the cathedral.

Senlis provides an excellent example of the superimposition of a Christian city upon the framework of a Roman castrum – originally called Augustomagus but later Silvanectis, from which the name Senlis has derived. The royal château was built upon the site of the Roman praetorium, the Hôtel de Ville on that of the forum and the Cathedral of Notre-Dame upon that of the Temple of Jupiter.

The château became one of the principal strongholds of the Carolingian dynasty. It was here, in 987, that Hughes Capet was elected King and the Capetian dynasty began. Louis VI made important additions to the fabric of the châteua. Philippe-Auguste made much use of it and provided the city with an outer ring of fortifications. In the late fourteenth century Charles V made further additions to the château and designated Senlis as the official residence of his children. Here, in 1420, was celebrated the marriage between Henry V of England and Catherine of France. The last king to stay at the château was Henri II. Henri IV was often at Senlis, but he put up in a house in the town. It was from here, on 21 March 1594, that he set out for Paris to win his Kingdom and to become the first Bourbon on the throne of France. The fact was commemorated by the last of the Bourbons, Charles X, returning from the last coronation at Reims. He ordered a bust of the *Vert Galant* to be placed on the façade of the Hôtel de Ville. For a small town, Senlis enjoyed an unusually close connection with the royal family.

In spite of the many hazards of history, Senlis had preserved, perhaps more than any other town in the Ile de France, its character of an old cathedral city, insulated and introspective. It is as if its ramparts had somehow protected it from contact with the outside world. 'No one thinks of it today,' wrote Gerard de Nerval, 'and its inhabitants seem to take little interest in the rest of the universe.' This is, of course, no longer true; nevertheless some of the old atmosphere lingers on in its crooked, cobbled streets which preserve much of the charm and most of the hygienic defects of their medieval past.

From the Rue aux Flagearts the *abside* of the Cathedral rises magnificently from its scaffolding of flying buttresses above the brown roofs and old, grey walls of what used to be the Bishop's Palace. Senlis, in fact, has not been a diocese since the days of the Revolution, and the Bishop's Palace now serves as the *Tribunal Civil*. But from the east side the scene has not lost anything of its original character; one would not be surprised to see a figure in an episcopal *soutane*, breviary in hand, pacing up and down in the trim little garden to the north. The houses around, charming and irregular, are typical of the architecture of a Close. It is here more than anywhere else that Senlis throws back the echoes of its past. It is here, as Edmond Pilon so charmingly puts it, *'où la vieille France est la plus vénérable, la plus parfumée, la plus douce'*.

At the north end of the Bishop's Palace is a tower which was part of the Gallo-Roman fortifications, for the Cathedral was set only just within the line of defence. Next to the tower there is a glimpse of the east end, with two apsidal chapels in the simple, transitional style of the mid-twelfth century. It would be difficult to say if it was Gothic or Romanesque. Above it is clearly Flamboyant with its tall slim lights and the fretted tracery of the parapets. It is at once clear that Senlis has been much rebuilt: only its history can provide the key to an understanding of its fabric.

In 1153 Bishop Thibault began the new Cathedral on a site which had hitherto provided space for three separate churches. Nevertheless, by Gothic standards, Senlis Cathedral is small. It was, however, too large for the revenues of the diocese. Within three years the funds had run out and Louis VII signed letters of recommendation to a team of *Quêteurs* (Collectors) who went round the neighbouring dioceses to raise funds. By the time that they had returned Thibault was dead; he was at least spared a disappointment because the results were not encouraging. Bishops Henri and Geoffroy, successors to Thibault, consecrated a large proportion of their revenues to the workshops; kings and popes supported the project, but Senlis progressed slowly. It was not until 1180 that we have any evidence of completion, for at that time we learn that three lamps were burning continually 'at the entrance to the Sanctuary, before the altar of the Virgin Mary'. A building programme which Suger had accomplished in just over three years was completed at Senlis in just under thirty.

The process of building followed the usual pattern. Slight developments of style indicate that the choir was built before the nave and the north tower before the south tower. On 16 June 1191 the Cathedral received its solemn dedication. Guillaume de Champagne, Archbishop of Reims, and the Bishops of Meaux, Noyon, Soissons and Laon, all of whom were engaged in rebuilding their own cathedrals, were present at the ceremony.

All we know is that, although ready for use, Notre-Dame de Senlis was by no means finished. Guillaume of Reims addressed a letter to the religious leaders of his province telling of the great sacrifices made by the clergy of Senlis for the building of their Cathedral, explaining that from want of proper resources it was still incomplete. He of course invited offerings, adding an indulgence to all those who would come to the new Cathedral in the following years on St John's day and make a donation.

The Cathedral as it was first built was much lower than it is now, and it had no transepts. We can still see, in the westernmost bay of the nave, above the organ, the original height of the vaulting. It was only eighteen metres. East of the first bay is a narrow bay with a quadripartite vault and two sturdy piers which were needed for the abutment of the towers. From this point eastwards the whole nave and choir proceeded without interruption, a regular alternation of *pile forte* – *pile faible*, making a total of four double bays each of which carried a sexpartite vault. The last bay opened into the apse which is elongated into the form of a horseshoe. This narrow vessel was flanked with a single aisle on each side which curled into an ambulatory round the apse and bellied out into five little chapels which were scarcely more than niches.

The second bay from the east on either side was extended, as at Sens, into a sort of false transept by the addition of double bays to each aisle. To the east of these were staircase towers by means of which one gained access to the tribunes. The interior façade was of three storeys only, for the triforium was omitted. Each bay was divided into two halves by the *pile faible*, thus providing two arches of the great arcade. Above each of these arches a single aperture opened into the tribune which was in turn surmounted by a single lancet in the clerestory. The architecture throughout was strong and simple, but it must have been poorly lit.

Marcel Aubert, the chief historian of the Cathedral, records an extraordinary tradition that the columns in the *pile faible* were moulded in a composition that included not only hard stone, bricks, tiles and glass, but 'incense, mastic, bulls' blood and vinegar'. According to Jean Vaultier, who wrote as early as 1598, François I made a special journey to inspect these pillars. They are, however, made of a hard limestone from quarries quite near Senlis.

Contemporary with the nave was the west front of the Cathedral, which was finished in about 1185. In many ways it reflected that of St Denis, but the architect seems to have had a problem posed by the smaller scale of his building. As at St Denis, there are three doorways marking the entrance to the nave and to the two side aisles. The nave being broader than the aisles, the central portal of St Denis is larger than the other two, but it is not very much larger. At Senlis it was decided that there was only space enough to give full development to the central embrasure. In order to make room even for this single portal, the architect has enlarged the façade of the nave at the expense of those of the aisles. It will be seen from the ground plan that the buttresses which flank the nave façade are not in line with the pillars of the nave, but have been pushed to north and south by the opening of this portal, with the result that the doorways to the aisles are much smaller in size and correspondingly simpler in treatment.

The reduction, for decorative purposes, of three portals to one posed another problem: what was to be the subject of the statuary? The decision was made, we know not how, to devote the only portal to the Virgin, who appears here for the first time on an equality with Christ. Marcel Aubert was right when he described the tympanum of Senlis as 'the Triumph of the Virgin'. It depicts that subject and it represents a new level in the cult of mariolatry. The figures of Christ and his mother are both the same size, both equally near the centre; the curious double-lobed arch in which the scene is framed seems to emphasise the equality of the two figures. On the left hand of the lintel the Virgin is depicted as having departed this life, with an Angel carrying her soul to Heaven, while the right hand side portrays her resurrection.

This scene is in a far better state of preservation than the other and it reveals the work of a real master of his art. There is a wonderful rhythm about the Angels as they crowd round to get a look at the reviving figure of Mary. Around them, in the archivolts, are the figures of a Tree of Jesse. Corresponding with each of the four archivolts are four statue columns on either side which were badly mutilated in the Revolution and horribly restored in the nineteenth century by the sculptor Robinet. Mouldings were made, however, of five of them before the work of restoration began. These are now in the Musée du Trocadero. Marcel Aubert, by comparing these with their corresponding figures at Reims and on the north porch of Chartres, has been able to provide the clue to their identity. On the left Abraham, Moses, Samuel and John the Baptist prefigure the sacrifice of Christ. On the right Simeon, holding the infant Christ, Jeremiah, Isaiah and David foretell the Passion.

*

In the thirteenth century, Senlis seems to have been a little more prosperous. Gifts are continually recorded of money, houses and even corn. By 1240 the Chapter clearly considered that it could afford to undertake a considerable programme of building. This resulted in the building of the spire and the separation of the nave from the choir by the interposition of a proper transept.

The aesthetic problem presented by the construction of a spire arises from the fact that an octagonal spire is more elegant than an attenuated pyramid. But the tower on which it stands is nearly always square. An octagon rising from a square leaves the four corners of the square projecting awkwardly against the skyline. At St Denis, where the north tower was originally crowned with a spire, the problem had been solved by placing triangular pinnacles on the four corners of the square. Each pinnacle consisted of a tall, pointed roof upheld by the slender columns of an open arcade. It was not an entirely satisfactory solution. Triangular pinnacles can look most peculiar from certain angles.

At Chartres, where the date 1164 is inscribed on one of the pinnacles of the south spire, a more ingenious means had been devised to mask the transition from square to octagon. The architect – who may have been the Harman who inscribed the date – evidently decided to tackle his problems one at a time. The passage from the square to the octagon is achieved by the addition of an eight-sided storey to the tower. Since the walls of this were still vertical, there was no difficulty in constructing the four pinnacles which fill the four corners of the square. From each facet of this octagon rise the pointed roofs of these pinnacles and the slender gables of the windows with which they alternate. Behind these gables and roofs the architect has effected the next transition – from the vertical of the tower to the inclined plane of the spire. 'The transition between the square tower and the polygonal spire,' wrote Emile Mâle, 'is imperceptible. There results from it a continuity in the upward movement and a unity of impact which are not to be found elsewhere.'

It has to be admitted that the architect of the spire at Senlis has achieved a far less felicitous result. He has made use of the intermediary stage of an octagonal tower, as at Chartres, with open-work pinnacles at the corners, as at St Denis. But this octagon tower takes up too much of the total elevation and the actual spire which grows out of it is relatively small. But even here, the tapering lines of the spire are largely concealed by a ring of lofty dormers with slender gables which continue the vertical lines of the octagon.

At the same time that this work was being done on the spire, the interior of the Cathedral was profoundly modified. The third and fourth bays from the east were taken down and a transept, the full height of the nave, was inserted. The evidence for this reconstruction is given by the stones themselves. On each of the great piers west of the crossing can still be seen the capitals from which sprang the arches of the main arcade as it continued towards the choir. The great piers east of the crossing have no such capitals and are thus identifiable as new constructions. The pier to the north of these two has the clustered columns of the thirteenth century, but its corresponding pier to the south has the simple grooving typical of the Renaissance. Between the eastern piers of the crossing there used to be a screen or *jubé*. Guillaume Parvi had it painted, or more probably

Senlis—Chartres: Comparison of Spires

repainted, in 1533 and set up his coat of arms on it. When the King attended divine service here he was seated on top of the *jubé*. This placed him in the same position relative to the congregation as for a coronation at Reims.

On one occasion, according to Müller, Henri IV was being preached at by a certain curé named Chauveau, who warned the King of the Judgment of God that he would incur if he did not forbid duelling. The King sent for him after the service and congratulated him on his outspoken address; *'Continuez à parler de la sorte et à dire la verité,'* he urged the preacher; *'c'est ce que doivent faire les prédicateurs aux grand, comme aux petits.'**

It was not until the sixteenth century that the Cathedral was completed. The reign of François I was a period of very great architectural activity. Much of it was secular and concerned with the introduction of the new ideas from Italy; but a considerable amount of the building programme was devoted to the great cathedrals of the twelfth and thirteenth centuries, many of which had remained unfinished. The later Middle Ages, with their long chronicles of English invasion and peasants' revolt, had not been a period propitious for building. Senlis itself had been involved in siege and counter-siege and at one moment had been in the hands of the Jacquerie. It took France several generations to recover. And now in 1515 a young, handsome, vigorous and ostentatious King, François d'Angoulême, ascended the throne. He was a man of considerable accomplishment, both in the art of war and in the arts of peace. Owing to the careful thrift of his predecessors he was extremely rich and could afford to indulge the costly art of building. It seems that he was one of the main contributors to this resurgence of cathedral building. He took for his badge the salamander – the very emblem of renaissance – and these creatures, together with the capital F for François remain on many cathedral walls.

It is less easy to judge the contribution made by the Church. France, and indeed Europe, was at a low ebb spiritually. A number of bishops were moved with an admirable zeal for reform, but the worldliness, viciousness and corruption of the Church was so deep rooted that it was often a short step from reform to Reformation. The Church of France, always a little independent of Rome, might well have gone under François I the way the Church in England went under Henry VIII. But it drew back, only to plunge France into half a century of religious war even more devastating than the English invasions of the Middle Ages.

* 'Go on speaking like that and saying what is true . . . it is what the preacher ought to do to great and small alike.'

It is at any rate certain that the renaissance in cathedral building in no way reflected a revival of faith within the Church. At Meaux the reforming Bishop Briçonnet had found only fourteen of his clergy competent to fulfil the responsibilities of their office and he asserted that 'no honest woman would have dared to set foot in the Cathedral Close'. A study of the Chapter of Senlis tells an all too similar tale. There are the usual *histoires* of non-attendance at divine worship. The strict regulations obliging the 'half-prebendaries' and chaplains to attend the services only reveal the reluctance to do so on the part of the canons themselves. The bishop was sometimes left to celebrate 'in pontificalibus' assisted by three or four vicars only.

But there was worse than this. On 15 February 1510, the Bishop, Charles de Blanchefort, protested to the Parlement about the lax morals of his Chapter, most of whom lived openly with concubines 'to the great scandal of the Church and people'. The Dean himself, Louis Labelle, was living in open sin with somebody else's wife and brought her publicly to the Cathedral with him. The Cathedral Close was known in vulgar parlance as 'the warren of whores'. These recriminations did nothing to improve relations between the Deanery and the Palace, then as always *plus ou moins tendues*'. In July following the Bishop's complaint, two choirboys were sent, as was the custom, to offer him Holy Water. They were repulsed with the words, 'I don't want any, damn you!' and were denied the customary gratification. It was the last time the Chapter offered Holy Water to their Reverend Father in God.

It appears that the members of the Chapter were drawn mostly from local families; the names which are listed for prebendaries coincide frequently with those which occur in the municipal deliberations. Sometimes a canonry was used to provide an income for a high-born bastard. Technically his illegitimacy should have debarred him, but, as so often with the Church of Rome, the matter could be arranged for the appropriate fee. On 5 February 1500, the bastard Jean de Montmorency was received as a canon, having duly produced letters of dispensation 'super defectu natalis'. The Montmorencys of Chantilly were one of the greatest families in the country; the Church could not afford to disoblige them. This was particularly true of a church as poor as Senlis.

The poverty of Senlis is a recurrent theme in the history of the Cathedral and is only equalled by its apparent proneness to accident. A letter from Charles VI, dated 27 April 1413, shows that the roof and spire were sadly in need of repair, and he remits a payment of 100 livres which the Chapter were owing him. Four years later there was a disastrous fire which burnt off the newly leaded roof. 'The molten lead,' writes Jaulnay, 'flowed through the streets in abundance'.

In 1413 the Bishop, Jean Raphanel, was taken prisoner by the English. The diocese was unable, or unwilling, to pay his ransom. In June 1504, a much more serious fire threatened to destroy the Cathedral completely. Once again, says Jaulnay, the lead flowed through the streets *'comme l'eau dans les grandes lavasses de pluie'*.

The Chapter wrote at once to the King – Louis XII – to describe the disaster and hoping that he would have *'pitié et compassion de la pauvre église de Senlis'*. The bells, they told him, had melted and the belfry, 'which is large, magnificent and one of the most singular in all the realm' was in danger of collapse. They ended with the reminder that Senlis was *'la plus pauvre et petitement fondée'* of all the cathedrals in his Kingdom.

The first task was to invite workmen from other building sites to come and give their advice. This brought Martin Chambiges from Beauvais, Pierre de Meaux from the Town Hall at Compiègne and Jehan Gobereau who came *'avec son varlet'* to determine the damage done to the leadwork. They received in all twelve livres for their expenses. The latter signed their names to the receipt, but Martin Chambiges was apparently illiterate; he signed with a cross. Curiously enough it was the bells that received first attention and the belfry was made sound immediately. On 7 December in the same year the bells were recast, all the clergy of the Cathedral being present *'en costume de Fête'*. The Canons at Senlis wore red cassocks and the choirboys green.

The King replied to the appeal by the gift of about 1000 livres per annum in the form of a levy on the sale of salt, but the Church was not inactive in trying to raise its own funds. The usual methods were employed, but permission to eat butter in Lent was applied on a sliding scale: *'pour les riches et les nobles'* a payment of two sous was exacted, but *'pour les marchants'* a sum of only twelve deniers.

In 1507 Bishop Blanchefort founded a Confrérie de la Vierge – as it were, the 'Friends of the Cathedral' – to assist with the raising of funds. Money began to flow in. Chanoine Pierre Legier, who kept the accounts, makes the entry soon after the fire: 'From a notable man who does not wish to be named: 23 écus'; less self-effacing, but more generous was Geoffroy Bouvilliers, bourgeois of Senlis, who contributed 400 écus. The financial resources of the Chapter were soon sufficient to pay for the elaborate façades of both the transepts and for some very fancy vaulting in the chapels and outer bays of the aisles.

Martin Chambiges' façades are more or less miniatures of what he built at Beauvais. We know that the many niches of Beauvais were originally peopled with statuettes: it is highly probable that the same was true of Senlis. The Chambiges, father and son, were among the last great exponents of the Gothic style. Already, by the accession of

François I, the impact of the Italian Renaissance was making itself felt in the architecture of the Loire Valley. Under the influence of the Montmorency family it soon spread to the churches of the Ile de France. But at Senlis new ideas were not encouraged. In 1514 the pillars of the choir and nave were elevated to receive the new vaults. On 3 March 1514, the Chapter resolved 'that appropriate windows shall be opened under the new vaults, according to the advice of Monsieur Lescot, in the style in which they were accustomed to make them formerly'. As at Sens, so at Senlis, the earliest and the latest phases of the Gothic may be seen in their perfection.

CHAPTER FIVE

Laon

Before the great days of the University of Paris, Chartres and Laon had pride of place in the intellectual world. Laon had been the capital of the Carolingian monarchy and had, on occasion, shared with Reims the distinction of being the Church of the Coronation. Situated at the intersection of two great roads and perched on the high ridge of limestone which dominates the surrounding plain, Laon was a natural fortress. Now, in the early twelfth century, it had become a stronghold of learning – Abelard's *'citadelle de la connaissance'*.

Guibert de Nogent, the local chronicler of the period, wrote to Bishop Barthélemy: 'God has given you two eyes more brilliant than stars.' These were the brothers Anselme and Raoul, the two great Masters of the Cathedral School. Anselme was perhaps the more distinguished of the two – *'la lumière de la France et du monde'* – and such was his reputation that merely to have been his pupil was held equivalent to possessing a degree. It was here at Laon that his precocious and turbulent pupil Abelard began his controversial career – the *Historia Calamitatum* – as he called his autobiography.

Already in the twelfth century the intellect of Christendom was set upon the road that was to lead to the great encyclopaedias of Vincent de Beauvais and Thomas Aquinas. The pursuit of logic and the appetite for debate had endowed scholasticism with a brilliant façade of method. The goal for which they strove was the unity, harmony and interdependence of all knowledge. It was this that provided the intellectual context to the Gothic style. 'While the Schoolmen were constructing this 'cathedral' of the intellect, which was to enshrine the whole of Christianity, others were building our Cathedrals of stone which formed as it were the visible image of the first.' In these words Emile Mâle sounds the keynote of the Cathedrals' Crusade. He may not be saying any more than that the sort of mind which produced scholastic thought is the same sort of mind that would express itself in Gothic architecture.

The philosophers of Scholasticism were deeply concerned with the relationship between the parts and the whole, between the general and the particular. Their treatises were subdivided into *parts*, their

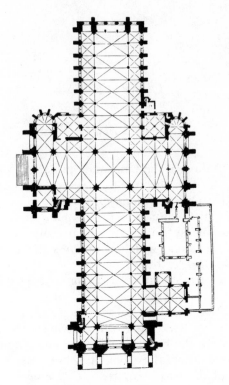

Ground Plan of Laon

parts into *members*, their members into *distinctions* and their distinctions into *articles*. As Erwin Panowski puts it: 'they felt compelled to make the orderliness of their thought and logic palpably explicit'.

The comparison between the thought and the architecture of the twelfth century is taken a stage further by François Cali in his study *L'Ordre Ogival*. He has sought to demonstrate the method by which the structures of medieval thought were realised in the construction of a medieval cathedral. 'The Clerics, trained by Scholasticism to trace effects back to causes, to analyse an abstract principle into as many logical consequences as it can have, discovered in the interior elevation of the new Cathedrals – tracing the columns back to the vaults – the most perfect image of what they were taught; the image of a unity which is good because it begets a multiplicity, and of a multiplicity which is beautiful because it coheres in a unity.'

This unit in multiplicity and multiplicity in unity is particularly in evidence at Laon. For Notre-Dame de Laon is the best preserved example of a twelfth-century cathedral in France. It was nearly

48

completed according to its original design and has suffered less in the way of later alterations than its compeers. In the distance Laon raises that many-towered silhouette which was often intended – as at Chartres and Reims – but seldom achieved. The views of the Cathedral as one climbs the steep ascent from the north-east are really dramatic – and this is by far the best way to approach the building. Inside it has retained a noble unity of style which is set off to perfection by the beautiful white stone of Chermizy. If there is something deeply satisfying to the mind in the contemplation of the interior, it is because the original design had satisfied one of the most distinguished minds of the age.

Laon was the creation of one of the great scholar bishops of the twelfth century, Gauthier de Mortagne. Educated at Reims, he had risen to be Ecolatre at Laon, and after his consecration to the episcopate he always retained his academic title. Louis VII used to address him as 'Maître Gauthier, Evèque de Laon'. He was made Bishop in 1155 and immediately set about rebuilding the old Cathedral, beginning with the sanctuary. By the time of his death in 1174 he had achieved the first phase of the construction, a choir of three bays ending in a polygonal apse, together with the east wall of the transepts.

It is almost certain that Gauthier planned the whole Cathedral as we see it today, for some of the sculpture of the south doorway in the west front has been assigned by Emile Mâle, on stylistic ground, to the same date as the choir. There is but one conclusion possible: the whole plan, including the iconography of the west front, had been established and the workshops were preparing the statues in readiness for the west front. The same can be shown to have happened at Reims and Notre-Dame de Paris.

In 1180, after a short respite, the work was renewed. The transepts were completed and the nave erected together with the west front and the towers. In 1205 the bequest of a quarry at Chermizy brought a new supply of particularly beautiful stone to the new works and the choir was extended to its present dimensions, but finished with a rectangular east end. At the same time flying buttresses, which the builders of St Rémi de Reims had recently added to the repertoire of the architect, were inserted throughout the Cathedral.

This work was completed by about 1220. It only remained to carry the transept towers up to their full height and to fill in the spaces between the nave buttresses with chapels to attain, in about 1230, the shape which the Cathedral retains today. In the early fourteenth century the rose of the south transept was replaced by a large light filled with decorated tracery. The same was planned for the north transept, but the work caused cracks in the tower and had fortunately to be abandoned. Laon has therefore retained its north rose and lost its south one. The stained glass of the east, north and west façades is still *in situ*, though in some cases much restored. Only three of the roundels of the west rose are original.

In approaching the glass, as with the architecture and the sculpture, we must seek to penetrate the thought of the times. The wise man of the twelfth century, wrote Emile Mâle, 'rises to the seen from the unseen; in reading Nature's book, he reads the thoughts of God.' Science, therefore, did not consist in studying things for their own sake, but in discovering the teaching which has been put into them by God for our benefit. 'Every creature,' said Honorius of Autun, 'is a shadow of the truth.'

To men of such an outlook even the seasons had their mystical significances. What was winter but the twilight of the human soul before the revelation of Jesus Christ? What was spring but the promise of new life implicit in Baptism? Medieval man did not just experience externals; summer spoke to him of the radiant light of eternal love and autumn of the final Harvest when each man shall reap as he has sown. But autumn is to the Seasons as evening to the times of day. The westering sun also reminded him of the final harvest, and windows depicting the Last Judgment usually faced the west. To this particular rule Laon was no exception. The rose over the west doors represents Heaven and Hell as the ultimate destiny of human souls.

The rose of the north transept depicts the Seven Liberal Arts – with Medicine added to make up an even number – forming a ring round the central figure of Philosophy. It was a theme dear to the mind of Gauthier de Mortagne. The windows were set up in 1190 and came from the school of the *maître verrier* Pierre d'Arras, who made also the south rose at Lausanne. Only two of the roundels – those devoted to Rhetoric and to Music – are modern replacements.

The east windows form a magnificent group, with a large rose surmounting three tall lancets. They are known to have been in place by 1228. The right hand lancet is a treatment of the Nativity, looking back at the Old Testament predictions of the Virgin Birth with the Burning Bush and Gideon, who has the appearance of a Knight in the Bayeux Tapestry. The left hand lancet combines the story of Stephen with the ever popular narrative of Theophilus. But it is the central lancet, representing the scenes of the Passion, that dominates the group. In this window Florival and Midoux – the great historians of the glass of Laon – see the most finished piece of work in the Cathedral; 'the colours are brighter and yet more closely blended, they are richer and more harmonious. The hand is more skilful and the touch more sure.' Above these the eastern rose is dedicated to the Virgin. She represents the Church after the Last Judgment. The imagery is taken from the Apocalypse, with the Twelve Apostles occupying the inner roundels and the Twenty-four Elders the outer ring. These east windows were of course those which a worshipping congregation faced. As they turned to leave the church they were confronted by the solemn reminder of the west rose with its depiction of the Last Judgment.

The west front marks an important advance in the development of the Gothic portal, the Gateway of Heaven prefigured by Suger at St Denis. Both Sens and Senlis had followed up the idea of the triple doorways, making the central one very large and the side ones almost insignificant. Noyon raised the side doorways to the same height as the central one but half concealed the whole behind a porch which projects from the façade like a *porte cochère*, in the form of a triple archway with its parapet treated as an openwork balustrade. The common failing of these three west fronts is the absolute dominance of the great buttresses necessitated by the towers. The lateral façades of Senlis seem to be just squeezed in between the massive upright shafts. At Noyon there are three almost identical façades completely separated by the buttresses.

At Laon, for the first time, the whole façade is treated as a single, gigantic composition and an entirely successful effort has been made to overcome the dominance of the buttresses. It was achieved by balancing the vertical with the horizontal elements. At ground floor level the architect has screened the façade by a triple archway which frames the three portals behind. It was originally free-standing. In the nineteenth century it was found necessary to increase the abutment of the towers by attaching this screen to the façade, forming three deep, but separate embrasures.

The second storey is lit by the magnificent rose window set between two large but simple lancets. Above these the architect has repeated the theme announced by the porch in a triple arching which again forms a screen behind which the buttresses are concealed. Above this runs a colonnade, providing a strong horizontal accent, but because the size of the rose window makes the central arch higher than the two which flank it, this colonnade is stepped up in the middle with the result that its horizontality is not oppressive. The vertical lines of the buttresses are apparent at this level, but they appear as pinnacles which begin to form the transition between the façade and the towers.

These towers attracted the particular attention of the thirteenth century architect, Villard de Honnecourt, who left a drawing of one in his album. 'I have been in many lands,' he writes, 'as you may see from this book: nowhere have I seen any tower such as that of Laon.'

The first storeys of the towers are square in plan. The second storey of each is octagonal, but the passage from the square to the octagon is dissimulated by the provision of four corner turrets in the light, openwork form of superimposed arcades. As Villard de Honnecourt's drawing reveals, the central octagon was intended to become a spire, with four smaller steeples at the corners supported by these arcades. Only the south spire was built, but it was taken down in the Revolution. The extremists wanted to take down the towers as well, *'les clochers étant contraires à l'égalité'*. This Leveller's philosophy could have been disastrous for Laon, had not a pedantic argument arisen as to the exact meaning of the term '*clocher*'. The Conseil du Directoire, Bouxin informs us, referred the matter to an engineer named Becquy de Beaupré who took the opportunity of strengthening the towers instead of destroying them.

At the base of the second arcade of each corner tower stand two enormous oxen, sixteen in all, looking outwards from the Cathedral and inwards towards each other. There is, of course, a legend attaching to these oxen. It is preserved by Guibert de Nogent. 'A certain clerk, charged with the conveyance of materials for repairing the roofs, was making the steep ascent of the hillside, when one of his oxen collapsed with fatigue. As he was trying in vain to find another to replace it, he suddenly saw one running up who offered himself of his own accord to lend his assistance to the uncompleted task. Thanks to this reinforcement the waggon was speedily conveyed to the church. On his arrival the poor clerk was in some embarrassment, not knowing to whom he should return the beast; but he, no sooner than he was freed from the yoke, without waiting to be led or driven, returned immediately to the place from which he had come.'

Guibert de Nogent was writing of a period earlier than the construction of the present Cathedral, but there is no reason why the legend, once established, should not have been transmitted to the later building. Whatever the truth of it, the oxen are there and have been since before Villard de Honnecourt did his drawings. Oxen had, after all, made no mean contribution to the building of the Cathedral. It is estimated by Pierre du Colombier that a single yoke of oxen could accomplish a journey of about fifteen kilometres, there and back, in the course of a day. Between them they could manage a load of some fifteen thousand kilos, which works out at about one cubic metre of stone. No wonder that we hear that at Sainte-Foy de Conques, there were teams of twenty-six yokes labouring to deliver stones up the steep gradients of the escarpment. One has only to undertake the long ascent that leads to Laon to appreciate the importance of oxen to the success of the enterprise.

There was an old saying: 'chastel abbatus est demi

refez' – meaning that a castle that had been knocked down was already half rebuilt because the stones did not need to be fetched. Undoubtedly the carriage of stone accounted for a great part of the cost of a medieval cathedral.

The west towers served as the belfries and in the thirteenth century housed nine bells, reputed to be the most melodious in France. The last one, acquired in 1268, was the great bourdon Guillemette, which was only used on the most solemn occasions. But during a thunderstorm – a phenomenon thought to be caused by the Devil – all the bells were sounded *à toute volée* to frighten the Devil away. It was for this reason that medieval bells often bore the image of Ste Barbe, the saint whose protection was invoked against thunderstorms.

The great bells of Laon did not survive the Revolution. On 5 November 1792, Melleville informs us, sixty-nine of them were collected in the courtyard of the Bishop's Palace ready to be taken off and recast as cannons. *'Il est tèmps de transformer en bouches terribles qui puissent sonner nos victoires . . . cette multitude de cloches inutiles, instruments de l'orgeuil et du fanatisme.'**

In what sense a church bell was an 'instrument of pride' is not clear. In medieval thought, according to Guillaume Durand, the bell symbolised the voice of the preacher. The beam from which it hung represented Christ crucified – the subject matter of the preacher; the three strands of the bell rope stood for the triple interpretation – moral, historical and allegorical – employed by the preacher, and the activity of the bellringers served as a reminder that the proper response to preaching was action.

The Middle Ages were strongly symbolic in their outlook and an understanding of their symbolism is necessary to any appreciation of their architecture. At Laon it is in the sculpture of the west front and in the stained glass windows that we should look for illustrations.

The west portal suffered much in the eighteenth century. As at Notre-Dame de Paris, the canons had the lintel and the tympanum of the central doorway removed to allow for the passage of the canopy held over the Blessed Sacrament as it was carried out in procession. The Revolution removed the statue columns and mutilated many of the figures in the architraves. Enough of these remain, however, to reveal the exquisite quality of the workmanship and to bring us abruptly up against the problem of symbolism.

Following the example of Senlis, the central archway is dedicated to the Triumph of the Virgin. The inner architrave is filled with the choir of Angels; the next three are given over to a Tree of Jesse – the

---

* 'I is time to transform this multitude of useless bells, instruments of pride and fanaticism, into the terrible mouths of canons which can sound forth our victories.'

genealogy of the Virgin – and the outer ring to the Prophets. To the right, or south, of this is the portal of the Last Judgment. It is all fairly obvious. In the second architrave Angels carry the souls of the elect to the bosom of Abraham. The medieval artist took a literal interpretation of the text: 'except ye become as little children ye shall not enter into the Kingdom of Heaven' and he represented the elect as infants. In the fourth architrave the elect, now restored to maturity, are seated and crowned.

In the outer register are the wise and unwise Virgins; at the top of each row the last scene represents a gateway. It is closed to the foolish and open to the wise. The symbolism of the gates of Heaven being open or closed is easily divined.

It is the north embrasure which really poses the problem. It is devoted to the Virgin with the usual scenes of the Annunciation, Nativity and Adoration depicted in the tympanum. In the architraves are first the customary Angels and then the apposition of Virtues and Vices which was already traditional. But the two outer architraves contain figures and scenes whose symbolism was only decyphered by Emile Mâle in 1902. Daniel killing the Dragon; Daniel in the Lion's den and being fed by Habbakuk; Gideon and the fleece; the Burning Bush; the Arc of the Covenant; a girl with a unicorn; a man, more recently identified by Suzanne Martinet as Virgil; Balaam; Simeon, Nebuchadrezzar, Shadrac, Mechac and Abednego; the Sibyl of Erythraea. Some of them have inscriptions, or the remains of inscriptions, attached. There is at first sight no common ground on which all these figures could unite.

Most of the figures are, in fact, explained in a book of sermons by Honorius of Autun called the *Speculum Ecclesiae* or Mirror of the Church. They are predictions of the Virgin birth. For instance Gideon's fleece on which the dew fell represents the Virgin impregnated by the Holy Spirit, while the ground remaining dry shows her virginity intact; Habbakuk passing food into the lion's den without breaking the seal prefigures how Christ 'left his mother's womb without breaking the seal of her virginity'. The Sibyl of Erythraea was supposed, since the days of Augustine, to have provided a pagan prediction of the Last Judgment and the coming of the King of Kings.

The inscriptions beside these figures are of particular interest because some of them correspond with the text of a manuscript preserved in the library at Laon which constitutes the libretto of the enacted liturgies with which the Church celebrated Christmas.

They started on Christmas Eve with the *Fête des Prophètes*, more commonly known as the *Fête de l'Âne*. This began with the procession into the Cathedral of a donkey, richly caparisoned, to an incantation punctuated by the Chorus: 'Hé! Sire Âne! Hé!'. It was meant to resemble the braying of an ass and required a somewhat uninhibited performance. When the donkey had reached its destination the procession of the Prophets began. Each was impersonated by one of the canons in theatrical costume; each was introduced by the Master of Ceremonies from the top of the choir screen and as he emerged he further identified himself with a sentence from Scripture – the same that was inscribed by his statue on the portal. Thus Balaam announced: 'there shall come a star out of Jacob' and Simeon: 'Lord, now lettest thou thy servant depart in peace'. The moment had now come for the re-appearance of the donkey, this time ridden by Balaam and having one of the smaller choirboys concealed in its caparison. The famous scene with the angel and his flaming sword was then re-enacted with the choirboy supplying the voice of the donkey. His words were greeted by a loud braying from the congregation amid general rejoicing in the course of which wine was freely distributed.

In the twelfth century one of the Canons bequeathed two vineyards to the Chapter, capable of producing seventeen *muids* of wine – that is to say 4250 litres – to be distributed at the *Fête de l'Âne*. It is scarcely to be wondered that the festivities of the medieval Church were popular in both senses of the word – they were festivals of the people and they were well liked.

Sometimes it was the stained glass which reflected the high moments of the liturgy. On Christmas Even the scene was enacted of the Shepherds at the crib, but the text was taken from the Apocryphal Gospel of St James. This added to the dramatis personae of the Nativity two midwives, Zélémie and Salome, one of whom appeared, alongside the more orthodox figures, in the window of one of the lancets in the choir which was devoted to the Nativity.

On the morning after Christmas, the Feast of Stephen, another dramatisation took place known as *Les Epîtres Farcies*. The Precentor read the Epistle in Latin from the top of the choir screen, while another cleric relayed it in doggerel French verse from below. For some reason Stephen had been raised to the peerage for the occasion and was hailed throughout as 'Saint Étienne le Baron'. The successive scenes of this drama are the subject of the glass of the left hand lancet of the east end.

By the happy survival of these manuscripts in the Library we can see how closely the decoration of the Cathedral was used to illustrate its liturgy. 'The symbolism of the cult,' wrote Emile Mâle, 'made the congregation familiar with the symbolism of art.' The carvings of the west porch assume an entirely new significance when they are thus related to the popular festivities of the Church.

A new theme is taken up in the surrounds to the two great lancets on either side of the west rose window. They represent respectively the Mirror of Science on the north side and the Mirror of Nature on the south. Later in the thirteenth century Vincent de Beauvais was to set down in literary form what had been the thinking of the Church for some time. In his own great Mirror, the *Speculum Majus*, he divides all knowledge into four categories: the Mirror of Nature, the Mirror of Science, the Mirror of Morality and the Mirror of History. He provides the key to much of the decoration of the great cathedrals.

The Mirror of Nature was divided under the headings corresponding with the six days of Creation – the Elements, the mineral world, the vegetable world, the animal world and finally Man. This is the theme of the southern lancet on the west front of Laon. It begins with God in deep thought – for all creation was held to proceed from Divine thought – and reckoning on his fingers how long the Creation should take. Then follow the stages of the Creation, culminating in the seventh day, when God 'like a good labourer, who has used well his working day, sits down to rest, leaning on his stick, and goes to sleep'.

The Mirror of Science is the subject depicted in the northern lancet. The Seven Liberal Arts, corresponding with the seven gifts of the Holy Spirit and with the seven days of the week, were deemed to be Man's contribution to his own redemption.

The symbolism whereby these forms of study could be represented pictorially derives from Martianus Capella and had already been exemplified in the *Portail Royal* at Chartres. Here at Laon the theme appears twice – in this northern lancet of the west front and also in the glass of the rose window of the north transept – but in each it received a slightly different treatment.

In the carvings of the north lancet and in the central roundel of the rose, the Liberal Arts are presided over by Philosophy, who can be seen with a ladder, which represents the degrees of learning which the student had to mount. He is portrayed with his head in the clouds. This was not intended to suggest the nebulous quality of his thought, but rather, following the description by Boethius, the sublime height to which the human intellect can reach – *'ipsum etiam coelum penetrabat'*.

Grammar receives an unusual treatment. It is depicted as a woman with a single pupil; she rests one hand gently on his shoulder while with the other she indicates a word in the book before them. The more common representation of Grammar appears in the roundel of the north rose window, where she is wielding a birch rod, eloquently described by Florival as 'stimulant habituel de toute étude en ce temps-là'.

56

Guibert de Nogent has an interesting reminiscence on the subject. One day, on his return from school, his mother asked him if he had been beaten; seeking to protect his master, he replied that he had not. But the marks upon his back told another story and his mother became indignant, declaring that she no longer wanted him to become a cleric if it meant enduring such chastisement. But the young Guibert took another view: 'In spite of these brutal beatings,' he wrote, 'I loved my master almost as much as I loved my mother. For although he treated me with the greatest severity, it was evident that he loved me as he loved himself and he looked after my interests with the greatest solicitude.'

The other sciences are represented with traditional symbolism. Dialectic has a serpent round her waist to signify subtlety in argument; Rhetoric raises her hand in an oratorical gesture; Arithmetic holds up both hands, the right hand holding the *boules* of an *abacus* or counting machine; Geometry is distinguished by a compass, Astronomy by an astrolabe, while Music hammers on a peal of bells or *tintinabulum*. These are all represented again in the glass of the north rose window, but here they are joined by Medicine. The symmetry of the window required one more subject to fill the eight roundels and there was at that time a flourishing school of Medicine at Laon.

It is not only in the iconography of its ornament that Laon provides so perfect an example of a twelfth-century cathedral. It represents also an important phase in the development of the Gothic style. Sens, Senlis and Noyon remained faithful to the logical system entailed by sexpartite vaulting – the alternation of a massive pier and a relatively slender column, '*pile forte – pile faible*'. Noyon and Soissons had obtained an increase in altitude over Sens by adopting the system of tribunes, which provide solid abutment up to triforium level. The four-storey façade of arcade, tribunes, triforium and clerestory is nowhere better exemplified than at Noyon. The next development was to reduce the amount of stone separating the nave from its aisles. The *pile forte* formed a very considerable barrier, and the nave only communicated with its aisles as it were at intervals. It was at Laon that the next step was taken.

In the last two bays of the nave (the first to be built) the old formula has been usd. The *pile forte* is a cylindrical column flanked by colonettes, each of which relates directly to one of the vault ribs. But in the next bay, and thereafter throughout the Cathedral, the colonettes have been omitted. The great arcade is composed of a series of cylindrical columns which are surprisingly slender; the aperture between them is correspondingly large and opens the aisles more adequately into the nave. This, together with the beautiful pale cream stone, accounts for the sense of airy lightsomeness and elegance which is one's first impression of entering Laon.

The alternance is still expressed. It will be noticed that the pillars of the great arcade of the nave stand on bases which are alternately square and octagonal. This difference is repeated in the abacus where the reason becomes apparent. The *pile forte* has to accommodate five vault ribs – the vaulting arch, the two transverse arches and the two wall ribs. It therefore needs a wider abacus on which they may rest. The *pile faible* does not receive the thrust of any trasverse arch and only has three colonettes to support. This development was taken a stage further at Notre-Dame de Paris; the last of the great Gothic cathedrals to use tribunes, it was the first in which flying buttresses were introduced, a technical advance which ultimately rendered tribunes obsolete. It was at Chartres that the decisive formula was reached: quadripartite vaulting throughout and the three-storey façade. The use of quadripartite vaulting was already widespread. It was the normal formula for the square bays of the side aisles. At Noyon it was used for the oblong bays of the choir, which is very short and hardly provides room for the alternating bays of a sexpartite vault. It was also, and probably for the same reason, employed in the transepts. This arrangement is found also at Laon.

The development of the transept provides another theme in the progression towards a classical formula. Sense and Senlis were both conceived as simple naves with aisles but with no transepts; Notre-Dame had very shallow transepts; Bourges had none at all. Noyon and Laon made the transept an important feature of the design. This was taken up at Chartres and incorporated in the classic formula. The purpose of a transept was not simply to provide the church with a plan that was cruciform. Suzanne Martinet has drawn attention to the connection between the development of the transept and the increase of pilgrimage. At Laon the High Altar was at first placed under the canopy of the crossing, before the western entrance to the choir. Most of the reliquaries and other objects of devotion were exhibited in an arrangement in which the altar had pride of place. This was the point of convergence for the endless streams of pilgrims who flowed into Laon, many of them en route for St Jacques de Compostella. The ample doorways at each extremity of the transept enabled a constant procession of the faithful to file past the altar without unseemliness and to accomplish their devotion of the relics with sufficient decorum.

For the twelfth century was the age of the relic. The Protestant and the unbeliever must make a conscious effort to understand the spiritual psychology of such a cult. To feel oneself in the presence of an object – even of the fragment of an object – which had been associated with Jesus Christ Himself, was a stimulant to devotion beyond price. Not far inferior were the mortal remains of heroes of Christianity who had won, through torture and hideous death, the glory of a Martyr's crown. For those engaged in worship – that is to say, for those trying to bridge the gulf between time and eternity – an unspeakable joy was derived from the august presence of the embalmed body of one who had achieved that passage in so triumphant a manner.

It was a noble coinage, but it was quickly debased. The commercial exploitation of the relic was one of the less edifying achievements of the age. The number of heads said to belong to any particular saint began to increase; France alone claimed three, all purporting to be that of St Quiriace. Portions of the True Cross and of the Virgin Mary's linenwear began to proliferate. Phials appeared on all sides, each allegedly containing a drop of the Saviour's sweat or a *soupçon* of his Mother's milk.

Although one would have thought authenticity to be the first requirement of a relic, it was untypical of the medieval mind to reason in this way. One of the few voices of incredulity came from Laon, from the chronicler Guibert de Nogent. 'How is it possible to imagine,' he asked, 'that the Virgin, who was humble, could have dreamt of collecting her milk for posterity? And how improbable, in any case, that the milk should have survived for so long!' He was referring in particular to one of the relics of Laon – a dove made of crystal and gold with eyes that had the glassy stare of carbuncles. Within the bird was a cavity containing the 'milk'. The whole was housed in a reliquary of ivory decorated with vermilion. It was exposed on the High Altar on 25 January, the festival of the Virgin's Milk.

The relics of Laon were of great number and variety. Hundreds of them dangled from the huge iron chandelier that hung in the centre of the crossing. It formed two great circles of light, each supported by an iron wheel, beautifully worked in arabesques. Thousands of other candles, in various branches and candelabra, provided a brilliant illumination to this lavish display of gold and precious stones. Some of the saints were housed under golden roofs capacious enough for a man to hide beneath – a circumstance to which at least one canon owed his life during the insurrection against the tyrannical Bishop Gaudri.

There is much about the inventories of Laon which calls to mind the fulminations of St Bernard. 'The eye is dazzled (and the purse is opened) by the golden roofs offered for the covering of relics; the Saints are modelled beautifully, and are thought to be the more venerable the more they have been gratified with colouring. The faithful go to kiss them; they are incited to make donations; they regard more the beauty of these statues than they do honour to the virtues of the Saints. They place in our churches not coronets but wheels, ornate with Jewellry . . . What are they trying to evoke? The repentance of the guilty or the admiration of the onlooker?' Now comes his famous condemnation: '*O vanité et plus encore folie que vanité! L'Église scintille et le pauvre a faim; les murs de l'église sont couverts d'or, mais ses enfants sont nus.*'*

The history of the Chapter provides a sorry example of the impossibility of serving God and Mammon. The number of canons, originally twelve, steadily increased and by the end of the twelfth century had reached eighty-four, which it remained until the Revolution. The canonries were well endowed and much sought after. In the thirteenth century it was found necessary to forbid the appointment of boys under the age of twelve, but the practice continued. Such juveniles were known as '*chanoines mineurs* and sat with the choirboys in the Cathedral. They could not exercise the privileges of their position until they had attained their majority.

In spite of their comfortable incomes, Melleville informs us, the canons had to be paid extra to fulfil the principal function of their position – the saying of the offices in the choir. Two pieces of silver were received for attendance at Mattins, one for staying on for Mass and a further one for Vespers. In 1232 it was agreed that there should be an issue of forty "jallois" of cheese for these who kept up their worship in Lent. A jallois was normally a measure of corn which varied between fifty and sixty litres.

In 1266 Guillaume de Troyes, Bishop of Laon, complained to his Provincial, the Archbishop of Reims, of the laxity of his canons. This produced a new *Réglement*. The canons were forbidden to sing the Offices '*avec précipitation*'; to talk or '*babiller à haute voix*' in the Cathedral; to go from stall to stall during the course of divine worship; to talk to anyone '*du sexe suspect*'; to carry arms – or bouquets of flowers; to sell merchandise in the Cathedral, to hear causes pleaded or to accept bribes.

As it was only six years since they had last been forbidden to behave in these and similar ways, we can only conclude that such actions were normal. In 1260 Jean de Courtenai, Archbishop of Reims, launched an attack of the Chapter in the solemn language of an anathema: 'Ecclesiam, quae domus orationis esse debet, locum negotiationis fieri prohibemus'. 'The Church, which ought to be the House of Prayer, we forbid you make a place of negotiations'. The

* 'O Vanity! and even more madness than vanity! the Church is resplendent and the poor are hungry. The walls of the church are clothed in gold but her sons are naked.'

constant reiteration of statutes to ensure the decorous behaviour of the canons in medieval cathedrals only illustrates how indecorous that behaviour usually was.

Hostilities between Chapter and Bishop were endless. In the twelfth century Bishop Barthélemy had resigned in despair as the result of them; in the early thirteenth century Bishop Roger de Châtillon attempted to assert his authority. The Chapter retaliated by saying all the Offices in an inaudible voice.

There was a strange custom appertaining to the enthronement of a Bishop of Laon. By tradition he spent the night before at the Abbaye de St Vincent. Having entered the city by the Porte Martée, he went to the Church of St Michel where his shoes and stockings were removed by the Vidame. He then processed barefoot beneath a little canopy to the Church of St Martin by the Cathedral, where his footwear was restored to him. Before the west doors of the Cathedral the whole Chapter was arrayed to meet him. The Abbot of St Vincent introduced him to them with the words: *'Messieurs, je vous présente votre évêque vivant; vous me le rendrez mort.'** This was in pursuance of the right of the Abbey to provide the burial ground for the bishops.

Whenever the Bishop celebrated at a major festival, he had to present each of his officiants with an eighteen-denier piece enclosed, for some reason, in a ball of green wax known as a *'boulette'*. On the first day of Advent he sang the Magnificat at Vespers and by tradition presented three *muids* of wine to the Chapter. A *muid laonnois* was about 250 litres. As the Dean, the Treasurer, the Archdeacons and the Master of the Hôtel Dieu did the same on the following days, the Advent Fast was liable to become a time of heavy drinking for the Canons.

The Magnificat was also the cue to one of the more picturesque rituals of the time. The great day for the choir boys was the Feast of St Nicholas. On the eve of this festival they appointed one of their number to be the Boy Bishop – *'l'Evêque des Innocents'*. On the day itself, when they came to the words in the Magnificat 'deposuit potentes de sede, et exaltivit humiles', the boys drove the dignitaries from their seats and they then proceeded to occupy them themselves for the rest of the festival, served by the dignitaries. After the service they broke out into the town, dancing, singing and doing whatever occurred to them to entertain the people. In the evening they were regaled by the Chapter with eight pots of wine. This custom lasted until the sixteenth century.

Even more riotous was the *Fête des Fous*, held on the eve of the *Fête*

* 'Gentlemen, I present your bishop to you alive. You will return him to me dead.'

des Rois or Epiphany. On this occasion the Chapter elected a
'*Patriarch des Fous*'; they all dressed up, performed '*les farces les plus
indécents*' in the Cathedral and then processed round the town. The
custom appears to have been derived from the Roman *saturnalia*
when the social order was reversed for one day and the underling put
in control. The *Fête des Fous* continued to be celebrated until 1560
when it was abolished, but right into the eighteenth century the
custom continued on this day of distributing a crown of green leaves
to the congregation. It started as a piece of genial good humour,
probably based on sound psychology, in which the Church could
safely indulge because it was secure in the strength of its spirituality.
It ended as a piece of pointless bad behaviour which was dangerous
to a Church which was in spiritual decline. *The Fête des Fous* was in
most places abolished by the sixteenth century.

The great age of the Cathedrals' Crusade had left Laon with a
magnificent Cathedral which was in every way a fitting monument to
the intellectual and spiritual vitality of the era. The following century
merely obscured the strong outlines of the façade by filling in between the buttresses with a series of chapels. These were probably the
foundations of wealthy bourgeois anxious to purchase their own
salvation by the endowment of Masses for their souls. Private privilege dictated the architecture of the late thirteenth and early fourteenth centuries, rather than popular piety. It was an unworthy
theme and it received an undistinguished expression. The chapels do
not merit our attention.

The Renaissance, however, another period of intellectual and
spiritual vigour, endowed the Cathedral with its last important
additions – the delightful sequence of open screens which enclose the
offending chapels of the fourteenth century. The dates inscribed
upon them range only from 1572 to 1575. It looks like a comprehensive and deliberate plan to mask a series of piecemeal alterations. It is entirely successful. The pierced arcading and openwork
ornament above the colonnade to either side of each door, is of an
extraordinarily delicate workmanship, which provides a delightful
contrast with the austere simplicity of the twelfth-century Gothic.
There are many traces of gilding and polychroming still to be seen in
the narrow fluting and deeply chiselled recesses of these screens, from
which one may infer that they provided a colourful, not to say garish,
enrichment to the Cathedral.

It is one of the great differences of taste in Mankind: the love of
bright, primary colours in bold and striking apposition to each other,
and the love of quiet subtle tones, against which the occasional dash
of brilliant colour is effective. Aldous Huxley, in his interesting little
study entitled *Heaven and Hell*, has tried to analyse this love of pure,

bright, primary colours. 'For the Greeks and the men of the Middle Ages, this art of the merry-go-round and the waxwork show was evidently transporting. To us it seems deplorable. We prefer our Praxitiles plain, our marble and our limestone *au naturel*. Why should our modern taste be so different, in this respect, from that of our ancestors? The reason, I presume, is that we have become too familiar with bright and pure pigments to be greatly moved by them. We admire them, of course, when we see them in some grand and subtle composition; but in themselves and as such, they leave us untransported.'

If today we enjoy the naked beauty of the stone, if we like to see revealed the white bones of its medieval skeleton, if we admire Laon for its calm, uncluttered elegance and for its quiet, intellectual proportions, we must remember that we are seeing it through the eyes of an age of sophistication. We have made a distinction between the 'fine' arts and the popular art of the merry-go-round. The mind of the twelfth century made no such distinction. Scholar and peasant alike were satisfied by the structural coherence and gaudy fineries of Laon Cathedral.

CHAPTER SIX

Notre-Dame de Paris

Laon had been the capital of the Carolingian kings. With the election, in 987, of Hughes Capet a new dynasty was founded and with it came a new dynastic centre – the old Lutetia, a name which had given place somewhat uncertainly to that of Paris.

It is not possible to form any picture of what Paris looked like at the beginning of the twelfth century, but during the reign of Philippe-Auguste a considerable expansion took place and by the end of the century many of the familiar landmarks could already be seen that were to figure in the earliest portraits of Paris – the miniatures of Pol de Limbourg and Jean Fouquet and of the illuminator of Froissart's Chronicle. They show a city completely contained within its curtain wall. The transition from town to countryside was immediate; the grey walls rose from the green meadows; only a few paces separated the narrow jostling streets from scenes of rural beauty still dimly enshrined in such names as St Germain-des-Prés, St Martin-aux-Champs and St Symphorien-les-Vignes. The proximity of Notre-Dame to the countryside is something that needs to be remembered when we consider its decoration.

The ramparts of Philippe-Auguste enclosed an area of little more than six hundred acres on the north bank; it was set about with thirty towers, placed at intervals of about sixty metres, and its entrances were guarded by six gatehouses. Above this long, embattled wall the skyline was spiked and pinnacled with the high pavilion roofs and pointed poivrières of the royal and military establishments and with the spires and belfries of some fifty churches. Pre-eminent among them was the tall, lean tower of the Templars. The statelier buildings were roofed in fine blue slates while the humbler dwellings contented themselves with the russet-brown tiles made outside the city wall in the tile yard or Tuileries.

One of Philippe-Auguste's motives, according to Guillaume le Breton, was to encourage building – 'that the whole city may be seen to be full of houses right up to the walls' – and he set his fortifications wide for that purpose. The original settlement, the Ile de la Cité, had expanded along both banks of the Seine, the *Arts et Métiers* to the north and the student population to the south. The King's Palace occupied the western extremity of the island. It remained the official residence of the Monarchy until the sixteenth century.

The Ile de la Cité was connected with the north bank by the Grand Pont or Pont au Change, beneath whose arches water mills had been accommodated where the city's corn was ground. In line with this, the Pont St Michel spanned the narrower arm of the river to the south bank. A little to the east of these were two more bridges, the Pont Notre-Dame and the Petit Pont. It was by means of the latter that one gained access to the quarter reserved for students, the *Quartier Latin*. The Montagne Sainte-Geneviève – hitherto the vineyard of Paris – was progressively overrun by their establishments which were so numerous that Rigord describes Paris under Philippe-Auguste as 'civitas philosophorum'.

In the early twelfth century Guillaume de Champeaux was the 'gloire rayonnate' of the school of Paris, but soon his pupil Abelard took over the lead and, to escape from the discipline of the Chancellor of the Cathedral, took his school across the Seine to the Mont Sainte-Geneviève, which in due course became the University. Thomas à Becket, Edmond of Abingdon and John of Salisbury – later to be Bishop of Chartres – all completed their studies here. When John of Salisbury was forced to leave England in 1163 he was delighted with Paris and exclaimed 'happy the exile to whom such a place is offered' – *felix exilium cui locus iste datur*. But among so many names distinguished for their piety and erudition there was one of particular importance to the future of Notre-Dame; Maurice de Sully.

Born the son of a peasant, he was sent by his mother, Humberge, to Paris to study. The Church in those days offered unlimited opportunity for advancement to men of humble birth and natural ability. Maurice may have lived by begging or as the servant of one of the richer students. It is not know at which school he studied, but his great attachment in later years to the Abbaye de St Victor may suggest the gratitude of a former pupil to his *alma mater*.

All that is known is that he was so successful that in 1159 he became a Canon of Notre-Dame and later in the same year Archdeacon of Josas. A year later, on 12 October 1160, Maurice de Sully was consecrated Bishop of Paris. Although a suffragan to the Archbishop of Sens, the Bishop of Paris was one of the richest and most influential people in the country. Maurice de Sully was to hold this position, and to hold it with great distinction, for thirty-six years.

He brought to the job that combination of scholar and administrator which so often forms the qualification for the episcopate. As his obituary claims, 'he greatly multiplied the revenues of his See'. But he appears to have been a man of little personal ambition and much personal humility. A large proportion of his wealth was consecrated to the rebuilding of his Cathedral. As the Chronicler of Anchin states: 'he erected this monument less by relying on the liberality of others than on the revenues of his own stipend'. In fairness to the others, it should be noted that Eudes de Châteauroux claimed that 'the Cathedral of Paris was built largely on widows' mites'. This was, however, no discredit to Maurice. 'His light shines before men,' continues his Chronicler, 'by his knowledge, by his preaching, by the liberality of his almsgiving and by the ubiquity of his good works. His presence in the Cathedral is frequent, or rather continual. I have seen him on a feast day, which was not a solemn one, at the hour of vespers. He was not seated in majesty upon his episcopal throne, but down in the choir, intoning the Psalms with a hundred of his Clergy.'

He early determined on the rebuilding of his Cathedral on far more grandiose lines and in the new style evolved at Saint-Denis, Senlis and Sens. To start with he had to clear the site. It was not unusual for churches which were designated as the cathedral or seat of a bishop to be built in threes – one in honour of the Virgin, one of St Stephen and one, which was the Baptistry, of St John. So, on the site of Notre-Dame there had previously stood an earlier Notre-Dame, the Church of St Etienne and that of St Jean-le-Rond. This latter was already in ruinous condition and was pulled down together with a number of canons' houses.

The first stone of the new Cathedral was laid in 1163, possibly by Pope Alexander III who was in Paris during the spring of that year. By 1177 the choir and apse were sufficiently advanced for the chronicler Robert de Torrigni to record his astonishment and admiration. 'The east end is already finished, except for the high roof. When this work is complete there will be no building this side of the Alps which will bear comparison with it.'

Robert de Torrigni speaks for the majority of his contemporaries. One voice was raised against the whole policy of cathedral building. It came from the Precentor of Notre-Dame, Pierre le Chantre, whose *Somme Ecclésiastique* was published in 1180. In it he attacks the great builders of the age. 'It is a sin to construct churches as is at present the custom. The sanctuaries of our churches ought to be in a humbler style than the main body, and this because of the mystical idea which they symbolise; for the same Christ who is the head of humanity, the "sanctuary" of the Church, is more humble than that humanity. Today, on the contrary, the sanctuaries of our churches become higher and higher.' Moreover, this epidemic of building was sometimes achieved by dishonest means. 'Cathedrals are constructed today with the usury of avarice and the ruse of untruthfulness.'

Maurice de Sully must have been aware of the protest of his Precentor, but it did not deflect him from his course.

He was one of those people who can visualise on a grand scale. His new Cathedral was to be five times larger than its forerunner and worthy of a city infinitely greater than Paris before the days of Philippe-Auguste. He was also a man capable of moving with the times and of adapting to circumstances. Every advance in technique and in style was quickly incorporated into the building of Notre-Dame. That the building was conceived as a whole is beyond doubt. The existence of a single, comprehensive master-plan can be inferred from the fact that the carvings for the west front were begun at the same time as the first buildings of the choir. This was, in fact, the normal practice. It can be seen in some of the decorative details. For instance, in the tympanum of the Porte Sainte-Anne not only is Maurice de Sully himself represented, but the capitals and bases of the colonnettes which uphold the canopy over the Virgin and her mother are identical with those in the tribunes of the choir.

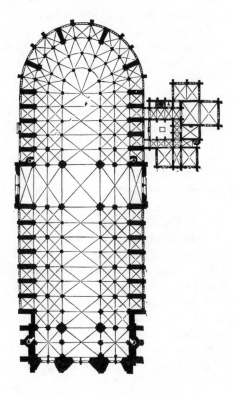

Ground Plan of Notre-Dame de Paris

Basically the plan of Maurice de Sully's Cathedral was extremely simple: a choir of two double bays and a nave of four, ending in a deep narthex beneath the towers of the west front; the whole surrounded by double aisles except at the crossing, where two shallow transepts interrupted the sequence without projecting beyond the outer wall. The choir ended in an apse and the aisles curled round into a double ambulatory with no radiating chapels. This was an original conception.

The idea of the ambulatory had first been conceived, so far as is known, in the charming little Romanesque church of Morienval on the edge of the Forêt de Compiègne. Here it is so narrow as to be useless liturgically and is thought to have been built to provide abutment to the apse, which was slipping. But a single ambulatory will only support a relatively low building. Maurice de Sully was dreaming of a vault 108 feet off the ground – thirty feet higher than that of Laon. Such an apse would require two tiers of abutment, and this is what the double ambulatory provided.

A section of the choir at once reveals the system. The inner ambulatory is built in two storeys – the upper storey being the tribune, a solid vaulted corridor running right round the building immediately above the great arcade. This gives abutment to the spring of the vaulting arch and itself receives abutment from the outer ambulatory. With the two sloping roofs of the tribune and outer ambulatory, the profile of our section resembles the outline of a gigantic buttress.

But it must be remembered that the medieval builder was preoccupied above all with the interior of the church. In many cases the exterior was obscured by other buildings which crowded round it. The west front and the lateral entrances were given special treatment, but Ruskin was right when he said 'the outside of a French Cathedral, except for its sculpture, is always to be thought of as the wrong side of the stuff, in which you find how the threads go that produce the inside, or right side, pattern'.

If we now translate this system into terms of internal architecture we find that it produces a four-storey façade. The great arcade is surmounted by the tribune and above the tribune is a space beneath the clerestory windows. This space is the upright side of a right-angled triangle of which the tribune roof is the hypotenuse. The steeper this roof, the taller this space becomes. At Noyon and Laon this space is occupied by the triforium, a colonnade masking a passageway for the convenience of workmen. At Notre-Dame there was no triforium but a series of roundels which opened into the roof tent of the tribunes.

Perhaps the most penetrating appreciation of Notre-Dame comes from Jean Bony in his brief but precious *'essai sur la spiritualité de deux Cathédrales: Notre-Dame de Paris et St Etienne de Bourges'*.

First he draws our attention to the 'cellular' aspect of the structure. 'The building is only able to gain height in so far as it is boxed in between two cages of small vaulted cells, square in plan, stacked in two tiers along the nave.' This produces two contrasting units of space – *'un vide total et audacieux au centre; un vide cloisonné et sans danger sur les côtés'*.*

Next he analyses the impact of this design. On entering the building by the *portail de la Vierge*, the visitor is immediately faced by a double perspective of the twin aisles north of the nave; *'deux longues fuites qui se perdent dans le pénombre'*.† To the right the great emptiness of the nave and beyond, the repetition of the two side aisles. 'It is an impression of immensity in depth and of multiplicity which is almost infinite.' These long perspectives all converge upon the sanctuary – for it is not in the vaults or above the vaults that God is to be found, but close to the ground, level with man, on the altar. *'Tout l'édifice est organisé et conçu en fonction de cette présence.'*

But this multiplicity of perspectives is broken between the nave and the choir by the shallow breach of the transepts. *'C'est le coup de génie de Notre-Dame de Paris'*. Without it the building would be too enclosed, too difficult to comprehend. By intersecting thus his long perspectives, the architect enables us to see the whole design in section. The transepts give us the full vision of ordered grandeur, after which the movement of the masses is continued until they arch in upon each other in the great hemicycle behind the altar.

It was a noble inspiration but in detail it is open to criticisms. The clerestory windows were small and the proportions of the façade top-heavy. Out of a total height of 108 feet the great arcade accounted for only thirty. Inevitably the building was badly lit. Denise Jalabert has pleaded the cause of badly lit churches: *'il faut reconnaître que cette demiobscurité nous touche profondément, et ceux qui viennent penser et prier à Notre-Dame trouvent un demi-jour favorable au receuillement'*.‡

Such, however, was not the attitude of the thirteenth century, for in about 1220 it was decided to suppress the roundels and extend the clerestory windows downwards, thereby increasing considerably the area available to the glaziers but reducing the interior façade to three storeys, thus making it more top-heavy.

* 'a bold and empty space in the middle; a space that is safely partitioned on either side.'
† 'two long receding flights which lose themselves in the half-light.'
‡ 'I have to admit that I find this half darkness deeply moving, and those who come to meditate and pray at Notre-Dame find a half light favourable to recollectedness.'

There was clearly a break in the continuity of construction between the building of the choir, which was complete and consecrated in 1182, and the subsequent construction of the nave. Numerous stylistic differences bear witness to this, but perhaps the most obvious is in the treatment of the grouped colonnettes against the outer walls which receive the thrust of the aisle vaults. In the choir these stand out in full relief, their bases set at the appropriate angles to receive the vault ribs; in the nave they are recessed into grooves, as if the architect had wanted them out of the way.

But between the two campaigns of construction a new and important technical device had been added to the repertoire of the Gothic architect – the flying buttress. It was at the church of St Remi de Reims, begun in 1170, that the flying buttress made its first known appearance as a visible feature constructed above the roof of the tribune. Shortly after its construction, the apse began to show signs of instability. It had to be shored up and piles of masonry were raised round the ambulatory which reached across by means of quarter arches to prop up the faltering fabric. The effect is not exactly beautiful, but looks like the makeshift solution to an urgent problem. The application of the same system, possibly by the same team of workmen, to Notre-Dame-en-Vaux at Chalons was presumably later, for here the flying buttress has already been turned into an ornamental feature. Gothic architects were skilful in making a virtue of necessity.

It was the architect who built the nave of Notre-Dame who seems to have been the first to think of incorporating flying buttresses into his original design. They had not been used for the choir and apse, but when he came to the nave, built between 1180 and 1200, they were intended from the outset. We can still see from the one remaining double flying buttress on the north side of the choir nearest the transept what these earliest attempts looked like – for all the rest were replaced in the fourteenth century by the single, slender arches which now span the whole distance in a single, graceful flight.

As the last cathedral to use the tribune formula, Notre-Dame stood at the end of a tradition. In one important respect it stood at the beginning of a new development. The vaults of Sens and Laon were supported on arches of unequal height, the diagonal ribs rising well above the boundary arches. The result was a canopy of roof which was more than slightly domed. Such a vault exercised a considerable thrust upon the lateral wall, which needed in consequence to be sturdy – its masonry thick and its windows small.

It was, however, the special virtue of the pointed arch that it enabled the builder to elevate the boundary arches to the same

70

height as the keystone of the vault, but in the earliest essays this possibility had not been fully realised. It was the builder of the nave of Notre-Dame who first took this important step.

The effect of constructing a vault with a more or less horizontal section is that the thrust is taken off the lateral wall and transferred to the piers that support the vault ribs. This enabled the wall to be reduced in strength and the windows to be increased in size. At the same time it necessitated the flying buttress to receive the increased thrust at the spring of the arch. This made possible the elimination of tribunes, which had hitherto provided the abutment, and the consequent reduction of the façade to three storeys. The fully developed system appeared for the first time at Chartres and, in a very different form, at Bourges.

There is one other feature of Notre-Dame that is of interest in the development of the style. It is sometimes suggested that there was a certain 'honesty' inherent in Gothic architecture, as if the builder had felt a *moral* obligation to make visually apparent that which was structurally true. If this was the rule, Notre-Dame provides a significant exception. The main arcade presents a regular procession of cylindrical columns of equal girth which retains no trace of the alternation *pile forte – pile faible* which is the logical expression at ground level of sexpartite vaulting.

The same equality in the drums of the piers had been achieved at Laon, but here the alternance is stated immediately above the capitals – the *pile forte* carrying five colonnettes and the *pile faible* three. This makes visually apparent that which is structurally true. The five colonnettes represent the five vaulting shafts – one cross rib, two transverse ribs and two wall ribs. The *pile faible* only carries one cross rib and two wall ribs.

At Notre-Dame, however, this further evidence of sexpartite vaulting has been suppressed and the *pile forte*, like the *pile faible*, made to support only three colonnettes. This is achieved by making the wall ribs discharge their thrust on to the topmost capitals right up at the spring of the vaulting arch. It is only at this level, when the vault can already be seen to be sexpartite, that the device is apparent. Undoubtedly 'structural truth' has been sacrificed to an uninterrupted uniformity. Only in the nave aisles is the alternance *pile forte – pile faible* retained, with the *pile forte* represented by a column ringed round by colonettes. These columns support the flying buttresses above.

The developments and modifications made in the course of construction in no way obscured the master plan, which, as we have seen, included a fully thought out scheme for the west front. This was unfortunately the part of the Cathedral to suffer most from the

Notre-Dame: Original System of Buttressing

vandalism of the eighteenth century, both before and during the Revolution.

The original scheme of Maurice de Sully, however, is perfectly clear. Viollet-le-Duc, in his great work of restoration in the mid-nineteenth century, was able to re-establish the original iconography. It was, for instance, possible to infer the identity of each of the statues from the little figures crouched at their feet. These little figures had escaped the fury of the *sans culottes*. Balaam, somewhat obviously, surmounted an ass, while the Queen of Sheba had a negro under her feet clasping a casket containing costly presents from Ophir.

The plan for the three west porches followed the tradition of placing the Last Judgment in the middle and flanked this with a *Portail de la Vierge* on the left or northern side and a *Portail Sainte Anne* on the right or south.

The iconography of the Cathedral, here as elsewhere, was clearly executed by artists working to the precise brief furnished by a theologian. Only in the floral sculpture were they allowed a free hand. In availing themselves of this liberty they revealed their own genius. Left to their own devices, as Emile Mâle so charmingly puts it, *'ils regardaient le monde avec des yeux émerveillés d'enfant'*. Later in the same passage he considers the accurate observation which informed their art. 'They gathered buds and leaves which were just unfolding and looked at them with that tender, passionate curiosity which we feel in our first childhood and which the real artist retains throughout his life.' There is a vitality and energy about the spring which matched the audacity and creativeness of the Gothic style – the whole weight of a vault upheld by a single budding water lily. 'The capitals of Notre-Dame, especially the earliest, are made of these Spring plants, swollen with their rising sap, which strive in their upward movement to raise the abacus and the vault above.'

Viollet-le-Duc has pointed out that the development of the Gothic reflected the seasons of the year in its representation of plant life. So in its first appearance of Sens and Laon and Notre-Dame, the buds are just opening, the fronds beginning to unfurl; it is the springtime of the style. By the beginning of the thirteenth century the shoots have opened out but not yet lost their prime; by its end they are in full flower – branches of leaves, sprays of roses, tangles of vine. The artists of Notre-Dame were unambitious in their choice; they looked no further than the fields and forests of the Ile de France. Plantain, celandine and ladies-smock could all be observed within an easy walk of Notre-Dame. They may be seen in the capitals of the great arcade, the tribunes and in the decoration of the porches.

When Maurice de Sully died in 1196 he had had the rare satisfaction of seeing his Cathedral for the most part erected. Only the west front and a few bays of the nave remained to be completed. In 1182 he had seen his choir consecrated and the regular round of divine worship, which was the *raison d'être* of a cathedral, had been established.

The worship of Notre-Dame was enriched by a musical tradition which had at the time no rival in Europe. Both in the development of its music and in the excellence of its performance, Notre-Dame led the Catholic world. The choir, known as *la maîtrise*, consisted only of twelve boys and six men, known as *machicors*. The expenses of the boys were paid from one of the prebends which was kept vacant for the purpose and known as *'la prébende morte'*.

The boys were formed into a choir school under a *Maître de Chapelle* who was responsible for their training in music and general deportment. Discipline was strict. Its object was explicit since the *règlement* of Jean Gerson in 1408: the boys were to behave in such a wise that people would say of them *'ainsi sont les anges de Dieu'*. No less could be accepted of those whose duty and privilege it was to sing before the Virgin *'dans son église la plus célèbre du monde'*. Misdemeanours in church were naturally regarded as the most heinous and were apparently expiated on the spot. It was decreed that the Magister Puerorum should 'carry rods in the church and during processions in order that the transgressions of the boys might be punished immediately'. Major offences were liable to incur not only beating but imprisonment.

In pursuance of this angelic image the boys were insulated from all contamination by the world. Parents were only allowed to visit once a month and no one else allowed to enter the premises except those who came to teach the various musical instruments. The boys' mothers were the only women that they ever saw. Thursday afternoon was their only holiday, but even then their liberty was confined to the *Terrain*, an open space within the Cloître at the eastern extremity of the island, or to rare excursions under the close supervision of the Master who had orders to talk to them only *'de choses utiles et de discours édifiants'*. The Master was assisted in his duties by the senior choirboy, known as the Spé, who had the status of a prefect and enjoyed considerable privileges. His badge of office was a golden rod and he was always dressed in black.

The uniform of the others was laid down by statute in 1349. Each boy was to be provided with 'a new robe of red cloth, with a little cape of red cloth over the shoulders; a jacket of blue serge, together with an old robe and jacket to preserve the new one and to change into; a black cloak with a cape to wear in church and a square "bonnet" for use by day and another white one for use at night.' This was because

74

the boys received the tonsure and was to protect them from colds. Twelve boys would be regarded as a minimum in any English cathedral today, and great care was taken of their health lest they should be obliged to miss any of the services.

They were worth the care, for the music which they sang set the standard for the whole of Western Europe. The high period of the Notre-Dame School coincided with that of the Cathedrals' Crusade – the second half of the twelfth century and the first half of the thirteenth. 'Under the two great *maîtres de chapelle*, Léonin and Prévotin,' writes Wilfred Mellers, 'they evolved an elaborate form of polyphony which is the musical counterpart to the greatest achievements of Gothic architecture and scholastic philosophy.' This polyphony was kown as *organum* and was used at festivals to replace the solo portions of the every-day plainsong. 'The composers,' continues Mellers, 'had become fascinated by the possibilities of combining elaborate and subtle countermelodies with the plainsong bass . . . Like plainsong it suggests a dissolution of the senses, a mystical contemplation of the divine.'

Our English word 'tenor', Dom Anselme Hughes reminds us, stems from the *organum*, 'where the notes of the lowest part were *held* (in Latin *tenere*) while the other part or parts moved forwards. If there was a third part it was called the *triplum* from which the English "treble" is derived.' A contemporary account by Giraldus Cambrensis describes the simple form of *organum* as 'a harmony in their singing, but in only two different parts, one murmuring below, the other soothing and charming above.' In its more elaborate form, under Prévotin, it often multiplied to four parts, providing, as Mellers says, 'a mature and indeed sophisticated convention which exactly complements the combination, in the Gothic Cathedral, of soaring, heaven-seeking movement with a mathematical logic that alone keeps the building from falling to pieces.' Unfortunately the music of this era cannot be performed with confidence today. Mellers thinks that the voice production of the time 'would probably make the music sound, to our ears, more Asiatic than Western'.

The Choir School was all part of a large complex of buildings and institutions which centred on the Cathedral. It has been christened by Henri Leclercq *'la Cité Cléricale'* but it was more usually known as Le Cloître – though it had no cloister in the architectural sense of the term. The area lay to the north and east of the Cathedral and contained some forty lodgings for the Canons – or *Messieurs de Notre-Dame*, as they were called. To the south was the Bishop's palace – distinguished in early portraits of Paris by one extremely high tower. Here was another 'Cloister' where the scholars of the Chancellor's School were lodged. Louis VII, du Breuil records, 'prided himself on having passed his childhood in this Cloister, as in a mother's womb'. The concept of a school as an *alma mater* was already current.

To the south and west were the Hôtel Dieu and a Foundlings Hospital known as *Les Enfants Trouvés*. Both were maintained at the expense of the *Messieurs de Notre-Dame*. There was a certain delicacy to be observed with 'foundlings' and the Commissaire was not expected to go himself to collect the child 'fearing derision and suspicion that the child was of his own gettting'; to avoid such embarrassment the *Dame des Enfants Trouvés* went on his behalf.

The whole area governed by the Cathedral enjoyed considerable privileges – not the least of which being immunity from the King's Justice. The officers of the Châtelet were not permitted to enter the Cloître. Nevertheless the portal of Notre-Dame was used as a place of judgment and of punishment. Major criminals, dressed only in a shirt, were brought to a scaffold erected on the *parvis*, where they knelt, holding a candle that weighed two pounds, before being taken to the Place de Grève for execution. This practice was known as the *Amende Honorable*.

Lesser offenders were punished on the spot. Du Breuil records how, in 1344, a certain Henri de Malestroit, convicted of *lèse majesté*, was processed round the streets in a tumbril with a chain round his neck and finally placed on top of a ladder before the west front of the Cathedral *'où il fut longtemps mocqué et injurié du peuple'*. Du Breuil himself could remember a priest being thus pilloried 'propter fornicationem'. In the bass reliefs to the left of the Porte St Etienne one of the panels depicts a woman thus exposed to popular ridicule.

Owing to the relative privacy of the Cloître, it was the west front of Notre-Dame with which the Parisians were most familiar; this was the face which the Cathedral presented towards its city. Appropriately, it is one of the most important achievements of the Gothic age. Started in 1200 and only completed fifty years later, it has retained an astonishing unity of style which argues an original master plan faithfully followed by a later generation. The west front of Notre-Dame stands, historically, between those of Laon and of Amiens and it differs from both in its simplicity and repose. In spite of a rich decoration, the architect has allowed us to enjoy a considerable amount of plain, smooth stonework – and this leads to one of the subtle attractions of the façade. The courses of masonry are clearly visible, and as they are all of the same depth, they give the scale of the whole building. It would be possible to judge the height of a man at the top of the façade by counting the courses of masonry that made up his height.

The façade without the towers is an approximate square with a side of some forty-two metres. The diagonals intersect at the base of the rose window – that is to say at the feet of the figure of Our Lady who occupies thus the place of honour on the west front.

The repose of the composition depends to a certain extent upon the upward progression from massive masonry to the airy fretwork of the topmost arcade. The ground floor, carved into cavernous recesses in its three portals, has a ponderous solidity. Above this the façade is alleviated by the lighter treatment of its larger openings and especially by the delicate tracery of the lovely rose window. The third storey is more airy still; it consists of a balustrade in the form of a tall and slender colonnade which masks the lower part of the towers and the gable of the nave roof.

Since the Cathedral has been restored by André Malraux to its pristine whiteness it can be seen today very much as it was first built, but with one significant exception: the gilding and polychromy of the statues. In 1489 the Armenian Bishop Martyr of Arzenjân wrote an all too brief description of Notre-Dame. He describes the figure of Christ in the Judgment Porch as 'placed upon a throne of gold and all adorned with ornaments of gold leaf'. Beneath him were Prophets, Patriarchs and Saints 'all painted in different colours and enriched with gold'. It was this that impressed him most about the whole Cathedral – *'cette composition représente le paradis qui enchante le regard des hommes'*. It has been well said that the west front of a medieval cathedral had some of the brilliance of an illuminated manuscript.

The *Galerie des Rois*, which forms at Notre-Dame a complete horizontal break in the façade between the portal and the first-storey windows, is a new feature. It is repeated at Reims and again at Amiens. Learned opinion has differed as to the identity of these Kings.

In the nineteenth century, the theory was evolved that these were the Kings of Judah. Emil Mâle, the greatest authority on the symbolism of medieval sculpture, insists that these 'Kings' are, in fact, a Tree of Jesse. At Notre-Dame they number twenty-eight – a figure which corresponds with the twenty-eight names from Jesse to Joseph listed by St Matthew. At Reims there are fifty-six, which can be made to correspond with the names in St Luke from Abraham to Jesus Christ inclusive. This is an unconvincing argument; since Luke's genealogy goes back to Adam, it is somewhat arbitrary to start counting from Abraham. A Lucan Tree of Jesse would yield forty-three figures. But in any case the mind of the Middle Ages did not feel tied to any statistical accuracy on such matters. At Amiens the Kings number twenty-two.

Against this theory Georges Durand, in his great work on Amiens Cathedral, urges the legitimacy of the age-long tradition that they are Kings of France. The earliest evidence of the tradition comes from an unexpected source. A manuscript of 1284 entitled 'Twenty-Three Tricks of Villains' tells how cut-purses would point out the statues to unsuspecting visitors: 'Ves là Pépin; ves là Charlemagne' – and while their attention was thus engaged, relieved them of their money.

The argument was brought to an abrupt conclusion in April 1977, when the mutilated fragments were discovered in the course of excavations. The last figure was that of the Virgin Mary: the *Galerie des Rois* was a Tree of Jesse.

The tradition that they were Kings of France, however, was so securely established that the statues had to suffer accordingly. First they lost their crowns. On 10 September 1793, an *entrepreneur de bâtiments* named Bazin was detailed by the Revolutionary Committee of the *Section de la Cité* to remove all 'epitaphs, coats of arms and other marks of feudalism'. He erected a scaffolding before the west front, where his purpose was, quite simply, '*de supprimer les couronnes*'. This was done and the heads sufficiently repaired with plaster to receive, in place of the crowns, '*le bonnet de la Liberté*'.

Later in the same year another builder named Varin was charged with the removal of the statues from '*la Galerie cy-devant ditte des Rois*'. Twenty-eight figures 'of a very hard stone', each some ten or eleven feet high, had to be removed. They first had any projections knocked off 'to facilitate their passage behind the colonnade', and were then hurled down on to the *parvis*. It was a somewhat stupid procedure, for it took twelve men a day's work to repair the damage thus done to the *parvis*. At some point the statues were deliberately decapitated. The phrase '*tranchée des têtes*' occurs over and over again in the accounts. What the guillotine was achieving in the Place de la Révolution, Bazin and Varin were echoing on the façades of Notre-Dame.

Above the *Galerie des Rois* is the great Rose Window. It is one of the most satisfactory ever built, for it manages to combine a maximum of strength with a minimum of masonry. The proportion of open space to stonework is $1: 1.146$. It is the highest ratio of glass to stone ever to be achieved.

If we compare the west rose of Notre-Dame with its closest contemporaries, the Collegiate church of Mantes-la-Jolie and those of Jean d'Orbais at Reims, it will be noticed that in the latter the tracery is made up of arches with their heads towards the centre. This design makes for a massive concentration of stone in the middle of the rose which is virtually only supported by the two mullions beneath it. At Notre-Dame the arches are turned with their heads away from the centre, producing a series of petal-shaped apertures. The weight is distributed more evenly over the whole area and the system of mutual, interlocking support is so good that this window has not suffered any deterioration of structure throughout the ages. Only a few stones that had been eroded by the weather had to be replaced by Viollet-le-Duc.

With the completion of the west front, the Cathedral first conceived by Maurice de Sully had been realised in all important respects, but in the second quarter of the thirteenth century certain profound modifications were made to this original structure. First came the enlargement of the clerestory windows and the consequent suppression of the roundels that had given light to the tribune roofs. We can still see, on the outside, the colonnettes that flanked the old clerestory windows and continue to mark their original height. Then came the replacement of the double flying buttresses with the single, airy arches which we see today.

During all this period, and right on into the fourteenth century, there was a steady proliferation of chapels, many of them contrived between the piers of the buttresses, which deprived the Cathedral of its original lateral façades. This filling out to the level of the buttress piers probably entailed the most important of all the later rebuildings – the north and south transepts. Maurice de Sully's transepts had been very shallow. Each formed a single, sexpartite bay to north and south of the crossing; their façades did not project beyond the outer walls of the nave and choir. Now that these walls had been carried out to the extremity of the buttress piers, the façades of the transepts were actually in retreat.

The new transept façades were begun, in the middle of the thirteenth century, by Jean de Chelles and completed after his death by Pierre de Montreuil. They brought to the Cathedral of Paris, which had played so important a part in the early development of the new technique, the finished Gothic style in its perfection. Pierre de Montreuil had already shown the way in his rebuilding of Saint-Denis, where the whole of the north transept is glazed and the enormous rose window made to form one continuous blaze of coloured light with the *claire-voie* beneath it.

The geometry of rose windows is the subject of a fascinating study by Painton Cowen. If we take the great rose of the north transept of Notre-Dame we will see that in the outer perimeter there are thirty-two trefoils. If we take the centre of one of these and draw a line from it to the centre of the eighth trefoil away, and continue this right round the clock, these lines will so intersect as to describe a circle which passes through the centres of the round medallions in the outer ring of petals. If we take the centres of these thirty-two medallions and repeat the process, but this time joining every eleventh point, we create two interlocking sixteen pointed stars. The intersections of their lines will be found again to describe a circle which passes through the centres of the medallions of the inner ring of petals. If we join the centre of each of these circles to the centre of the fourth roundel away, we draw four interlocking squares, the sides of which intersect at sixteen points. If these are joined so as to make a sixteen-pointed star, their intersections will describe a circle which is the central eye of the rose.

Beneath the rose windows the transepts were provided with portals almost as important as those of the west front. The south porch is dedicated to St Stephen, recalling the little church of St Etienne which had previously occupied the site. In the tympanum is a vigorous depiction of his martyrdom which was almost exactly copied in the south porch of Meaux. On the north transept two more

Rose Window, North Transept, Notre-Dame: geometrical scheme by Tad Mann
(from Painton Cowen's *Rose Windows*, Thames and Hudson, 1979)

portals were consecrated to the seemingly inexhaustible theme of Notre-Dame.

No one can ever understand the architecture of the twelfth and thirteenth centuries who does not appreciate the profound and passionate affection which was bestowed upon the Virgin Mary. One only has to read the sermons of St Bernard, the *De Laudibus beatae Mariae* of Albert le Grand or the *Speculum beatae Mariae* of St Bonaventure to feel the emotional intensity of this outpouring of a sublime and sublimated love. They none of them hesitated to apply to the Virgin the highly erotic imagery of the so-called Song of Solomon. Louis Battifol has pointed out in his *Histoire du Brévaire Romain* that this love-song was appointed in most thirteenth-century lectionaries for reading on the Feast of the Nativity of the Virgin. She was the Rose of Sharon and the Fleece of Gideon; she was Aaron's rod and Jacob's Ladder; she was the Rainbow and the Dawn that heralds the rising of the sun, the intermediary between darkness and light, between sin and salvation.

Every word connected with her was the subject of a devout and ceaseless meditation, so that St Bonaventure came to see in the simple 'Ave' a combination of the negative 'a' with the curse 'vae'. The triple malediction 'Vae! Vae! Vae!' of the Eagle of the Apocalypse was thus reversed by the triple recital of the *Ave Maria*. The Middle Ages were never very careful about their etymology.

Last but not least she was the Queen. She was Queen of Heaven and she was Queen of the Earth, where she frequently displayed her power by the working of miracles. Although these were innumerable, there was only one which found its way into the iconography of the medieval cathedral – the story of Theophilus.

Theophilus was the Dr Faustus of the age. He sold his soul to the Devil and witnessed the deed in a parchment signed in his blood. But he was overcome with remorse and implored the Virgin to compass his salvation. She accepted his repentance, forced the Devil to yield up the parchment and restored Theophilus to his sanctity. It was a popular subject for the Mystery Play, notably at this time one by Ruteboeuf, and the tympanum of the porch of the north transept, known as the *Porte du Cloître*, illustrates the main episodes. At the top of the composition a bishop is recounting the well-known, well-loved story to a group of delightfully attentive listeners.

In due course, the Virgin of the theologians became the Virgin of popular piety. The peasant who crossed himself on hearing the Angelus was innocent of any of the sophisticated symbolism of the Schoolmen; his devotion may have been none the less sincere for that. Instinctively, the artists of the epoch expressed this shift of emphasis. From representing the Virgin with all the lofty attributes of royalty in a stylised, archetypal figure, they moved towards an idealised femininity – the village maiden type of Madonna of the thirteenth century. As peasant women carried their babies on one hip, so the Virgin Mary was made to carry hers. It involved a lopsided stance known in French as *hanchement*, with all the weight on the left leg and the right knee slightly flexed. This offered endless opportunity for flowing drapery of which the medieval carver made the happiest use. The Virgin who stands between the twin doors of the *Porte du Cloître* is one of the most perfect examples. She has miraculously survived – the only full length statue of the whole ensemble.

When she was first set in her place against the impost the Cathedral of Paris had reached its high moment of Gothic glory. The Flamboyant and Renaissance styles did not leave their mark upon its fabric. The seventeenth and eighteenth centuries were to mutilate and disfigure the building as this statue was mutilated and disfigured by having her child dashed from her arms. Serene in the beauty of simplicity she has represented throughout the centuries the devotion of the Parisians and the dedication of their Cathedral to Notre-Dame.

CHAPTER SEVEN

Chartres (2)

In 1194 a terrible fire destroyed the greater part of the town of Chartres; Bishop Fulbert's Cathedral, with the exception of the new west front, was reduced to ashes. For two days it continued to burn and the inhabitants were in agonies about the fate of the precious relic, the Virgin Mary's chemise. On the third day the heat abated somewhat and there emerged from the crypt a procession of clergy who had been trapped in it throughout the conflagration. On their shoulders they carried the Reliquary.

An early inference that the destruction of her Palace argued a lack of protective care on the part of its Queen, was deftly turned by the Papal Legate into a conviction that her real desire was for a bigger and better Palace.* It was decided to rebuild.

It is sometimes objected now, as it was objected by St Bernard then, that the Church is more ready to spend in the service of architecture than in the service of mankind. But the decision to rebuild Chartres must not be seen narrowly as an unwarrantable extravagance on the part of a 'triumphalist' Church devoid of social conscience. The commercial well-being of the people of Chartres depended largely on the success of its four Fairs, which coincided with the feasts of the Purification, Assumption, Annunciation and Nativity of the Virgin. The customers at these Fairs were mostly pilgrims attracted by the sacred relic. Economy and religion, in fact, worked hand in glove; in medieval terms Chartres was not economically viable without its Cathedral. It was the Butchers, the Bakers, the Cobblers, the Drapers and Wine Merchants of the town, just as much as the Royal family and the dignitaries of the Church who paid for the reconstruction. Their contributions could be regarded as wise investment as well as pious gestures.

In return, the Church guaranteed the safety of the merchants and their wares. It went further and allowed some of the merchandise to be sold within the sacred edifice. This exempted the traders from the taxes levied by the Count; the cathedral in the twelfth and thirteenth centuries was the great adversary of the feudal system. Often this

---

* 'Beata Dei genetrix novam et incomparabilem ecclesiam sibi colens fabricari.'

trafficking in the nave led to such irreverence that action had to be taken. 'The many ordinances passed by the Chapter,' write Otto von Simson, 'to prevent the loud, lusty life of the market place from spilling over into the Sanctuary only show how inseparable the two worlds were in reality.'

Among the items to be purchased at these great Fairs, the relic loomed extremely large. Leaden figures of the Virgin, miniature representations of the chemise and full-scale copies to be worn by women in childbirth or, more improbably, by knights in armour, were bought by the thousand. For the protestant, the agnostic and the atheist, all this is hard to imagine. 'If you are to get the full enjoyment out of Chartres,' wrote Henry Adams, 'you must for the time believe in Mary, as Bernard did, and feel her presence as the architects did in every stone they placed and in every touch they chiselled.'

Besides being an economic necessity to the town, the Cathedral was of political importance to the King. The comte de Chartres, who, in the person of Thibault the Great, was count also of Blois and Champagne, was a dangerously powerful magnate and in alliance with England and Normandy. But the Bishopric of Chartres was in the gift of the King of France. This right of appointment gave the house of Capet an important means of infiltrating potentially hostile territory. The erection of a prestigious cathedral as it were under the nose of the Count was something upon which the King was prepared to spend lavishly.

Popular enthusiasm, also, broke out again, as in 1145, and teams of pilgrims harnessed themselves to the wagons that brought the stone from Berchères to Chartres. *Quêteurs* went with the relics round France and crossed over to England. A young English student, who had bought a golden chain for his fiancée, offered it instead to the Virgin Mary and was rewarded by a dream in which he saw her wearing his chain round her neck. It made no difference that England happened to be at war with France; priorities were different in those days. Richard I welcomed the *quêteurs* in person and insisted on carrying the reliquary on his own shoulders.

As the money kept coming in, the new Cathedral rose rapidly from its forest of scaffolding. The architect – to use the term in its modern sense – had been given a task which was at once daunting and exciting; daunting, because he had to use the foundations of Fulbert's Cathedral, with all the restrictions which that imposed, and exciting, because to meet the challenge he had at his disposal the full resources of the new technique.

Fulbert's choir had three radiating chapels of considerable length, each rounded off in a little apse. The new architect has brought his façade out so as to engulf these chapels, leaving only their apses forming three semi-circular projections to the perimeter. This gave him room for his two ambulatories, but it dictated that the dividing ring of columns should be unevenly spaced; the two bays on either side of the east chapel are noticeably smaller. The architect has made a virtue out of necessity and turned these bays also into little chapels, forming a slightly arched projection to the façade. Had a later architect not upset this symmetry by the insertion of the large Chapelle de St Piat, the whole ambulatory wall could be seen as one continuous, undulating screen of coloured glass.

The re-use of the old foundations imposed another important feature upon the new Cathedral. Since Fulbert's building had only a wooden ceiling it could afford to have a span of sixteen and a half metres to the nave. This would be the broadest area ever to be vaulted in stone. It would need to be proportionately higher and broke all records at thirty-seven metres.

The method of construction has recently been studied by John James, an Australian architect. He was driven by the extreme rarity of the documentation to see what could be revealed by a minute and attentive inspection of the stones themselves. They yielded a clear picture of successive teams of nomadic masons who came, laid a few courses of masonry and departed – perhaps because the financial resources of the Chapter were exhausted – and sometimes returned to lay a few more courses after other teams had come and laboured in their turn.

As John James became more intimately familiar with the stones, so he could begin to identify the idiosyncrasies of the different master masons – in the manner in which they treated the profiles of the apertures in the triforium passage, or in the cut of the masonry or the system of measurement and geometrical calculation which they used. He has detected more than forty campaigns of building, twenty-nine of them relating to the construction of the nave. Now the vault of the nave was celebrated in a poem by Guillaume le Breton which can be dated between 1218 and 1224. The Cathedral was begun in 1194 and vaulted in about 1222. This gives approximately one campaign of building to each year. Only nine different teams of masons can be identified, each returning on two or three occasions to the *chantiers* of Chartres.

In a further inspection of cathedrals and major churches in the Ile de France, John James was able to identify the work of the same teams – at Laon and Reims and Soissons and in the churches of Braisnes, Essommes and Orbais. And as they went from *chantier* to *chantier* they brought with them the latest developments in the art of Gothic building.

The supreme importance of the architecture of Chartres is that it set the fashion which most of the great cathedrals were to follow. There were, in 1194, five Gothic cathedrals in course of construction: Sens, Senlis, Noyon, Laon and Notre-Dame. As a group they showed a quite remarkable variety. At Laon the aisles which flanked the nave and choir were single: at Notre-Dame they were double. Noyon and Laon had clearly articulated transepts: Sens and Senlis had none. Noyon and Senlis had chapels radiating from the ambulatories: Notre-Dame had two ambulatories but no chapels. Sens alone had no tribunes and Senlis no triforium. The one feature which they all possessed in common was the sexpartite vault, but whereas at Noyon, Sens and Senlis this was allowed to dictate an alternation of major and minor piers, *pile forte* – *pile faible*, at Laon and Notre-Dame the pillars of the main arcade were of equal size.

It was at Chartres that the decisive formula was reached: transepts were retained, tribunes abolished, quadripartite vaults were used throughout and a double ambulatory with radiating chapels provided for the choir but single aisles for the nave. Reims, Amiens, Tours and Beauvais were to follow this pattern.

But it was not just the decisive formula for the solution of a constructional problem; it was the attainment of an ideal of architectural beauty. Chartres, Reims, Amiens; it is impossible to choose between them. They represent, as Emil Mâle has phrased it, *'trois moments d'une même pensée'*. Three moments of a single thought. 'They are quite admirable, all of them: Chartres – robust, restraining a force which seems to be trying to rise higher: Reims – perfect, balanced in all its members: Amiens – sublime, reaching that point beyond which lies only the impossible.'

Robust was the right word for Chartres. On the exterior, the architect has produced a nave in which beauty and strength go hand in hand. The flying buttresses consisted originally of only the lower two arcs joined together by the sturdy little cartwheel arcades. One of the few developments of style at Chartres can be seen in the replacement of this rather Romanesque decoration by the pointed tracery of the flying buttresses round the choir and apse. Both in the nave and the apse the topmost arc was a later, and possibly superfluous, addition. If these can be removed by the historical imagination, the façade can be visualised in all its early purity of style.

Nearly everything that was done at Chartres had been done before, but much of it had been done in a tentative and more or less experimental fashion. Now, for the first time, the new style, drawing together the essential elements of its construction, steps confidently into its own. The builder seems to be fully aware of the resources and potentialities at his disposal.

He used it to obtain a maximum area of glass. This seems to be the controlling principle of the design, and indeed it was this that led him into what could be considered as his only defect. The roses that surmount the twin arches of the clerestory are too large to fit into a pointed arch. They necessitate the use of a round arch for the wall rib, which has to be raised on stilts to attain the same height as the pointed arches of the nave vault. This in turn twists the inward facet of the vault into the shape of a ploughshare.

Apart from this minor defect – if it is a defect – the architecture of the interior has a classic beauty which has only been equalled at Reims and Amiens. Piers, buttresses and arcading make up a vast openwork skeleton of stone, almost devoid of walls, which could stand on its own, as no doubt for a time it did. But the open spaces between these ribs and bones were destined to receive what is undoubtedly the finest set of stained glass windows to have survived so nearly intact.

When walls had been a structural necessity, the medieval builder had sought to obtain the rich effect which he desired by mural painting. But the smallness of the windows so reduced the lighting as to render most of his efforts disappointing. With the elimination of the wall it became possible to replace the flatness of pigment with the lovely luminosity of glass.

To enter the Cathedral, especially on a day of splintering sun, is to enter Aladdin's cave. It appears at first as darkness, but a darkness which is glowing with opalescent colour. One hundred and seventy-three windows, totalling an area of two and a half thousand square metres, contribute to this overwhelming impact. Then, as the eye becomes accustomed to the darkness, the architecture begins to emerge – clustered columns rising upward in stately unison until they part company and arch out into the ribs of the great vault one hundred and twenty feet above our heads, framing the glorious galaxy of glass. This was the experience of the sculptor Rodin. *'D'abord l'extrême éblouissement ne me laisse percevoir que de lumineux violets; puis mon regard peu à peu distingue une arcade immense, sorte d'arc en ciel ogival qui apparait au ressaut des piliers. La mystère s'évanouit lentement, lentement l'architecture se précise. Et l'admiration s'impose irrésistiblement.'*

To see these windows thus is to appreciate them at one level, as a glowing, vibrant constellation of colour; to gaze at them is to be transported, like St John the Divine, to a Paradise where the streets

---

* 'At first I was completely dazzled, so that I could only dimly see a luminous purple. Then, little by little, I began to make out an immense arcade – like a Gothic rainbow, appearing at the spring of the vaults. Slowly the mystery fades; slowly the architecture begins to emerge, compelling irresistibly my admiration.'

are 'pure gold, as it were transparent glass', to a city whose foundations are garnished with sapphire and emeralds and amethysts and pearls, which had 'no need of the Sun, neither of the Moon, for the glory of God did lighten it'.

But with a pair of binoculars – an equipment necessary for a visit to Chartres – one can see the windows at another level; the detailed viewpoint of the glaziers who made them. For this Paradise, this translucent evocation of the Heavenly City, is made up of hundreds of thousands of tiny scenes, many of them depicting the most humdrum daily life. It was in his everyday routine that medieval man was taught to glorify God.

Take, for instance, the second window from the west in the north aisle. It was given in memory of a Bishop called Lubin by the wine merchants and publicans of Chartres on the somewhat slender pretext that when Lubin was a monk he was reputedly Cellarer of his Monastery. It is the sanctification of viticulture – an offering to God of the labours of those engaged upon the production of wine 'that maketh glad the heart of man'. Most of the window is descriptive of the production of wine; the rest depicts the life story of Lubin. In the circular panel in the centre of the light we can see the Cellarer drawing his wine from a green barrel. Two circles up from the bottom on the right, in an incomplete roundel framed in red, is a scene from Lubin's childhood. When he was a shepherd boy a monk, thinking him to be rather bright, decided to educate him. In order to give him his alphabet he cut the letters into his belt – and the actual letters can be seen (with binoculars) in this roundel.

The windows were all gifts to the Cathedral. Many of them came from the richer clergy – and some of these were very rich indeed. Lord Clark has reckoned that the Dean's private income would have been some £250,000 a year in modern money. Forty-four windows were given by the royal and noble families of France; forty-two by the Trades Guilds of the City of Chartres. These guilds have mostly appended their 'signature' in the form of a few scenes of their typical activities at the foot – that is to say the most easily visible part of the window. Thus a lady is seen trying on a dress in the Drapers' window and in another a Cobbler is depicted threading the laces into a new-made shoe.

In the Chapel of the Blessed Sacrament, formerly the Chapel of the Holy Martyrs, the extremely lovely central window shows the stoning of Stephen. The window to the left of this was the gift of the Stonemasons and at the bottom, on the right hand side, they can be seen at work on the Cathedral; above their heads are the models from which the profiles of the architecture are to be copied. In one scene the apprentice is watching his master at work and learning thus the secrets of his art; in the next the apprentice has taken over the work while his master stops for a drink.

Some of the windows have a particular interest for the English. The fifth from the west on the north side can be judged from its style to be by the same hand as one of the windows in Lincoln Cathedral. At the east end, immediately to the right of the entrance to the Chapelle de St Piat, is an absidial chapel of which the right hand window commemorates St Thomas à Becket. When he was murdered some of his blood fell upon a young cleric who accompanied him. This young cleric was John of Salisbury, later to be Bishop of Chartres. He brought with him the precious relic of the new saint's blood.

There was no overriding theme to which the donors of windows were asked to conform. Each was allowed to express his own personal faith in the way which he chose. What matter that among so many there should be five windows dedicated to St Nicholas and four to St Martin – not to mention the twenty which rendered homage to the Virgin Mary?

But in the great rose windows of the transepts, each with its five lancets beneath it, we do find a coherent iconography. This is no doubt due in part to the fact that each ensemble is the gift of a single donor. The windows of the north transept were given by Blanche de Castille, the mother of St Louis; those of the south transept by Pierre de Dreux, duc de Bretagne.

The north rose, with the loveliness of a water opal and the complexity of a snowflake, is distinguished by the bold and effective introduction of squares into the design. In the very centre are the Virgin and Child surrounded, in the inner ring, by doves and angels. The square panels depict the Kings of Judah and the half circles round the circumference the Minor Prophets. Beneath the rose, in the central lancet, the infant Virgin is seen in the arms of her mother, St Anne. Time has dealt harshly with the latter; it has so darkened her visage as to make her resemble some Parsee princess.

On either side of St Anne, Melchisidek, with his bread and wine, prefigures the Eucharist and Aaron, with his budding staff, the Virgin birth; David predicts the Passion, and Solomon the Adoration of the Kings. It was an opportunity to present Solomon in all his glory. In fact he is represented in the full regalia of a French king at his Coronation – and he bears a suspicious likeness to the known portraits of St Louis at the age of about sixteen.* His mother, Queen Blanche, who paid for the window, was not going to miss the oppor-

* He was described by Fra Salimbene of Padua as *gracilis, macilentus et angelica facie*.

tunity of eternalising the son she adored and of glorifying the Capetian dynasty which he represented.

In the south rose window, the risen Christ occupies the centre roundel encircled by the worshipping chorus described in the Book of Revelation. In detail the twenty-four musicians provide important information on the state of evolution of musical instruments at that time. In the lancets below is a deeply theological statement expressed by the mounting of the four Evangelists upon the shoulders of four Prophets. Outside left, as one looks at them, is Luke on Jeremiah; inside left Matthew on Isaiah; inside right John on Ezekiel and outside right Mark on Daniel.

It is a strange theology which seems at first to invert the importance of the Old and the New Testament. It was an attitude, however, not uncommon in the School of Chartres. Of their respect for Greek Philosophy the *Portail Royal* bears witness; but looking at these Evangelists riding upon the Prophets one is reminded again of the words of Bernard: 'We are dwarfs mounted on the shoulders of giants.'

At the bottom of the panel are members of the Royal house of Dreux, descendants of Count Robert of Brie, the younger brother of Louis VII.

The north and south façades to the transepts should be seen in close connection with their stained glass, for their sculptured porches reflect the same themes as their windows. The north portal, or *Portail de la Vierge*, was begun in 1197, only three years after the great fire. Artistically and theologically it shows a considerable evolution of style, technique and thought since the days of the *Portail Royal*. The latter had inspired a similar west front at Senlis but already by then the Church had elaborated its doctrines concerning the Virgin. At Senlis we see for the first time her full, and largely imaginary, life story: her genealogy, her birth, her 'falling asleep' and her assumption and coronation as Queen of Heaven.

These ideas are all incorporated into the north portal of Chartres. In the central bay the tympanum is devoted to the Coronation of the Virgin, while to either side of the doors the statue-columns show a new conception of the sculptor's art. Essentially the move is towards a greater realism. The figures are no longer motionless and mummified like those of the west front; the postures are more varied, the folds of the drapery more natural, for the underlying anatomy has been considered. From left to right they present a progression from patriarchs to prophets to apostles; from Melchisidek to St Peter.

The figure of Melchisidek is particularly striking: there is a wonderful sense of strangeness and dignity about this representative of the eternal order of Priesthood as he stares out into the future, holding his chalice and his loaf close to his breast. It is all somehow conveyed by the simple, harmonious lines of his loose, light rayment and the curling rhythmic furrows of his beard. Next to him is Abraham with Isaac, still bound, in front of him. Both are looking past Melchisidek towards the Divine voice which saved Isaac and provided the ram, depicted at their feet.

Answering them on the right of the doorway are John the Baptist and St Peter, who used to hold a chalice reflecting that of Melchisidek. What a wonderful contrast this pair affords – the weird, wild look of the 'voice crying in the wilderness' and the solid respectability of the Rock upon which Christ was to build his Church. There is something almost baroque about the sweep of the Baptist's beard, while Peter bears a strong, and surely intentional, resemblance to Melchisidek; his brow is slightly furrowed and he has the same far away look.

Against the central doorpost is a figure of St Anne with the infant Virgin in her arms. In 1204, the year before the completion of the north portal, the comte de Blois had sent from Constantinople to Chartres another breathtaking relic – the head of St Anne. *'La tête de la mère,'* runs the account in the Cartulary, *'fut reçue avec grande joie dans l'église de la fille'.**

In the series of arches above this central bay the theme is the Creation and Fall of Man. In medieval thought the Creation was the achievement of the *Word* of God – and so of Christ, the Word-become-Flesh, who thus appears in each scene. The subject can therefore, by a simple process, be enrolled into service in honour of Christ's mother. So also, when we come to Adam and Eve in the right hand archivolt of the central arch, the thought is that since through woman came sin, through woman also came the redemption from sin. The figure of Adam, one knee on the ground, right elbow resting on his right knee and the hand supporting his head, is the very picture of dejection after the event.

On either side of the central door the left hand bay is devoted to the Annunciation, Visitation and Nativity, to the accompaniment of a procession of virtues and vices; while to the right a selection of worthies from the Old Testament gives the place of honour in the tympanum to Job. The artist seems to have chosen for his text chapter 2 verse 7: 'So went Satan . . . and smote Job with sore boils from the sole of his foot unto his crown.'

These two flanking bays are the last sculptural ensemble of the Cathedral, for between the completion of the central bay of this north porch and the beginning of its side supporters, the whole of the south

---

* 'The head of the mother was received with great joy in the church of the daughter.'

portal was undertaken. This, like the rose window above it, was the gift of Pierre de Dreux, duc de Bretagne. This nobleman was a great grandson of Louis VI and thus represented a younger branch of the House of Capet. But he had achieved an independent status by his marriage to Alix de Thouars, through whom he became duc de Bretagne. Both the statuary and the stained glass of the south porch were paid for by him, and he and Alix appear at the feet of Christ on the central doorpost of the portal.

The theme is the Last Judgement, with the Martyrs of the Church in the left hand bay and the Confessors in the right. These figures mostly seem just to lack the vital spark of inspiration, but one scene is a work of genius – the separation of the sheep from the goats immediately above the central doors. It is not without humour. The figures of the condemned seem more disappointed and disgruntled than dismayed, let alone appalled, at their predicament. Significantly they number in their throng a king, a bishop and a monk. But the impact of the scene derives from the dynamic rhythm of the harvesting angels above their heads. Moving with the unison of a well-coached crew they sweep their victims to their damnation.

The façades of the two transepts are flanked by towers which do not rise higher than the top of the rose windows. On the south side there is a further tower over the last bay of the side aisle before the ambulatory. The symmetry of the plan dictates that there was to have been another answering this one on the north façade. Had these six towers been completed with spires the silhouette of Chartres would have been an exciting, many-towered skyline such as was only achieved at Laon. Instead it has but two – those on the towers erected by Geoffroy de Lèves which rise to either side of the *Portail Royal*.

The south tower was the only one to be completed according to its original design. Otto von Simson has shown in his profound study of the Gothic cathedral that this tower was constructed on a complex system of harmonic proportion to which St Augustine himself must needs have given full approval. It is a model of strength and simplicity and nothing could be more admirable than the way in which the architect has used the ring of tall, attenuated gables to mask the transition from the square to the octagon and from the octagon to the spire.

The solidity of the tower is attested by the fact that there were, up till the Revolution, two great bourdons weighing 13,500 and 10,000 kilograms respectively. It took eighteen men to swing them. In 1793 they were melted down to provide canon for the revolutionary army. They were an irreparable loss, these great bells whose sonorous tones boomed out the authentic voice of the Middle Ages. '*Ce sont des siècles, ce ne sont pas des heures,'* wrote Auguste Rodin, *'que sonnent les cloches de nos grandes Cathédrales.'**

Victor Sablon, the seventeenth-century historian of Chartres, records that in the first floor chamber of the south tower there was a mill and a bread oven for use in the event of a siege. It must be remembered that during the Wars of Religion, Henri IV laid siege to Chartres and a canon ball passed through the rose window of the west front. A year later he chose to be crowned in Chartres Cathedral instead of Reims.

Up till the year 1506 the north tower was crowned with a steeple of timber and lead, but in that year it was struck by lightning and burnt out. It was decided to rebuild in stone and the task was allocated to Jean Texier, usually known as Jean de Beauce. His spire is an amazing structure, as unlike its opposite number as possible. For in the south tower and spire there is an apparent austerity and simplicity behind which lurks a deeply intellectual theory of proportion, whereas Jean de Beauce has relied for his effect upon a fantastic over-ornamentation. His short spire rests upon an octagonal tower of two storeys which rises from a square continuation of the old tower. But the whole is so bristling with pinnacles, so cusped and crotchetted, so criss-crossed by fretwork balustrades and intersecting gables as to defy description. As a *tour de force* it must elicit our astonishment if not our admiration. But whatever our judgement on their respective merits, we can see in the two towers the beginning and the end of the French Gothic.

Having constructed his Flamboyant, open-work spire, Jean de Beauce proceeded, in 1520, to build a low clock-tower on the north façade of the tower. It is a purely Renaissance structure, reminiscent of the style of Chambord. No one standing in the little *place* to the north of the Cathedral could possibly be expected to guess that the spire and the clock-tower were by the same hand.

In 1514 Jean de Beauce was also commissioned to construct the elaborate screen that separates the choir from its side aisles. It was still unfinished at his death in 1529, but during those fifteen years he had shown his ability once more to move with the times: a great master of the Flamboyant Gothic, he was young enough in his old age to convert to Renaissance ornament. It has to be said, however, that his earlier Flamboyant work, that which is situated nearest to the crossing, is by far the finest.

Essentially he was providing exhibition space for a number of tableaux of the life of Christ. These scenes are in full relief and run

* 'It is not the hours, it is the centuries which are sounded by the bells of our great Cathedrals.'

93

right round the ambulatory. They contain some two hundred figures and took two and a half centuries to complete, the last figures being set up in 1789. They range from the Presentation in the Temple, just to the left of the iron grille on the south side, carved by Jean Saules whose characters, arranged as if acting a mystery play, are in the everyday clothes of the reign of François I, to Renaissance figures in classical draperies and those heavy specimens of muscle-bound masculinity so unaccountably dear to the Italian painter. In the scene of the Transfiguration by Thomas Boudin the figure of Moses is undisguisedly copied from Bernini. Over the north entrance to the choir the Crucifixion, carved by Nazières in the early eighteenth century, reflects in its composition a painting by Rubens.

The decision to undertake this choir screen caused a situation which throws an interesting light on the financing of such undertakings. The Bishop, Evrard de la Marck, refused to contribute. The Chapter registered a protest with the King. 'The Lord Bishop will not make any contribution whatever to the expenses of the Church, to the rebuilding of the spire or the enclosure of the choir; to which, however, he is obliged by reason of his dignity and on account of the revenues which he receives'. Their appeal was successful and the wealthy Bishop was ordered to contribute the sum of 20,000 francs. One may surmise, however, that relations between the Palace and the Deanery were not thereby improved.

The enclosure of the choir by this elaborate screen was the last significant addition to the Cathedral. By 1520 Chartres was substantially the building which we know. In place of the roof, which has assumed the flat uninteresting green of copper oxide, we need to imagine the greys and whites produced by silver lead, in closer harmony with the warmer grey of newly quarried stone. We need to replace in our mind's eye the gilded polychroming of the sculptures; we must allow for a certain darkening of the painted glass. But essentially the completed Cathedral was what we see today.

What we do not see is the original context. A real effort of the imagination is needed to recapture the astonishing contrast between the splendour of the Church's architecture and the drabness of the structures by which it was mostly surrounded – of dwellings which at the worst were little more than hovels with walls of mud and roofs of blackened straw that matched what Aldous Huxley called 'the dirty whites, the duns and goose turd greens' of rustic clothing.

Since the Middle Ages Chartres has only been altered in one important respect and that was by the replacement of the lead roof by copper, which has of course turned green. One of the earliest eulogies of the building comes from Guillaume le Breton in 1220. 'Finished with a vault which one might compare with the shell of a tortoise,' he wrote, 'the Cathedral of Chartres has nothing more to fear from fire from now until the Day of Judgement, and it will save from the eternal fire numerous Christians who by their gifts have contributed to its reconstruction.'

Unfortunately he was wrong about the fire. The roof was still of timber and in 1836 it was completely burnt out. The beams were replaced by iron girders and a copper roof was laid upon them which was meant to be temporary but is still *in situ.*

The destruction of the timbers was a great loss. Like almost everything else at Chartres they were of superb quality. Vincent Sablon, writing in 1697, gives a vivid picture: 'nothing could be more admirable than the timbers of the Cathedral – one might almost say "the forest" because of the great quantity of beams and the long avenues as far as the eye can see. These beams are still as sound as when they came out of the forest from which they were taken; there is not the smallest worm hole nor the least sign of decay.'

The roof tent also provided magnificent echoes and Sablon found it 'an indescribable pleasure to go up and sing there or play the flute or trumpet'.

A last detail may be added, which only too easily escapes our attention. The floor is as excellent a piece of workmanship as any in the building. It slopes down some eighty centimetres from the crossing to the west doors. This was to facilitate its washing, which was no doubt a frequent necessity. In 1531 it became imperative to forbid 'vagabond pilgrims' from sleeping in the Cathedral 'as they have been accustomed to do, in order to avoid the inconveniences, infections and ordures which they import'.

In the middle of the nave floor is a labyrinth – a sort of miz-maze of inlaid marble. Its track is two hundred and ninety-four metres long and was called 'the Road to Jerusalem'. It is thought to have been one of the penances of the pilgrims to negotiate its entire length upon their knees. It is more than possible that in doing so they managed to obliterate the name of one of the greatest architects the world has known. It became traditional, as at Reims and Amiens, for the names of the architects to be inscribed in the inner sanctuary of the labyrinth. No name has survived at Chartres and we shall probably never know who was the author of this dream-made-real. His great work has inspired the tributes of men throughout the ages, but perhaps the most perceptive compliment was that paid by Napoleon. 'Chartres,' he observed, 'is no place for an atheist.'

The most remarkable property of the building, however, is its inexhaustible capacity for inspiring our interest. We can return again and again and always re-experience the same initial thrill. The last word must be left to Rodin. 'I have often visited it, this Cathedral.

But today it appeared to me in a new light, more beautiful, more brilliant than ever and I set myself to study it as if I were seeing it for the first time.' This experience is the hall-mark of a true appreciation of its greatness.

CHAPTER EIGHT

Bourges

At the same time that the new nave and choir were being built at
Chartres, an independent – and in many ways very different –
venture in Gothic architecture was taking place at Bourges.

It is important to remember that Bourges occupied a significant
and in some ways unique position in the politics of the Capetian
kings. It had been purchased by Philippe I from the vicomte in about
the year 1100. This acquisition represented a considerable extension
of the Capetian domain – whose natural frontier might well have
been the Loire – towards the south of France. It was a wedge driven
between Burgundy and Poitou.

The significance of this infiltration was greatly enhanced by the
special position of the Archbishop of Bourges. Not only did he
number among his suffragans such dioceses as Limoges, Cahors and
Albi, but he enjoyed a primacy over the Archbishop of Bordeaux and
his suffragans. The Archbishop of Bourges was now a vassal of the
King of France.

But Bourges was more than the nerve centre of a complex network
of political powers – it was a rich and beautiful city at the heart of a
beautiful and opulent land. The Province of Berry was described in
1567 by Nicholas Nicolay, 'Geographer and Valet-de-Chambre to
King Charles IX'. He divides the country into three categories; first
were the little valleys – *'terres grasses et rougeâstres'* – which produced
the cereals; then there was the dry and rocky soil 'producing
abundance of very good wine'; finally there were the treeless uplands
which provided pasture for immense quantities of sheep, which,
'because of the mildness and sweetness of the air, which make the
grasses tasty and delicate', produced wool of a far finer quality than
any other part of the kingdom. This was the true Golden Fleece
'which makes the province very famous and rich'.

Situated towards the north of this attractive and productive
countryside, *'fertile et delectable'* and which 'produces an abundance of grain, vegetables and cloth and all manner of excellent
fruit; wines that are delicate and delicious and which keep well;
game, poultry and all freshwater fish', was the capital and cathedral
town of Bourges, *'cité antique et moderne'*.

Under the Romans the original town of Biturica had been one of the most important in the Empire, covering an area of thirty-eight hectares – some hundred acres. But in the general decline in urbanism following the fall of the Roman Empire, the faubourgs had been abandoned and the city had withdrawn within the walls of its high citadel.

By the end of the twelfth century, this process had been reversed. The city had overflowed into new faubourgs and these had been encircled by Philippe-Auguste with an outer wall 'built of great blocks of very hard stone, rusticated on the exterior' – that is to say with each stone faceted for the better deflection of cannon balls. On the highest ground of the medieval city stood the Grosse Tour, a massive *donjon* which proclaimed by its strength and its severity the rule of the King.

But the dominant feature of the old town was of course its Cathedral. Nicolay found it *'fort grande, haute à merveille, et construite avec artifice admirable et dépense inestimable'*. The word 'artifice' today suggests a device or trick. In the Middle Ages, as we have seen in the chapter on Sens, the word 'artifax' was used of God as the Creator. It is probable that Nicolay meant that the master plan of Bourges was something which evoked his admiration.

The new Cathedral was certainly the product of a single master mind. Robert Branner, the most important authority on Bourges, has christened him *'le Maître de Bourges'* and it is a title which befits him. Whatever specification was laid down, whatever theological requirements were stipulated by the Chapter, whatever contributions were made in the way of technical advice or aesthetic suggestion, it was in the mind of the Master and in his mind only that the whole, huge, intricate conception was evolved. We know nothing of him but the monument which he has left behind him. There is reason to suppose that he served his apprenticeship and formed his taste in the area which centres on the river Aisne. He began to create his masterpiece simultaneously with the Master of Chartres.

It is interesting to compare the approaches of these two great architects. Both started with the same inheritance; both were tackling the same task – and each produced a different solution. Chartres was to set the fashion for the two great Cathedrals of Reims and Amiens; Bourges was to inspire the beautiful hemicycles of Le Mans and Coutances. The builder of Beauvais, while obviously following the Chartres-Amiens tradition, incorporated also some of the insights of the Master of Bourges.

It would be an over-simplification to say that the Master of Chartres was concerned for the structure of his solids and that the Master of Bourges was preoccupied with the relationship of his

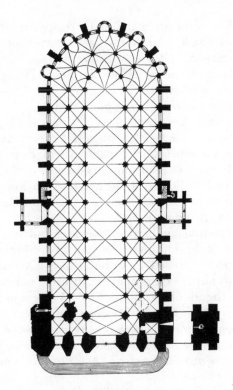

Ground Plan of Bourges

spaces – but that is basically the difference between their respective approaches.

The point of departure for both was the newly finished nave of Notre-Dame, with its built-in flying buttresses; both of them saw immediately that, because of the flying buttresses, it was possible to dispense with tribunes. Both of them therefore adopted the three-storey façade of great arcade, triforium and clerestory – but each did so in an entirely different manner.

The Master of Chartres reverted to the three-storey façade of Sens, while greatly increasing its height. This provided considerably larger windows for the aisles and clerestory. The Master of Bourges retained the small clerestory and put all the extra height gained by the abolition of the tribunes into his great arcade. The immense height of the main columns is the first impression of which the spectator is aware. Seen on its own, the nave façade is dispro-portionate – like a figure on stilts. But it is not meant to be seen on its own and it cannot be seen on its own. It is meant to be seen in relationship with the second façade, that of the inner aisle. Through each of the arches of the great arcade there appears the three-storey façade of the inner aisle, with its own great arcade, its own triforium and its own clerestory. The two together make a five-storey façade. This effect was the specific legacy of Bourges to Beauvais. Instead of producing larger windows, as at Chartres, the Master of Bourges produced three tiers of windows in place of two.

The spectator in the centre of the nave is thus at all times conscious of the façades behind the façades; the aisles are always contributing to the all-pervading impression of spaciousness. In the same way, the spectator in the aisles is at all times conscious of their relationship with the central nave. Thanks to the height of the inner aisle – and it carries its vault at twenty-one metres – the main clerestory can be seen from almost any point in the Cathedral.

This special relationship between the nave and its aisles is built on the cross-section of the building; it needs also the dimension of length for its full effect to be realised. Five double bays of sexpartite vaulting, extended by two bays of quadripartite vaulting beneath the towers, together with the double ambulatory of the apse provide the impressive array of one hundred free-standing columns. There is no transept, no interruption. '*La combinaison monumentale de ces hautes nefs,*' wrote Louis Gonse, '*se développant sans arrêt et semblant prendre leur élan vers le mouvement tournant du sanctuaire, produit un des plus beaux tableaux d'architecture qui se puisse voir.*'*

'There is no trace here of the "cellular" structure of Notre-Dame,' writes Jean Bony; the advent of the flying buttress had opened up a new possibility – '*de vider de l'intérieure la masse pyramidante de Notre-Dame de Paris et de n'en conserver que l'enveloppe.*'† It was for this reason that there was no need at Bourges for transepts. If, as Bony suggests, the transepts of Notre-Dame were necessary to expose the whole system in section, no such need could be claimed in the open, airy hollowness of Bourges. Here a transept would have been a break in rhythm – an interruption in that 'triumphant triple avenue at the end of which is God'.

For Bony compares the spirituality of Bourges with that of the mystical technique known as Augustinian contemplation. 'In this great vision of wholeness, and completeness, matter loses much of its substantiality, the impression of multiplicity begins to fade, rather like individual persons in Augustinian contemplation. The One,

* 'The monumental grouping of these high naves, extending without interruption and seeming to gather their momentum towards the circular movement of the apse, produces one of the most beautiful architectural compositions that it would be possible to see.'
† 'to hollow out from the interior the pyramidal mass of Notre-Dame and to retain only the outer shell.'

absorbing all things into itself, empties them of their substance and of their solidity.' One of the most simple and beautiful expressions of this form of ecstasy is to be found in the writings of Jan van Ruysbroeck: 'when we transcend ourselves and become, in our ascent towards God, so simple that the naked love in the height can lay hold of us, where love enfolds us above every exercise of virtue . . . then we cease and we and all our selfhood die in God.'

Since the vault is sexpartite, the eye looks instinctively for the rhythm *pile forte – pile faible*. It will be seen that an alternance does exist. It is only really noticeable at triforium level, where the *pile forte* carries five colonnettes and the *pile faible* three. Once one is looking for it one can see that the *pile faible* is slightly more slender. It is clear that the Master of Bourges did not want to interrupt the steady progression of his forest of pillars by any too obvious distinction in their girth. He has slimmed down the *pile forte* as much as he dared in order to maintain as fully as possible the open communications between the nave and its aisles.

This vast cage of stone, with its three tiers of windows, was of course intended to receive a full complement of stained glass, as at Chartres. An inventory of the contents of the Cathedral made in February 1794, lists five crates of glass 'taken out at various times to give a more abundant lighting to the choir.' The dim but richly coloured lighting of the Cathedral in the Middle Ages would have enhanced the mystery without taking away from the majesty of the design.

The architecture of the exterior is largely dictated by the requirements of these interior dispositions. One of the best views of the Cathedral is from the public gardens to the south-east. It is an awe-inspiring sight. The first impression is that created by the unbroken length of the single vessel – lying like a great ship turned turtle in the middle of the town. The historical imagination must immediately remove the series of double pinnacles which surmount the buttress piers. All the early drawings and engravings show these piers to have ended in the simple, roof-like copings just above the junction with the main flyers. The decorative parapet and delicate pinnacles beneath the roof are also later additions. If, in the mind's eye, we can remove these nineteenth-century baubles, we can appreciate the original austerity of the design.

It was not always thus. In the fourteenth century a false transept was added, breaking the continuity of the roofline, and a flèche was erected at the point of intersection. These were finally removed after Viollet-le-Duc's survey in the mid-nineteenth century.

The overall effect is much closer to that of Notre-Dame than to that of Chartres, but the most striking difference to both of these is in the treatment of the flying buttresses. Owing to the narrowness of the inner aisles, the slope of the great flyers is more steeply inclined, and although intermediary piers are used, they do not rise above the line of the flyers which thus present a straight diagonal, striking out from the façade like the oars of a gigantic galleon. This system achieves a considerable economy in stone. The buttress piers of Chartres are simple but massive. Robert Mark, who has made a specialised study of the two Cathedrals, estimates that at Chartres each pier, exclusive of its foundations, weighs 1000 tons. At Bourges on the other hand, the much lower buttress piers weigh only 400 tons.

Robert Mark has applied the most up-to-date techniques of recording dead-weight and wind stresses to the engineering of the Gothic cathedrals. A model of the main structural elements – piers, columns and flying buttresses – is made in epoxy plastic and heated to 150° Celsius, while being subjected to pressures designed to equal maximum wind conditions. The lowering of the temperature back to normal locks in any deformations due to excessive loading, which will show as contour lines when viewed in a polariscope. This process is known as 'stress freezing' and has a lot to tell us about Gothic engineering.

His deductions about Bourges are most interesting. 'We found that the vault thrust is entirely carried by the lower of the two flying buttresses that support each pier. The higher one must then have been placed to provide support against roof and parapet wind loading.' He reaches the conclusion that 'the light choir structure at Bourges, then, provides stability to the high roof that is fully comparable to that afforded by the much heavier Chartres buttress configuration.'

How the Master of Bourges, who almost certainly used Roman figures for his calculations with the severe limitations which these impose, could have arrived at such technical competence within a few years of the invention of the flying buttress is beyond imagination. When a second architect took over the construction of the nave, he appears to have been uneasy about his predecessor's daring. We can see at a glance that his flyers have a greater depth in elevation and rise to a point considerably nearer to the parapet. This obvious break in the system of abutment, together with a number of less obvious changes in the details of the decoration, have enabled Robert Branner, in his great work on Bourges Cathedral, to plot the successive stages of its construction.

It started in 1195 and continued for some sixty years. Henri de Sully, elected to the Archbishopric in 1183, was therefore the prelate at the time when the new building was begun. It is not known what part he played. There was, in fact, something anomalous about his position: one of the leading figures of the Church in France, he counted for very little in his own Cathedral. At his enthronement a curious little ceremony was introduced for the first time. Just before the singing of the Te Deum, the Dean advanced and bound the Archbishop's thumbs together with a piece of ribbon to indicate, so Canon Rousseau informs us, that in the Cathedral 'he had neither jurisdiction nor power and was no more, to all intents and purposes, than an ordinary canon.'

Henri de Sully was the brother of Eudes de Sully, at that time Bishop of Paris, and it is clear that Notre-Dame was by no means unknown to the Master of Bourges. But there is no direct evidence that the influence of Notre-Dame was mediated through the brothers Sully. It is even more uncertain what role was played by his successor St Guillaume – a man more distinguished for his piety and learning than for his gifts as an administrator. It is more likely that the Chapter were the real initiators and supporters of the building campaign. Curiously enough, after the single intrusion of Gérard du Cros, the next two Bishops came from the same two families: Simon de Sully, the nephew of Henri, and Philippe de Berruyer, nephew of St Guillaume. The five of them covered the whole period of the building of the Cathedral. The most that can be said is that, between them, they provided the administrative competence and the spiritual inspiration necessary for the construction of a cathedral.

In 1181 Philippe-Auguste had granted to the city permission to overflow beyond the line of the Gallo-Roman fortifications. This permission was extended also to the Cathedral. It is not known for what reason the decision was made to rebuild, but recent excavations have provided evidence of a fire which may well have afforded the pretext. As late as 1172 the Chapter were still concerned with the embellishment of the old fabric and a western portal, similar to the *Portail Royal* of Chartres, was being prepared by the workshops. By the time the carvings were ready, the decision to rebuild had been taken and the sculptures intended for the west front were used in the north and south porches of the new building.

The permission to extend beyond the Gallo-Roman wall was the determining fact about the siting and general disposition of the new Cathedral. The former building had reached the limit of the wall. Now it was possible to overflow towards the east, but beyond the line of fortification the ground fell away sharply. In order to maintain the existing floor level, the new apse had to be raised up on a sort of undercroft which is known as the crypt. Louis Gonse regards this crypt as one of the great architectural masterpieces of all time – 'the dawn of a triumphant maturity, but with all the unexpectedness and freshness of young ideas.'

Bourges: Original System of Buttressing

The first fresh and unexpected feature is the use of curved ribs for the ambulatory vaulting, which is repeated in the main church above in more elaborate fashion. The problem arises from the shape of the bays in the curving part of the ambulatory. Each of these forms a trapezoid. Two straight vault ribs joining the four corners of the trapezoid would so intersect as to form one very small vault web towards the inner circumference and a very large one towards the outer circumference. One way to overcome this problem – which was adopted in every other cathedral mentioned in this book – is to move the point of intersection to the centre of the trapezoid. This gives four ribs of more or less equal length, but it loses the continuity of the single diagonal drawn from corner to corner. The Master of Bourges had produced the ingenious alternative of joining the four corners with two curved lines. This moves the point of intersection nearer the centre of the trapezoid while preserving the continuity of the two diagonals.

We cannot leave the crypt without taking note of the full-scale design engraved upon the floor of one of the rose windows of the west front. It is not often that medieval architects of that date have left their cartoons behind them.

The building of the crypt raised the new apse to the level of the old Cathedral and at this stage an important modification was made to the design. Following the pattern dictated by the crypt, the hemicycle was to be composed of two concentric rings of six pillars each. The cross ribs which joined these pillars formed the radii of a semicircle and were abutted by six large buttress piers on the exterior. Between these, five smaller piers were placed to receive the lighter thrust of a zig-zag vault of the outer ambulatory. In about the year 1200 it was decided to perch five little horse-shoe chapels on these five smaller buttresses. Each chapel was to contain three lancets – a disposition which greatly increased the area available to the glaziers. By the year 1205 the whole of the outer ambulatory and the first straight bay of the choir had been completed, vaulted and roofed.

During the next three years the four further bays of the choir were carried up to the same height and began to envelop the nave of the old Cathedral. This half-demolished old building within the outer aisle of a half-built new one was a draughty arrangement and it was to prove fatal to the saintly Bishop Guillaume. In 1209 he determined to take part in the crusade against the Albigeois, but while he was preaching his farewell sermon he caught a fever from which he never recovered 'because the place in which he preached was exposed to every wind – omni vento erat expositus.'

In 1214 the whole choir was finished. A papal Bull of that year appointed the Bishops of Orléans and Auxerre to settle a dispute between the Dean and his Chapter. The subject of the dispute does not concern us, but the text makes it quite clear that the choir was by this time in full use for Divine worship. It is probable that the Master of Bourges never saw his choir completed. A change in the plan can be detected in the clerestory and high vaults which have been raised to nearly three feet above the level originally intended. So fundamental an alteration argues the likelihood of a change of architect.

Having built their choir, the Dean and Chapter now turned their attention to the glazing of the windows. These windows, most of which have happily survived, form three tiers – the inner clerestory, the second clerestory and the ground floor windows of the outer aisle. They can be dated with some confidence between 1215 and 1220. François Quiévreux has demonstrated, by a minute study of the brush strokes, not only that these windows were the work of two *maîtres verriers* working simultaneously, but that both of them had just completed orders for windows at Chartres. He assigns to them the cumbersome titles of *'le Maître du Vitrail de St Eustache de Chartres'* and *'le Maître du Vitrail de l'Apocalypse de Bourges'*. We will call them the first Master and the second Master.

It is fascinating to follow his argument in his minute observation of detail. In the faces Quiévreux has identified that the first Master leaves a space clear between the iris and the eyelid, while the second makes them contiguous; likewise the second Master indicates the little groove in the upper lip beneath the nose with a loop that almost resembles a nose-ring, whereas the first Master omits it. In the hands, the first Master indicates the finger joints with a single line and usually crosses the third and fourth fingers over the first two; the second Master indicates the joints with a double line, producing an almost skeletonic effect, and he keeps the fingers parallel. Differences can be detected also in the manner of representing the folds in the draperies, where each artist has a distinctive 'coup de pinceau'.

With these barely perceptible hall-marks, the artists have unknowingly 'signed' their windows.

Once able to identify the hand of each master, Quiévreux made an interesting discovery. Of the five little apsidal chapels, all except the eastern most have retained their original glazing; they alternate between the two Masters. If we now consider the windows in the ambulatory walls which flank these chapels, it will be found that each chapel glazed by the first Master is set between two windows glazed by the second, and vice versa, so that a regular alternance was established between the two styles. To this system there is but one exception: in the south-east chapel, where the lancets represent the patron Saint of the Cathedral, St Etienne, with two other Deacons, St

Laurence and St Vincent, to support him, the first Master was responsible for the latter two figures, while the depiction of the patron Saint was made over to the second Master. Five chapels could not be equally distributed between two artists, nor could the three windows in the fifth chapel be equitably apportioned. The second Master, we assume, was compensated for the smaller number of the windows assigned to him by the greater honour of portraying the Saint to whom the Cathedral was dedicated.

It has to be added that, although this theory is accepted by Jean Verrier and Marcel Aubert, it is not entirely accepted by Louis Grodecki, who is one of the great authorities on French medieval stained glass. He sees a third hand in these windows. But Grodecki has not the gift of lucidity and his argument defies abbreviation.

But if the symmetry of the authorship is not beyond doubt, at least the symmetry of the subject matter can be established. The single overarching theme is that of the Divine work of reconciliation between Jew and Gentile which finds its clearest expression in the second chapter of Ephesians: 'for He is our peace, who hath made both one, and hath broken down the middle wall of partition between us'. Significantly, it is the passage which leads up to the famous architectural simile which describes the household of God as 'built upon the foundation of the Apostles and Prophets, Jesus Christ himself being the chief corner stone; in whom all the building fitly framed together groweth unto an holy temple in the Lord'. At Bourges the stained glass complements the architecture as an illustration of this passage.

The subjects of these windows are so arranged as to answer each other across the apse. The first light on the north side states the opposition – for Dives was held in medieval thought to represent the Jews and Lazarus the Gentiles. The corresponding window on the south side tells the story of Joseph – but Joseph was held to prefigure Christ, who is thus introduced as the ultimate source of reconciliation.

In the next pair towards the east St Stephen faces St Thomas, the Apostle of India. The first illustrates the Gospel rejected by the Jews; the second the Gospel preached to the uttermost confines of the world.

As the arc of the ambulatory draws the windows on each side closer and closer to each other, so the theme of *rapprochement* intensifies. Thus in the fourth pair the Prodigal Son is opposed to the Passion. Again, in the teaching of St Gregory, the Prodigal represented the Gentiles and the second brother the Jews. In the lowest quatrefoil there is a striking contrast between the second brother labouring honestly with his oxen and the Prodigal riding off on a horse with his falcon on his wrist – a traditional symbol for seigneurial life. But in the topmost medallion the artist has gone beyond the parable and shown the two brothers being reconciled by God. Across the ambulatory to the south, the Passion window recalls the price at which that reconciliation was won.

Finally, with the innermost pair, the theme reaches its culmination in the New Covenant and the Last Judgment. The New Covenant is a complex theological statement that was presented by the butchers and *charcutiers* of the town. It tells of the sacrifice of Christ together with its prefigurings in the Old Testament. In the scene of Abraham's sacrifice the wood carried by Isaac has symbolically taken the shape of a cross. Above is depicted the Resurrection, with Elijah bringing to life the Shunamite woman's son and such symbolic figures as a lion and its cubs. The meaning of this is explained by Honorius of Autun in his Easter sermon *De Paschali*. The lioness was thought to give birth to still-born cubs which were brought to life on the third day by the roaring of the lion.

But the real point of the window is in its topmost roundel, where Jacob is seen blessing his two sons – Manasseh, who represents the Jews, and Ephraim who represents the Gentiles. The death of Christ was not for the chosen race alone, but for all men, to whom, in the opposite window, the Last Judgment comes impartially.

It was a theme to satisfy the subtle mind of a medieval theologian, and no doubt it provided the visual aids for generations of preachers. It looks as if the financial resources of the Chapter were fully engaged in the cost of the glazing, for building operations were only resumed in about 1225.

The nave, which is the work of the third architect of Bourges, follows closely the original master plan. Branner advances the attractive suggestion that the third architect may have been an apprentice of the first – he seems to have been thoroughly conversant with all the tricks of the trade of which the first *chantier* gives evidence. If this is so, we might see in the nave the work of a grateful pupil piously honouring the original intentions of his revered Master.

He does not, however, descend to slavish imitation. He has introduced his own amendments. In the clerestory windows the oculus is larger and rests on the point of the central arch, while the outer lancets have been made taller. In the high triforium he has inserted an oculus above the arcade but in the lower triforium he has departed altogether from the arcade, using instead a geometric progression of twin lancets surmounted by a roundel. But these are details. Our first impression upon entering takes no account of these. '*Dès le premier pas,*' writes Bony, '*tout l'édifice se révèle dans sa prodigieuse unité.*'*

* 'From our first entry the whole edifice reveals itself in its prodigious unity.'

If the interior of Bourges is something dynamically original and almost unique, the same is true of the west front. It is a composition far removed from Notre-Dame, for there the nave and its four aisles are disguised behind a façade with only three upright divisions. Bourges frankly expresses the fivefold disposition of the interior by offering the same number of portals. Notre-Dame presents a façade of great simplicity – Bourges appears to have a more or less bewildering complexity. It must be remembered, however, that the north tower collapsed in the sixteenth century and was rebuilt without any regard for symmetry. The original north tower was probably identical with that on the south.

But the architect of Bourges had problems peculiarly his own. He was apparently troubled by the extreme wideness of the nave in comparison with the side aisles, for he has almost imperceptibly tapered the nave towards the west. The same motive may be attributed to the positioning of the two inner buttresses of the façade, which have been moved closer to each other. The size of the central embrasure has thus been reduced at the expense of those to either side. In the same way the porches on the extremities of the façade were enlarged. This was to allow for a rather more ample treatment of the towers, which would have been too narrow if they had been confined to the exact proportions of the outer aisles.

But the real difficulty arose from the fact that the existence of inner side aisles made it impossible for the towers to buttress the central bay of the nave. There is behind the façade a system of vaulted chambers which provides for this abutment. The west front is really a screen behind which these chambers are concealed. Its upright members correspond to the fivefold division of the interior, while the horizontal divisions were dictated by the need for passageway communications throughout the building.

It is quite clear from the arrangement of buttresses and walls at the top of the south tower that it was intended to carry an octagonal spire. It is probable that the north tower would have been symmetrical. The spires were never built. The towers, in fact, gave the architects more trouble than any other part of the Cathedral. In 1313 the south tower was showing serious signs of fatigue and the large and ungainly *'pilier boutant'* was built to shore it up. The form of the building may have something to do with the fact the Dean and Chapter were in need of a prison and chose this buttress building to provide one. Such a prison was necessitated by the rights of *haute et basse justice* exercised by the Chapter over the Liberty of the Close.

The Close, or Cloître, was a little village on its own, with its own walls and its own gatehouses, containing some eighty dwellings. In 1174 Louis VII released the inhabitants of the Close from all lay

jurisdiction. They were also exempt from the authority of the Archbishop and directly subject to the Pope, a suzerainty which was
sufficiently remote to impinge but seldom upon their autonomy.
Within the confines of the Close the Canons of Bourges, known as
Messieurs les Vénérables, formed a state within the State – 'a little world
of its own,' as Canon Rousseau called them, 'jealous in the extreme of
its rights and immunities.'

The most usual infringment of these rights seems to have been the
arresting of one of the inmates of the Close by the civil authorities.
Two anecdotes will suffice to illustrate the tenacity of *Messieurs les
Vénérables.* In 1286 two thieves were arrested in the Close by the
King's bailiff and died in his prison. The Chapter insisted on its
rights and the bailiff had to produce two sacks of corn, representing
the two thieves, which were then solemnly tried, convicted and
sentenced to hanging – a sentence which was carried out in public.
The Middle Ages believed in the principle of the proxy.

Equally serious was the offence of Hughes Tordu, a former Prévôt
de Bourges, who struck one of the clergy in the Cathedral. On 26
December 1332, he was summoned to appear at three o'clock, *'sans
coiffe ni culotte',* dressed only in a tunic. Holding a waxen candle he
was solemnly processed round the Cathedral, escorted by all the
Canons, vicars and choirmen. Having completed the circuit, he gave
the candle back to the Dean, admitting his fault: *'j'ai mis témérairement
la main violente, en l'église de Bourges, sur Pierre Poillebin, clerc, et en fais
amende honorable par ladite torche.'** It was not unknown for offenders
against the dignity of the clergy to be 'beaten with rods' before the
altar.

The Canons of Bourges in the Middle Ages were no better than
they should have been. There were forty of them and they were not
required to be in more than sub-deacon's orders to qualify for their
stall, their prebend and their voice on the Chapter. Because of the
frequency of their professional incompetence, four more had to be
employed for whom it was obligatory to be in priest's orders and to
reside permanently in the Close – *'prébendé de résidence'.* As at Notre-
Dame, one of the prebends was kept vacant to pay for the choir.

Not very much is known of the medieval liturgy of Bourges, but
Canon Rousseau quotes a description of the celebration of the *Fête
des Rois* in which a star was made to move along under the vaults,
guiding the three Kings to the manger. It required a rope 720 feet
long. On 6 January 1519, Guillaume Pellevoisin, *'grand machiniste des
mystères célébrés dans l'église',*† received six sous for accomplishing this

* 'I had the temerity to lay hands violently, in the Church of Bourges, on Pierre
Poillebin, Clerk, and make due apology by means of this said light.'
† 'chief mechanic of the mysteries celebrated in the church.'

stage effect. It would be interesting to learn what his other duties were.

At the end of the fourteenth century the city of Bourges found a new and munificent patron of the arts in Jean de France, duc de Berry, brother of Charles VI. It was his wish that after his death a sumptuous memorial should be raised to him in the middle of the Cathedral choir. As it was to have a procession of '*pleurants*' it would have taken up far too much room and the Canons successfully resisted the project. The Duke then proceeded to construct a Sainte-Chapelle at the ducal palace to house his sepulchre. Built by Guy and André de Dammartin, it was one of the architectural gems of its age. The Benedictine dom Martène, writing in 1724 when appreciation of Gothic architecture was at a low ebb, exclaimed: "I do not know if it would be possible to see a more beautiful building.' Thirty years later the Archbishop, reluctant to pay for the upkeep of this redundant church, had it pulled down and the monuments of Jean de Berry and his wife finally found their way to the Cathedral.

They were placed in the crypt. They deserve a more distinguished housing, for the Duke was a benefactor of the Cathedral. In about 1370 the great west window – known as '*le grand housteau*' – was set up at his expense.

No doubt for this reason a miniature of the west front was included in the *Très Riches Heures du Duc de Berry*. The artist has only included the three central bays of the front, presumably because his primary interest was to illustrate this window. It is the earliest known depiction of Bourges and it shows that the buttresses were originally more richly ornamented than they appear today. In particular there was a statue of St Stephen poised above the central gable and on the face of each of the inward buttresses, each beneath an elegant little stone canopy, were figures of his executioners hurling stones at him from either side of the *grand housteau*.

The treatment of the same theme in the tympanum of the portal devoted to St Stephen – the one to the right of the central doorway – is less successful. It has no sense of grouping – just a row of figures, two of whom are in exactly the position of a footballer about to throw in. There is here none of the dynamic rhythm of the same scene as depicted at Notre-Dame and Meaux.

It must be remembered that the sculptures were very badly damaged by the Huguenots and that most of the figures are subsequent restorations. Certain statuettes from the architraves have survived and are in the Musée de Bourges or the Louvre. They show an impressive economy of detail and an effective use of bold and simple shapes. As they are in good condition it is not easy to see why the restorers of the early nineteenth century saw fit to remove them.

This restoration was carried out by Caudron between 1840 and 1846. It led to an outburst of anger and contempt from Didron. 'Time has already rendered justice to these restorations; it is not two years since they were executed, and already some of these sculptures in mastic have disappeared . . . all the rest are cracking and only need to be allowed to fall off.'

Nevertheless the central tympanum still contains one of the most accomplished of all the many similar depictions of the Last Judgment. Only the lowest of the three tiers was badly damaged, but enough remained for the original composition to be respected. It shows the resurrection of the bodies from their earthly tombs. According to medieval tradition all are resurrected at the age of Christ at the time of his death, that is to say, in the prime of life. All the figures are naked except for that of the Bishop, who is fully robed. The medieval mind was quite prepared to show a bishop among the company of the damned but apparently stopped short at uncovering his nakedness.

The artist has been at pains to express movement – of tombs bursting open and of bodies clambering out. He achieves it by means of angularity – the diagonal accents of the coffin lids and the legs and arms all crooked at a variety of obtuse and acute angles. If this sculpture can be seen illuminated by the afternoon sun, the figures all appear to be looking towards it, as if dazzled after their long sojourn in the tomb. There is something of the pathos of the Prisoners' Chorus in *Fidelo* about the scene.

In the tier above the artist has relied upon contrast for his effect. The central figure of the archangel presides, holding in his right hand the scales of justice while his left hand curls protectively round the head of a soul – traditionally represented as a child – for whom a demon is waiting eagerly. The archangel's wings express the duality of the situation. His right wing, on the paradisal side, is cupped in an attitude of retentive care, whereas his left wing, on the infernal side, is spread in a gesture of relinquishment.

On this sinister side the damned, still naked, form a scene of ugly and disturbing confusion, while to the angel's right all is order and decorum. The souls of the righteous are in the hand of God and they have become respectably dressed for the occasion. At the extreme left, beneath a trefoiled canopy, sits Abraham holding his capacious bosom open to receive the elect, while overhead angels form an angelic chain to pass along the coronets which are presumably the reward for kind hearts. One of the figures is already crowned – a tall and handsome king who holds a flower in his hand. The combination of royalty and sanctity immediately suggests St Louis, who had died only a few years before.

1. Beauvais: the tallest choir ever built

2. Sens: the nave and choir, showing the sexpartite vault and the alternance
pile fort—pile faible.

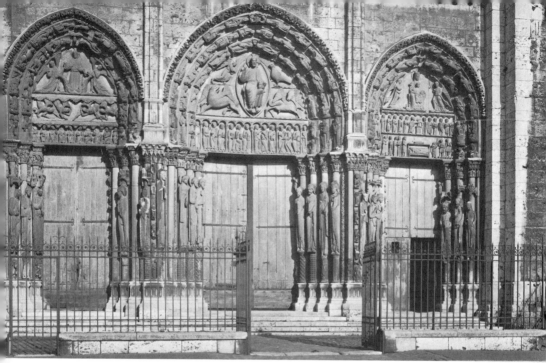

3. Chartres: a) The *portail royal*

b) Statue columns

4. Laon: the towers from the west

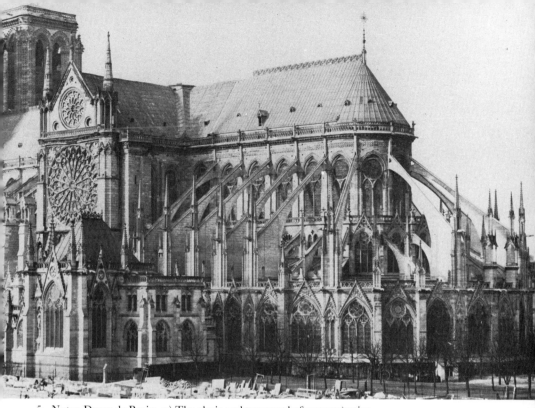

5. Notre-Dame de Paris: a) The choir and transept before restoration

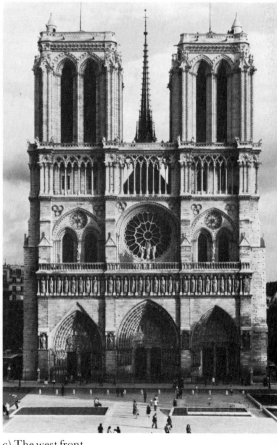

b) The nave and tribunes   c) The west front

6. Chartres: aerial view from the east

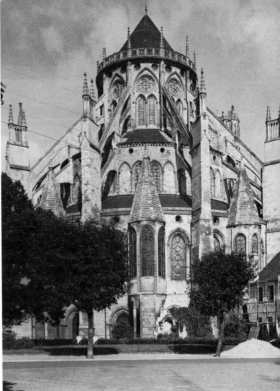

Bourges: a) The choir and aisles from the triforium b) The apse from the east

c) West portal: The Last Judgement

8. Le Mans: the choir and hemicycle

9. Le Mans: the choir and its aisles

10. Coutances: the apse from the east

11. Coutances: a) The cathedral from the north-east

b) The pillars of the hemicycle and ambulatory vaults

12. Reims: the west front

13. Reims: the choir and hemicycle

14. Reims: the Coronation, Louis XIV enthroned

15. Amiens: the nave, choir and hemicycle

16. Tours: the choir and hemicycle

In the upper section, the figure of Christ, half naked to reveal his wounds, holds out his hands as if to offer mankind the choice between life and death. Beside him four angels hold the instruments of his passion, while at the two extremities the figures of the Virgin and St John kneel in attitudes of supplication. As Auguste Rodin so beautifully puts it: *'Le geste de la prière gouverne de beaux plis dans les draperies'.**

In the sixteenth century the symmetry of the west front was destroyed by the collapse of the north tower. In 1504 the foundations were already moving. Experts were summoned from Albi, Blois and Gaillon to advise the Chapter. The tower was braced with iron bars while work on the foundations was put in hand. One of the Canons, Pierre de Costello, 'stimulated the workmen by his presence on the site', while the Chancellor went in person to seek oak trees in the forest of St Salais. It was all in vain. On the last day of December 1506 'a frightful crash proclaimed the fall of the tower and of one and a half vaults of the great nave'. Later in the day two more pillars collapsed and with them went another bay of vaulting.

This time Colin Biart, who had done important work on the châteaux of Amboise, Blois and Le Verger, was called in, together with Guillaume Senault, the master mason of Gaillon. Sixteen carpenters, under Bernard Chapuzet, *'maître charpentier de la Cathédrale'* were taken on and 'worked without respite, day and night' to shore up all that it had not been found necessary to demolish. By October 1508 all was ready and on the 19th the first stone of the new tower was laid. The number of *'compagnons'* rose to forty-three and of *'manoeuvres'* to forty-nine supplemented by nearly a hundred other workmen, making a total task force of 190. In 1518 the painting of the royal arms and those of the Cardinal Bohier upon the bosses of the new vaults marked the completion of the repairs to the nave; in 1540 the tower itself had been completed. The Cathedral of Bourges had assumed the form which we see today.

The later history of the Cathedral need not detain us long. The ravages of the Huguenots were confined to the decorations, although an unsuccessful attempt was made to mine the building as at Orléans. In the eighteenth century the Canons made their usual depredations in the name of good taste, removing the stalls, the altar, the choir screen and all the gilded finery of the Middle Ages, including a number of stained glass windows. Their own embellishments did not survive the Revolution. It was the 'constitutional' Bishop, a man named Torné, who himself gave orders for the spoliation of the choir.

It is to their eternal credit that all the Canons of Bourges remained

* 'The posture of prayer dictates the beautiful folds of the draperies.'

loyal to the Church into which they had been ordained. The record of the Chapter throughout the centuries had not been one of distinction, but in their last hour they rose magnificently to the occasion. On 12 July 1790, the law was passed for the suppression of Chapters. It was not published until 4 October. On that day the Canons met. They resolved unanimously to maintain their strict adherence to the Church of Rome, being ready 'with God's grace to give their blood and their lives' to this sacred cause. They behaved with great dignity and perhaps because of this they were allowed for the last time to celebrate the rites of Christmas and the Epiphany *avec la pompe accoutumée*. After that they dispersed. Canon Rousseau has written the chronicle of the terrible sufferings which they endured. In the whole history of St Etienne de Bourges, this is the finest page.

CHAPTER NINE

Le Mans

There is a certain obvious attraction about a building which is all in a single style. It offers the complete and perfect translation of the ideas of the architect; it has a unity which derives from its being an aesthetic whole. This impression is easily experienced at Bourges. But there is also an attraction no less powerful about a building which has been added to throughout the ages. Unity is here sacrificed for continuity, as generation after generation has left its own particular mark upon the fabric – its own unique expression of its faith. To those who come to worship, rather than merely to admire, this mixture of styles coheres because there is a common thread – a *fil conducteur* – in the living faith of the long procession of our ancestors, which each new phase in the architecture will represent in its own inimitable manner. A good example of such a happy medley of architecture is the Cathedral of St Julien du Mans.

And yet the main difference of style at Le Mans does not only reflect difference of generation but change in political affiliation. In 1205 Philippe-Auguste added Le Maine to his possessions and when, twelve years later, Bishop Maurice applied for permission to rebuild the choir and apse on lines so grandiose that they would project beyond the ancient city wall, it was specified that the architecture should be '*français*'. The normal term for the Gothic style throughout Europe at this time was *opus francigenum* – 'French work'.

For the existing Cathedral, although largely posterior to St Denis, had borrowed little from the Ile de France but was Angevin in feeling, the style associated with the Plantagenets. The new 'French' apse at Le Mans was a political assertion.

But the political and the religious were not nearly so distinct from one another then as they are today. Had not Suger insisted that the King of France bore in his person 'the image of Christ'? Did not the ceremony of the *Sacre*, for which the oil had been sent express from Heaven, proclaim the Sovereign of the House of Capet to be the Lord's Anointed? No separation of thought was necessary between the advancement of the Kingdom of God and the extension of the boundaries of the Kingdom of France. The *abside* of Le Mans – one of

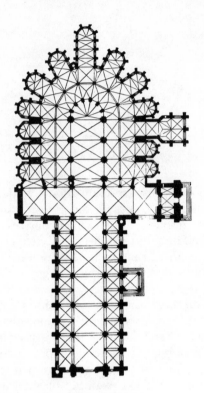

Ground Plan of Le Mans

the most perfect achievements of the Gothic architect – was an impressive assertion of both.

The contrast between the choir and the nave is very striking. Certain remote views from the north and south show the pronounced disparity of the two roof levels – the Gothic completely dominating the Angevin. From nearer to, seen from the little Place du Château to the north-west of the Cathedral, the juxtaposition of the enormous windows of the transept with the large expanse of wall – and correspondingly small expanse of glass – in the nave and aisle is also eloquent. It must be remembered that the flying buttresses were only added to the nave in the thirteenth century when the choir was being built.

Inside, the difference of scale is almost equally apparent, but it is compensated to some extent by the fact that the nave has its own beauty and its own distinction. For the nave offers a not unworthy example of a very different type of architecture.

It is at once obvious that there are here two phases of building which are superimposed one upon the other. The older is represented by the outer wall of the aisles, which often exhibit the alternance of dark stone and pale stone that was typical of the Romanesque. On the inner façades of the nave also the older masonry may be distinguished by its pinker colour. It is a local stone called *roussard* which was rejected by the later builders in favour of the creamy white stone of Soulitré. The outline of the older arcade makes it apparent that the original *ordonnance* was a regular procession of pillars of equal size and equal spacing which was replaced by the alternance *pile forte – pile faible*; for whereas the older arches spring correctly from the *pile faible*, they vanish awkwardly behind the massive masonry of the *pile forte*.

This older building was started under Bishop Vulgrin and finished under Hildebert de Lavardin. It was begun in about 1060 and consecrated on 25 April 1120 by Hildebert himself. There had been a certain amount of difficulty with William the Conqueror who had demanded, but in vain, the taking down of the towers which overlooked the Château in a manner which he felt to be potentially dangerous.

The first nave was only roofed with timber, and two successive fires underlined the necessity of a stone vault. This was realised by Bishop Guillaume de Passavant. In order to carry his great stone canopy he needed far stronger supports at every alternate column.

The new vaults, which were presumably completed in 1158 when the nave was consecrated, owed nothing to those already erected in the Ile de France. They represent the local style – '*la voûte angevine*' – of which the Cathedral of Angers affords, appropriately enough, one of the finest examples. The most typical feature of such a vault is its dome-like section. The keystone at Le Mans is nine feet higher than the apex of the vaulting arch.

The capitals in the nave present the variety of treatment that corresponds with the varying dates of its construction. They range from the crude and almost puerile grotesques of the eleventh century to the highly stylized acanthus leaves and volutes of the twelfth century that reveal their closeness to the Corinthian original.

But the medieval spirit did not easily content itself with stylisations. In some of these capitals faces peep out between the abacus and the acanthus fronds; birds rummage among the leaves; an owl stares blankly out from the foliage. But one can never be sure if such figures are merely artist's licence – an expression of the exuberance of the age – or whether they might not have some symbolic meaning and were carved according to the dictates of the presiding theologians. Emile Mâle has no doubt that this owl should be taken as symbolising the blindness of the Jewish race who rejected the Light of the World and preferred the works of darkness. Such, at any rate, is the significance given to the owl in the Bestiaries of the period.

Having constructed the nave in an architecture which took little or no notice of the style that was being born in the Ile de France, the builders of Le Mans then proceeded to adorn their nave with a porch which was virtually copied from Chartres. The scene in the tympanum of Christ surrounded by symbolic figures of the four Evangelists is almost identical with that of the central arch of the *Portail Royal*. It appears again in the little church of St Loup de Naud near Provins. Francis Salet, one of the great authorities on Le Mans, has made a special study of these portals and considers that of St Loup *'peut-être l'oeuvre la plus achevée, la plus harmonieuse que nous a transmise le douzième siècle'.*

Much the same progression of style can be observed in the windows of the nave. Enough fragments have survived to make it clear that the nave was once adorned with an important, if not complete, set of twelfth-century glass.

Of these the most distinguished is the 'Ascension' window in the second bay of the south aisle. It has suffered numerous restorations, receiving its present setting in 1956 from the *maître verrier* Max Ingrand. The groups of Apostles are set against plain backgrounds of alternate red and blue, and this alternance has been repeated by Ingrand for the empty panels. The exaggerated posturing of the figures and the rather geometric folds of their raiment links these windows with many of the wall paintings and illuminations of the west of France in the first half of the twelfth century.

The Ascension window is an unusually monumental composition – the groups extending across the full width of the embrasure. Its style is reflected, however, in the much smaller panels of certain other windows. A good example is the scene of the three Magi warned in a dream not to return to Herod. It is in a roundel at the top of the window dedicated to St Stephen which answers the Ascension window in the second bay of the north aisle.

The rest of the glass, which tells the story of St Stephen, is the best preserved example of a later style which clearly shows the influence of St Denis and the west front of Chartres. The lovely sapphire blue, the balanced grouping of the figures, the easy flow and harmonious lines of the draperies all suggest a close affinity with the great windows of the Passion and the Childhood of Christ in the central and southern lights above the *Portail Royal*.

The west window of Le Mans, also, at once recalls the central west window of Chartres. But the likeness was deliberately accentuated in

* 'perhaps the most perfected and harmonious achievement which the twelfth century has bequeathed us.'

118

the nineteenth-century restoration. This was carried out by Félix Gaudin in 1896. The large figure of the patron saint of the Cathedral, St Julien, is his own work and of the eighteen panels only twelve are original. The fact that they are not easily detected is evidence of the sympathetic care with which the restoration was effected. The panels now exhibit an alternance, resembling that of Chartres, between squares and roundels, but Louis Grodecki, the great authority on the glass of Le Mans, affirms that the original panels were all square.

Although most of the windows in the nave have suffered mutilation and although thirteen of them are modern, they still provide a beautiful ensemble and afford an interesting study of the progress of the art of stained glass during the twelfth century. Both in the later windows and in the sculptures of the south porch, the influence of Chartres – that is to say of the west end of Chartres as built by Geoffroy de Lèves – is conspicuous. It is conspicuous by its absence in the architecture, which remains true to the Angevin style.

In contrast to this the new choir and apse were, it was stipulated, to be 'French', but in 1217 that definition still allowed the architect a wide degree of choice. His taste was, in fact, eclectic. Obviously Bourges was his primary model, but he has greatly improved upon it. 'All the hesitations,' wrote Louis Gonse, 'all the deficiencies even, that can be noticed in the upper parts of Bourges, have all disappeared. The architect of Le Mans proceeds with an unfailing sureness of touch.'

But he is happy to borrow from wherever he finds a worthy model. From Picardy he has taken the deep apsidal chapels, each with its own articulated roof; from Normandy, the circular abacus, the rather sharply pointed arch and the lace-like delicacy of the carvings; from Paris, the composition of the intermediary piers and the crisp precision of the capitals. But this diversity of origin has not resulted in the least diversity of style. The mind of the maker has imposed its own unity upon the whole. The result may be, in general terms, impeccably French; in reality it is unique to Le Mans.

The architect, whoever he may have been, was a man of sensitive aesthetic imagination and of an apparently faultless technical ability – *'un homme dans la pleine maîtrise de son art'*. Despite the attacks of Huguenots and Revolutionaries; despite the occasional periods of neglect and the ceaseless erosions of Time, the *abside* has stood. 'Not a stone has given way in the whole, gigantic ensemble; not a movement, not a crack has occurred'. The bars of iron that were inserted in 1823 to tie the buttresses together were as superfluous as they were unsightly – a monument to the ignorance of the architect who ordered their erection. The first architect knew far better than he did. *'Au point de vue statique,'* continues Louis Gonse, *'l'abside du Mans est,* *avec celle de Cologne qu'elle précède d'un demi-siècle, la plus savamment conçue des absides gothiques'.**

The ground plan shows at once the most distinctive feature – the impressive array of thirteen chapels, each of them two bays deep except for the eastern one which has twice the depth. Three of them project at right angles from either side of the choir and are contiguous. The other seven radiate from the outer ambulatory. From the focal point of the apse, which is where the celebrating priest stands at the high altar, each chapel appears in its entirety in the interstice between the great piers. Thus the chapel altars are each related to the high altar. In order to achieve this correspondence there has to be a short space of ambulatory wall between each chapel. These spaces have been used for the insertion of six windows which greatly improve the lighting of the ambulatory. This internal disposition has a determining influence upon the design and form of the flying buttresses.

If we now look at the exterior, from the great Place des Jacobins below, we will notice that the outer buttress piers are grouped in pairs which stand to either side of the windows just described. But the intermediary buttress piers are single. The flyers, therefore, have to branch out from the single pier to both the outer piers. This gives the whole structure the shape of a capital Y from above.

If we now pass back into the Cathedral and see how this arrangement 'comes out' on the inner side, we will see that the triangular interstices caused by the intermediary windows reflect the same form of the capital Y in their vaulting.

Seen from the inside, the choir at Le Mans is one of the most astonishing achievements of the Middle Ages. Its architecture is the result of a noble vision faithfully realised – a building beautiful in its design and faultless in its execution. Everything is reduced to its essentials. The architect had no need of a triforium, so it is omitted; the pointed arches of the great arcade reach to the foot of the clerestory windows. Behind them the façade of the inner ambulatory exactly fits the archway of each bay, so that the smaller clerestory is framed in the actual arch; beneath it the triforium and main arcade occupy the interstices between the columns.

The height of the first ambulatory is thus dictated by its relationship to the central vessel. The high vaults are thirty-four metres to the keystone; those of the first ambulatory are twenty-two. The presence of a triforium in the first ambulatory in turn dictates the

* 'From the point of view of statics the apse of Le Mans is, together with that of Cologne, which it precedes by half a century, the most knowingly thought out of Gothic apses.'

much lower vault of the outer ambulatory, which is only eleven metres. All this had been done at Bourges, but at Le Mans the design has been perfected. The proportions are improved, making the clerestory windows considerably taller; the design of the triforium is much more satisfactory and the decorations more judiciously disposed. There is no sign of hesitation; nothing has been left to chance. The architect knew exactly what he wanted to do and how to do it.

The beauty and sheer technical perfection of the choir has long been recognised. It was only in 1908 that it was discovered that the aesthetic effect of the architecture is based upon a subtle and sophisticated use of counter-perspective. The *Architecte en Chef*, Pascal Vérité, had occasion to make a measured drawing of the plan. He has recounted in the *Bulletin Monumental* what was the unexpected outcome of his researches: 'I noticed that the three bays of the choir differ from each other in width, in depth and in height.'

The side walls are not parallel, but splay out slightly towards the east. It is only a matter of two feet, but the spread is so exactly symmetrical that it cannot be attributed to mere inaccuracy. Nor could it be dismissed as coincidence that the same gradual enlargement towards the east can be detected in a slight but steady rise in the height of the vault ridge. Finally, the bays of the choir reveal a progressive widening. There is but one explanation possible: the architect was determined to counteract the narrowing impression of perspective.

This optical illusion, worthy of the designers of the Parthenon, cannot be detected by the eye of the beholder except upon the floor. The black and white squares of the *dallage* (tiled floor) do not coincide with the lines of the choir stalls. Only the modern photographer, who can reduce the effect of perspective by using a telephoto lens, has surpassed the architect of Le Mans in creating a deliberate impression of 'build up', superimposing pier upon pier and vault upon vault and diminishing the sense of distance between the spectator and the tall, lean arches of the hemicycle.

There are certain other features which contribute to the general effect. The three great piers on either side of the choir are composite – a central core flanked with twelve colonnettes. On the inward side, these colonnettes rise without interruption, cutting through the capitals of the great arcade and through the sculptured cornice which underscores the clerestory. This unbroken vertical accent adds greatly to the majesty of the design.

It is interesting also to observe how the architect maintains a balance between symmetry and variety. In the apse the form of the tracery in both the upper clerestory and the triforium is regular and symmetrical. In the straight bays of the choir each is given a different and more, or less, elaborate treatment. But this variety is clearly intentional because it is in each case exactly reflected in the opposite bay.

Both within and without, the choir of Le Mans is one of the most perfect realisations of all that Gothic architecture sought to express – a cage of coloured glass upheld by a slender scaffolding of stone. *'Non pas du solide,'* wrote Paul Claudel, *'mais le poème du poids . . . Le Temple païen était en bloc; l'Église est un concert d'efforts.'*

At least in the upper storeys the brilliantly lovely glass, to house which this architecture was designed, has remained more or less intact. Looking up into the vaults of the sanctuary, we are looking back into the thirteenth century. It is something of a miracle that these windows have been preserved: the dangers by which they were threatened were many and formidable.

It was the elements and the Huguenots who did the greatest damage to Le Mans, but eighteenth-century "good taste" also played a considerable part in the work of destruction. In April 1562, the Protestants took possession of the Cathedral and began a terrible programme of pillage which lasted for three months. Tombs were violated, statues decapitated, reliquaries desecrated; the choir screen and stalls were so mutilated that they had to be demolished. We know from the *Plaintes et Doléances du Chapitre*, drawn up after the uprising, that fifty-seven windows in the apsidal chapels were broken, together with all the intermediary windows of the ambulatory. But the upper windows of the choir remained untouched.

In 1767 Louis-André de Grimaldi, a Bishop of the House of Monaco, began his series of equally disastrous 'improvements'. The high altar, dismissed as *'un amas confus de pierres et d'ornements de cuivre'* was swept away; the Medieval and Renaissance silver, of which the worthy Bishop would not even allow an inventory to be made, was condemned as *'vieilles et inutiles'* and sold. Finally the whole Cathedral was whitewashed. But Grimaldi did not do what the Chapter of Notre-Dame did: the upper windows of the choir remained in place.

During the Revolution an attempt was actually made to have the whole Cathedral pulled down in order to make place for buildings 'of a more egalitarian nature' – that is to say Tribunals and Prisons. The move was successfully countered by the Société des Arts. But the elements nearly succeeded where bigotry and barbarism had failed. On 9 November 1810, part of the vaulting of the south transept collapsed and the next day one of the high windows of the choir on the south side was blown in by the wind. It was taken down and portions of it used for the repair of other windows that had been damaged.

Each time that a disaster occurred – and there was another caused by a violent hailstorm in 1858 – the restorers seem to have taken bits of glass from one window in order to repair the damages of another, so that by the end of the nineteenth century the original series was confusingly shuffled. The remaining gaps on the ground floor were filled with contemporary glass described by Louis Grodecki as *'insipide et d'une rare mediocrité'*.

These re-adjustments and replacements, however, are fairly minor blemishes. The tout ensemble of the upper windows ranks with Tours and the Sainte-Chapelle as one of the finest arrays of glass in France.

It was a new style. Whereas at Chartres the upper windows are devoted to large-scale figures which can be identified from ground level, those of Le Mans, with the single exception of the east window, are divided into little scenes which can only be 'read' with binoculars. Whereas at Chartres the dominant colour is the famous blue to which it has given its name, that of Le Mans is red. Blue, as Claudel so perceptively described it, is the colour of darkness: red is the colour of flame. 'Over the altar,' he writes, 'we see precisely that long flame where the red intrudes upon the blue as if to devour it, as if to absorb it, producing that purple, that foxglove purple which is the glory of Le Mans. *Vous vous souvenez de ces grands tapis de pourpre lumineuse en face de la Sacristie?'**

They are unforgettable. Being orientated towards the north the windows 'opposite the Sacristy' are practically never penetrated by the sun. Jean Villette, in his study of the glass at Chartres, observes that when the sun is not out the windows reveal a greater unity; 'each window retains all the strength and all the variety of its colours'. Without the sun to enflame the reds and scarlets, the blues reassert themselves and produce this rich and vibrant purple.

The last window before the ambulatory on the north side of the lower clerestory provides an excellent example. It was presented by the Vintners and there is a story attaching to it. On 20 April, *dimanche de Quasimodo*, 1254, the choir was consecrated by Bishop Geoffroy de Loudun and the various Corporations of Le Mans were invited to attend the ceremony with torches. For reasons which we can only surmise, the Vintners arrived too late to perform this function. To atone for their failure they decided forthwith to offer to the Cathedral 'in place of flambeaux which only sparkle for a moment, a stained glass window which will illuminate the Church for all Eternity'. They provided one of the loveliest windows in the whole Cathedral.

The one exception to this series is the east window of the lower

---

* 'You remember that transparent cloth of purple opposite the Sacristy?'

clerestory, which alone reflects the later style of Chartres, recalling in particular the window dedicated to St Chéron in the north-east apsidal chapel. It shows St Gervais and St Protais – two martyrs especially venerated in France – on either side of the Virgin at whose feet the donor comte Rotrou V de Montfort, is holding up his window in a gesture of homage.

Rotrou de Montfort was one of those mentioned as having assisted at the Consecration. We know nothing of that ceremony except for a charming detail in the document preserved in the *Actus Pontificum Cenomanensis* which tells how the dust and debris of the builders was cleared away by voluntary labour, women of all ranks helping to remove sand regardless of the damage to their clothing – *'contra mulierum morem . . . vestibus non parcentes'* – and children holding up their tunics to make a pocket for the removal of dust.

The finished Cathedral had place for six thousand people – twice the estimated population of Le Mans at that date. The Chapter could not have undertaken so vast a project and completed it in so short a time without considerable financial resources. It is known that Queen Berengaria, widow of Richard Coeur de Lion and *'Dame douairière du Mans'*, provided considerable assistance.

We have slightly more detailed information about the financing of the transepts. We know from the *Nécrologie-Obituaire* of the Cathedral that Pierre d'Ardenay, Archdeacon of Montfort, who died in 1303, had given, during his lifetime the sum of fifty livres *'ad incipiendum opus in cruce . . . versus campanile'* – 'to begin the work of the transept . . . towards the bell tower.' This refers to the south transept.

It was not, however, until 1387 that the building of the south transept was begun. It was undertaken by *'maître Jehan le maczon [maçon]'*, his apprentice Henri Gillot, the sculptor Colinet le Blont and a team of seventy workmen – masons, plumbers, capenters and labourers. In spite of this rather large task force, the transept was not completed until 1397.

The south transept, ending as it does in the great tower, could not be given a south window. It was therefore the obvious place in which to position the organ. It was one of the finest in France, wrote the Chanoine Pioger, *'surtout par son harmonie qui produit un si bel effet'*.* The quality of the instrument is only matched by the excellence of its encasement. 'The organ-case,' writes another Chanoine called Marquet, 'is one of the most sumptuous bequeathed to us by the Renaissance'.

At the end of the fourteenth century Bishop Adam de Chastelain offered an organ 'in the German manner' to the Cathedral. It cost

* 'above all for its harmony, which produces such a beautiful effect.'

1500 écus. In 1519 the Cardinal de Luxembourg gave 200 écus to help make 'as well as the gilded organ, the beautiful great organ'. Perhaps the 'gilded organ' was the German instrument already installed. It is more than probable that the *'belles, grosses orgues'* were substantially the instrument which we see today, though it was only built ten years later, between 1529 and 1535. It was the work of Pierre Bert.

The buffet was ornamented with the cardinal virtues, with *Caritas* in the centre, bearing the inscription in Latin: 'the greatest of these is Love'. There were also inscribed verses from Psalm 98: 'sing, rejoice and give thanks. Praise the Lord upon the harp, sing to the harp with a psalm of thanksgiving. With trumpets also and shawms: O show yourselves joyful before the Lord the King'.

Its glory was short lived. In 1562, when the Huguenots attacked the Cathedral, the organ was wantonly and badly damaged. Two towers of *'grosses trompes'*, between twenty-four and thirty-two feet high, were demolished; many of the working parts destroyed and the statue of Love taken down and broken. Neither music as the food of Love, nor Love as the fountainhead of all morality were apparently valued by that rather dour religion.

The organ was not finally repaired until 1650. Subsequent restorations, writes Pioget, 'completely changed the character of the instrument. The organ builders suppressed a number of mixtures – sacrificed to the taste of the age – in order to replace them with *gambas, voix célestes* and *unda maris* in doubtful taste. As the result of this, and in spite of the addition of new *jeux*, the great organ has been deprived of its sonorous effects.'

Not long after the building of the south transept it was possible to begin work on its opposite number to the north. In 1392 Charles VI had an attack of insanity while at Le Mans and was looked after by one of the canons. No doubt this had something to do with the munificent donation made in the same year, *'pour la grande et spécial [sic] dévotion que nous avons pour Monsieur sainct Julian de Mans'*, amounting to ten thousand livres.

In spite of Charles VI's donation, considerable efforts had to be made to raise the funds necessary for the completion of the transept. The Dean and Chapter were patrons of some forty livings, and in each of these churches collecting boxes were placed. The offerings were sometimes considerable. In 1394 the Abbaye de Beaulieu declared the enormous sum of 1,544 livres. In 1403 the Canons of the Cathedral opened their own coffers to find only thirty-three livres, seven ounces of which were in counterfeit money. To make up for this they decided to set aside 10 per cent of their prebends. On top of this the Chanoine Jacquemin bequeathed twenty livres 'pro opera sumptuoso ecclesiae'. But it seems to have been the Archdeacons who really saved the situation. The Archdeacon of Montfort gave 400 livres only to be outdone by the Archdeacon of Château-du-Loir who gave 1000. But perhaps the greatest benefactor next to the King was Guillaume Fillastre, Archdeacon of Laval, later Cardinal de St Marc, whose frequent liberalities between 1423 and 1427 earned him the honour of having his portrait in the north rose window and his escutcheon on one of the bosses of the vault, near to that of the King.

The work was carried out by two architects, Nicolas de l'Ecluse and Jean de Dampmartin and seems to have been completed in about 1430. It is a very noble piece of architecture. As at Amiens, it retains the round arch to enframe the rose window which forms the upper part of the north light. Beneath this is an elegant triforium in which the tracery takes the form of a row of *fleurs de lys* – no doubt intended as a compliment to the royal benefactor. The transept in fact is normally referred to as *'l'oeuvre du Roi'*.

The text of a law suit between Bishop Adam de Chastelain and the Chapter, which refers to the royal donation, mentions also that the new transept was to be built *'au pareil de l'autre'* and the King's wish was clearly respected. No difference in style can be detected.

The determining feature of the new transepts is that they were built upon the foundations of the old. From the point of view of the ground plan they were in scale with the Angevin nave. Now they had to be accommodated in elevation to the scale of the Gothic choir. Their height is therefore out of all proportion to their width. There was no room to develop side aisles and so to repeat the architecture of the choir. There was therefore nothing to dictate the levels at which the façade should divide into arcade, triforium and clerestory – so the architects of both transepts have devoted almost the whole wall space to enormous windows which cover an area of 150 square metres each.

In order to maintain the stability of these vertical walls of glass the builders introduced an inner framework of iron ties. They held until 9 November 1810, when an exceptional gust of wind caused the collapse of part of the vaulting and blew in some of the windows. The damage was successfully repaired, but it is perhaps significant that no other builder attempted to emulate the tall and narrow transepts of Le Mans.

CHAPTER TEN

Coutances

There can be little doubt that Le Mans served as a model for the choir of the delightful little Cathedral of Coutances in Normandy. But whereas Le Mans was specifically imposing a 'French' style upon a former Plantagenet stronghold, at Coutances the Gothic structures of the Ile de France have been assimilated into an ensemble which is unmistakably Norman in tradition. It was the work of an architect, André Mussat infers, 'well up to date with the architectural movements of his time and strongly attached to the structural and decorative customs of his province'. The architect has gone behind Le Mans to the original inspiration of Bourges; he has been influenced by Burgos in Spain and by Pontigny in Burgundy; but his *abside* most closely resembles that of the great Norman Abbey of St Etienne de Caen. All these, however, have been fully digested and the Master Builder has produced a work of art that is entirely his own.

But if the choir reminds us from the inside of Le Mans and from the outside of Bourges, it resembles them in style rather than in scale. The vaults are less than half the height of those at Bourges. Coutances is thus a Gothic choir and apse in miniature.

It is in the nature of the miniature that it should be exquisite. In the enormous constructions of Reims or Amiens there is room for a certain level of inaccuracy, for certain negligences that will pass unperceived. In the smaller scale production of Coutances, where all the parts may be more narrowly scrutinised, everything had to be fully thought out and precisely executed. It is in this scrupulous care that the essential merit of Coutances resides. 'We are confronted here,' writes Yves Froidevaux, 'by one of the most perfect achievements of the Middle Ages.'

But the Master Builder did not begin with a clean state. He had to build on what had gone before. The genesis of Coutances follows the pattern which was by now becoming familiar. In 1204 Normandy was taken over by Philippe-Auguste. In 1218 the old Cathedral was destroyed by fire. It was immediately decided to rebuild. The reconstruction started with the nave, which is thus contemporary with the choir of Le Mans and was not influenced by it. But the

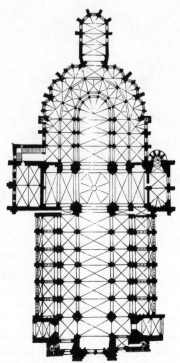

Ground Plan of Coutances

building of the choir and apse was a second and separate campaign which followed at a date late enough to derive its inspiration from Le Mans. This inspiration controls the general appearance of the hemicycle and the disposition of its aisles and ambulatories. But in detail the architecture is true to the decorative style of Normandy.

Certain features may be listed which are typical of the region. The arches of the main arcade are ornamented with a multiplicity of mouldings which begets a corresponding multiplicity of colonnettes; in the spandrels between the arches of the triforium are roundels carved with floral designs of a surprising delicacy, only surpassed in the exquisite cloisters of Mont St Michel. Also in Norman taste is the very large triforium, divided into twin bays. In the later parts – the transepts and the choir – a new feature becomes apparent: when twin arches are placed within a containing arch, the arcs of both are described from the same centre, so that the mouldings are parallel. A comparison between the nave triforium and the arcading in the lantern at once reveals this difference. Where the French influence is more apparent, the Norman features are more numerous.

The decision to append a choir with three tiers of windows on to a nave with the modest height of twenty-one metres posed a problem of proportion which seems to have caused the architect some concern. He could have copied Le Mans and built a choir and apse that were on an undisguisedly larger scale than the nave. It is perhaps more excusable to do this when the nave is an older building in an earlier style. Coutances is all in one style and a disparity in scale between the two halves would have been less acceptable. But it must have been the architect's decision to build the central octagon and spire which determined his solution of the problem. It would not be feasible to perch such a spire upon two buildings of unequal height.

Being therefore unable to raise the level of his vault ridge, the architect obtained the extra height he needed by lowering the level of the ambulatory some four or five feet. This enabled him to have an inner aisle of thirteen and a quarter metres and an outer aisle of seven and a half. The result did not satisfy him, for he subsequently lowered the level of the nave floor as well, thus revealing at the base of the columns a ring of rough masonry which was never meant to be visible.

We only need to recall that the inner aisle of Le Mans is the same height as the main vault of Coutances to see how tiny, in terms of cathedrals, the latter really is.

The nave was begun under the episcopate of Hughes de Morville. He was the nephew of Simon de Morville, one of the murderers of Thomas à Becket. Simon had died 'giving proof of a deep repentance' and Hughes consecrated one of the chapels in the north transept to the newly canonised martyr. In the window is portrayed the crime in which his uncle had taken part.

It may be no coincidence that the village of Morville, which is thought to have been the birthplace of Bishop Hughes, is very near the quarries of Yvetot which provided the stone for the Cathedral.

Whoever was the Master Builder was set a task circumscribed by the remains of the Romanesque Cathedral built under Geoffroy de Montbray in the early eleventh century. Not only did he have to build upon the old foundations; he had to incorporate much of the old masonry within the new construction.

Beneath the sloping roof of the nave triforium one can still see the Romanesque arcading of the former tribunes. Obviously they cannot have survived in mid air; their supporting pillars must have continued to underpin them. It is to be assumed therefore that these pillars remain encased in the new masonry of the great arcade. In one of the chambers of the north-west tower, also, is clearly a Romanesque survival. The older masonry never shows, but it is there and it must have dictated the proportions of the new building.

In order to appreciate the nave as it was first built, it is necessary to get behind the later additions. The triforium originally opened through twin arches into the roof space above the aisles. Towards the end of the thirteenth century each of the arches was subdivided into two, thus greatly reducing the aperture. Finally these inner archways were also walled in, leaving no communication between the triforium and the nave. In the fourteenth century the balustrade of roundels, for which no possible need remained, was inserted. It completely alters the proportions of the triforium.

The chapels, which were contrived between the buttresses of the nave, were also built in the course of the fourteenth century. They project well beyond the line of the original buttress piers, with the result that new piers had to be erected and the flyers extended to meet them. The insertion of these chapels placed the aisle windows at one remove further from the nave. To mitigate the loss of lighting caused by this arrangement, the architect had the happy inspiration of separating the chapels from each other by a series of openwork tracery screens. If these chapels are removed by the historical imagination, and the original windows replaced in their openings, the nave can be reconstructed in all its pristine purity of style.

The transepts and the choir form a second campaign of building which must needs have been the work of a second Master Builder. The difference in style is at once apparent in the triforium and clerestory. In the triforium the delicately carved roundel above the twin arches is replaced by a large trefoil. In the clerestory the wall rib now enframes a slender screen reflecting the tracery of the window. This feature is continued in the choir.

This separate treatment of the front and back of the aperture in the wall is one of the distinctive features of the choir. It is most clearly seen in the hemicycle, where the coupled columns provide an obvious expression of this duality. The inner ring of the arcade presents the concentric arcs of its multiple mouldings towards the choir; the outer ring presents the same towards the ambulatory; between these two archivolts, the inner surface of the arch is flat and undecorated. The same arrangement is found in the more complex piers of the straight bays of the choir. But perhaps the system is at its most effective in the clerestory of the apse, where the interstices between the windows and the wall ribs are provided with little quadripartite vaults.

This expression of the thickness of the wall gives a feeling of solidity to the choir at Coutances which is reinforced by the relative lack of height in its proportions. Even in miniature, it lacks the tall attenuation of Le Mans.

In other respects the apse of Coutances is closer to Le Mans than to Bourges. Both have six columns to the hemicycle, whereas Bourges has four; both make use of cylindrical columns, whereas at

Bourges they remain composite; both have only two storeys to the inner façade, whereas Bourges has three because it retains the triforium.

It has been suggested by Colmet Daage that the choir of Coutances might even be by the same hand as that of Le Mans. It is not a likely hypothesis. The architecture of Coutances is in some ways retrogressive. The Master Builder had made very little use of tracery, although the fully developed technique was at his disposal. He shows a distinct preference for the simple lancet. In the transepts he has made his largest lights by grouping lancets in a manner almost suggestive of Salisbury. While other cathedral builders were striving for a maximum display of glass, he seldom makes full use of the area available for a window and he devotes considerable space to the triforium at the expense of the clerestory.

One detail distinguishes the choir at Coutances from either of its French prototypes. At the point where the straight bays of the choir begin to curve round into the hemicycle there is a break in the balustrade which underlines the clerestory, and a little projection built out on corbels interrupts the rhythm of the vault ribs. This projection houses a spiral staircase which communicates between the clerestory and the roof. On the exterior these projections show as tall, square turrets capped with tall, square pinnacles of roof.

Seen from the south-east, from the gardens of the Bishop's palace, the *abside* of Coutances is small, simple and elegant. The whole composition soars to its climax in the central lantern – *'la plus belle et la plus originale de toutes celles qui furent élevées au treizeième siècle sur le sol Normand'*. To this great octagon tower the build-up of the successive tiers of the apse is entirely subservient. The east end of Coutances has thus a character of its own which distinguishes it at once from its French prototypes, Bourges and Le Mans, and links it with its Norman prototype, St Etienne de Caen.

There is an almost total absence of ornament. The architect has relied upon his structural forms for his aesthetic effect. The windows here are mostly simple lancets; the pinnacles are capped with pointed roofs; the clerestory is surmounted by the plainest of parapets. Compared with the sophisticated tracery, the cusped and crocketted pinnacles and the triple tiers of fretted balustrades at Le Mans, this is austerity indeed. In the straight slope of the overarching flyers and in the concentric rings of its ambulatory roofs, Coutances is much closer to Bourges.

But Bourges has no transepts; the streamlining of its roof continues without interruption to the western towers. In contrast to this the apse of Coutances is solidly backed by the transepts, which add four more pyramidal pinnacles to the skyline. From a certain angle these pinnacles form as it were the seven points of an arpeggio, culminating in the central lantern.

It is more than possible that the lantern was intended to provide a base for a spire, which would have brought Coutances much closer to the proportions of Salisbury, which is its contemporary. The supporting piers are adequate, and in 1477 Bishop Geoffroy d'Herbert proposed the superimposition of a spire. The Chapter, usually at loggerheads with the Bishop, opposed the suggestion and the money available was spent instead on the parish church of St Pierre.

If Coutances had been given its spire and if the spire of St Etienne de Caen had not collapsed in 1566, the similarities between these two *absides* would have been all the more striking. The build-up of the narrow towers, capped with their tall and slender pyramids of roof and backed by the sharply pointed spires of the west front, with their attendant group of elongated pinnacles, is truly dynamic. 'They thrust skyward,' writes Wim Swaan, 'with the energy of rockets leaving the launching pad'.

The spire of Coutances was never built. The octagon lantern, however, seen from within or from without, is a most accomplished piece of architecture which forms a more than adequate climax to the whole building. The tremendous piers which have to support it in the crossing, together with the upward movement created by the unbroken lines of their countless colonnettes give to the whole Cathedral a feeling of magnitude which its dimensions belie. From outside, the verticality of the tall window apertures combines with the upward thrust of the four attendant turrets or *'fillettes'*, again helping us to forget that this is a Cathedral in miniature. As a technical and aesthetic achievement, the lantern of Coutances is superb – an affair of the greatest audacity and elegance. A plunging view from the centre keystone of its sixteen-ribbed vault, which creates a truly kaleidoscopic perspective, shows that none of the masonry of the lantern is directly supported by the piers. It seems to hang in mid air. In the late seventeenth century, when appreciation for Gothic architecture was at a particularly low ebb, the great engineer Vauban visited Coutances and after gazing at the lantern exclaimed: 'Who is the inspired lunatic who dared to launch such a monument into the air?' It is probably more of a compliment than he meant it to be.

The finished Cathedral did not for long enjoy a peaceable existence. Too valuable as a *place forte*, the Cathedral and the Close became the objects of siege and counter-siege in the quarrels between the Harcourt family, supported by the English, and the King of France. It is interesting to note how important it was to the French King to have 'his man' at the Bishopric of Coutances.

132

In 1371 there was a respite and a restoration. Bishop Sylvestre de la Cervelle was enthroned and received a handsome royal subsidy to augment his revenues *'moult diminuées par le fait de nos dernières guerres'*. He immediately set about healing the wounds of the country and repairing the dilapidation of the Cathedral. *Quêteurs* were sent to all the 550 parishes and the clergy instructed to receive them with kindness – 'in ecclesiis suis recipiant benignitur'. Although it was a people impoverished by the ravages of war to whom the appeal was made, the response was generous. It is not men who enjoy security and abundance who are most likely to support a spiritual cause, but those who have learned in the hardest of schools the meaning of sacrifice.

It was not to last. Further hostilities led to further damage and in 1402 the Cathedral of Coutances was described as being 'about to fall into ruins'.

The year 1479 saw the beginning of a new renaissance under Bishop Geoffroy d'Herbert. It was he who felt confident enough to propose the building of the spire, but his confidence was not shared by the Chapter. He carried out some very necessary repairs to the fabric and refounded the Cathedral choir.

Coutances had a musical tradition as long as its history. As early as 1232, Toussaint informs us, it was laid down as one of the duties of the precentor or *chantre* 'to examine the clerks of the choir and to instruct them in music'. A century later another *ordonnance* instituted twenty-four clerks of the choir and six boys of twelve years of age. It was stipulated that these should be 'born in legal wedlock, have a sweet and sonorous voice, be graceful, good looking, well built and quick witted so that one might have high hopes of them.'

The choirboys seem to have been drawn from a fairly wide social spectrum. At least one nobleman's son is listed – Guillaume de Cussy – whereas another named Leliepvre received extra clothing from the Chapter *'à cause de sa grande pauvreté'*. Normally the choir parents were invited to contribute twelve livres towards warm winter clothing.

A book of ceremonial observed in the Cathedral in 1259 is described by Lecanu in his *Histoire du Diocèse de Coutances*. It shows that the rites were *'le pur Romain'*.

The attraction of the medieval liturgy was in the variety brought by the various festivals. The three days after Christmas provided the occasion for honouring the office of Deacon by giving them the leading roles in honour of St Stephen, their Patron Saint. Priests had their turn on St John's day and finally the choirboys took charge to celebrate the Holy Innocents.

The choirboys were given the female roles in the liturgical dramas.

One was to play Mary Magdalene in the Easter Procession. Lecanu has published the Coutances text:

1st Choir	Dic nos Maria, Quid vidisti in via?
Mary	Sepulchrum Christi viventis Et gloriam vidi resurgentis
2nd Choir	Dic nos Maria, Quid vidisti in via?
Mary	Angelicos testes, Sudarium et vestes.
3rd Choir	Dic nos Maria, Quid audisti in via?
Mary	Resurrexit Christus, spes mea, Procedet vos in Galilea.
Un Enfant	Magis est credendum Mariae veraci Quam Judaeorum Turbae fallaci.
All	Scimus Christum surexisse A mortuis vere.

Many of these ceremonies were discontinued in the sixteenth century when the Church was under Protestant pressure. At Coutances the *Jeu de la Nativité* and other popular embellishments of Christmas, were suppressed in 1592 by a rather puritanical Archdeacon. It was a time of plague and he judged it unseemly that a church so frequently in use for funerals should be given over to anything so frivolous. 'Frivolous' may be the wrong word. A church which leaves itself only the two notes of gravity and decorum condemns its worship to a dull monotony.

It has been pointed out by Louis Bouyer, in his excellent study entitled *'Architecture et Liturgie'*, that one of the tendencies of the Counter-Reformation was to do away with the enclosure of the choir and thus to open up the service to the laity. If that was the rule, the great cathedrals certainly provide a large number of exceptions. The *jubé* – in many cases badly mutilated by the Huguenots – was often rebuilt in Renaissance style.

Louis Bouyer traces the history of the choir screen. In the earliest Christian churches the clergy worshipped with the people: *'il n'y a pas un culte de Clergé mais un culte d'assemblée'*. There were two focal points in the earliest church buildings, one centring on the Scriptures, known as the *schola* and the other centring on the altar which was placed in the middle of the church.

In the later basilicas of Rome a new disposition was adopted. The Bishop's chair, no longer the *cathedra* of a doctor, was taken out of the *schola* and became the throne of a high functionary of the State. Like the seat of the Magistrate or the Governor, it was placed in the apse, where it was soon joined by the altar. The introduction of candelabra and incense enhanced the quasi-imperial status of the Bishop. His ministers, writes Bouyer, 'instead of providing, as formerly, the links that effected his solidarity with the whole people, tended to become a display of lacqueys, increasing his own dignity while separating him from the vulgar throng.'

This separation of the clergy from the laity came to be expressed architecturally by the enclosure of the choir and in particular by the *jubé* or pulpitum, which blocked the view of the sanctuary from the nave.

In the Middle Ages this exclusion of the laity from the place of worship was to a certain extent mitigated by the readiness of the clergy to come out and perform to the people. When these popular processions and liturgical dramas were suppressed in the sixteenth century, only the stark separation between clergy and laity remained. It was this that made the choir screens the object of Huguenot hatred and which brought down upon them the destructive forces of the Revolution. It was at Coutances that this opposition first became manifest. In 1791 the vicars of the newly established 'constitutional' church, now severed from Rome, petitioned the Municipality for the removal of the choir screen on religious grounds; 'The people would like the clearing away of the choir screen so that they could see the priest who prays for them'.

Three years later the Cathedral was condemned to further mutilation. It was considered too large for parochial needs and the two transepts were walled off to provide a municipal theatre to the north and a granary to the south. As the lead was stripped off the roofs to provide the army with bullets, neither of these new civic amenities could have been well suited to their function.

It looks as if these partitions were still in place in 1836. On 28 June of that year Victor Hugo visited Coutances and in the evening he wrote to his wife: '*J'ai déjà fait mon tour dans la ville, quoiqu'il soit onze heures du soir, et j'ai vu les beaux clochers assaisonnés d'un magnifique clair de lune*'.* The sight of those clustered pinnacles against a moonlit sky could not have failed to appeal to his romantic imagination. But a

* 'I have already made a tour of the city, although it is eleven o'clock in the evening, and I have seen the beautiful spires in the flattering light of a magnificent moon.'

proper inspection by the cold light of day on the following morning revealed a very different picture. *'Toute la Cathédrale crie au scandale!'*

One fourteenth-century arch had been disfigured by the erection of an absurd altar with a *gloire* 'like a golden sun'; there were two plaster walls across the transepts; worst of all the architect Duchêne was beginning to distemper the walls of the nave 'in a bright yellow, and the vaults white with red ribs'. But Hugo noted with satisfaction that a public outcry had stopped the architect *'au quart de sa bétise'*. Public opinion was beginning to play an important role.

Victor Hugo had already written in 1831 his great book *Notre-Dame de Paris* which did so much to recall his contemporaries to a proper appreciation of their Gothic inheritance. Contrary to what the title suggests, the original inspiration came not from Notre-Dame de Paris but from Notre-Dame de Reims.

CHAPTER ELEVEN

Reims

By the end of the twelfth century the number of cathedrals which were being built in the royal Domain of France was steadily increasing. Sens, Senlis, Noyon, Soissons, Laon, Notre-Dame, Chartres and Bourges were slowly rising from the scaffolding and debris of the master builders. The enthusiasm was contagious. Guillaume de Seignelay, Bishop of Auxerre, 'seeing that his church was suffering from the age of its construction and badly put together . . . whereas all the Bishops around him were raising Cathedrals of a new and most splendid beauty, did resolve to order a new edifice with the help of specialists skilled in the art of building, so that it might not be so wholly different from the others in its appearance and design'.

In this campaign of competitive construction Reims, the seat of the Archbishop of north-east France and the church of the coronation, was beginning to lag behind. The Archbishop was in a somewhat difficult position. Reims had, in fact, been one of the very first cathedrals to reflect the style of St Denis. In 1152 it is recorded that 'Archbishop Samson had the old tower pulled down when he enlarged his church by the length of two arcades and began to build a tower on either side'. In these words an anonymous canon has described what subsequent excavations have revealed – a narthex similar to that of St Denis. Samson was among those present at the consecration of Abbot Suger's building in 1144 and he was one of the first to take up the new style.

As at St Denis this narthex had been appended to a Carolingian nave and as at St Denis the choir was then rebuilt with an ambulatory and radiating chapels in the new Gothic style. Here Samson's building seems to have followed the design of the great church of St Rémi de Reims, erected by the Abbot Pierre de Celle between 1162 and 1181.

Thus in the early years of the thirteenth century Reims had a Cathedral with a nave of the tenth century sandwiched between an east end and a west end in the earliest form of Gothic, a form which was already out of date. Notre-Dame, Chartres and Bourges were pointing the way to something altogether more magnificent, both in grandeur of conception and in purity of style. Beside these, the

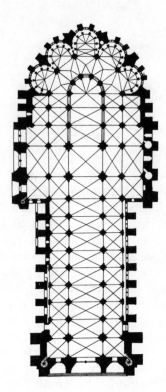

Ground Plan of Reims

Metropolitan and Coronation church of Reims was beginning to look quite inadequate.

Fate – if it was indeed Fate – intervened. On 6 May 1210, the Feast of St John before the Latin Gate, Samson's Cathedral was burnt to the ground. Anthyme Saint-Paul, in an article in the Bulletin Monumental of 1906, has tried to argue that the Archbishop Aubry de Humbert was himself responsible for the conflagration. The chronicler Alberic des Trois Fontaines does, however, specify that the fire was caused 'through negligence'; that was the official story and it is probably safer to believe it. The fire was, however, timely not to say opportune and Aubry immediately set about the reconstruction of the Cathedral on much more ambitious lines. A year later to the very day, he laid the first stone of the new building. The foundations were described as being 'magne profunditatis et latitudinis' – 'of great depth and width'.

It was nearly seventy years before the building was completed and the different phases of construction require the most painstaking unravelling. Scholars who have attempted the task have produced an astonishing diversity of interpretation.

But the very insolubility of the problem provides us with the most important fact about the Cathedral of Reims: the scrupulous and self-effacing care with which the subsequent architects respected the original, overall plan, thereby covering their tracks. Only the builder of the west front imposed a new design upon the old. Once inside the Cathedral the visitor is immediately struck with the noble unity of the architecture.

In the course of seventy years there had been many developments in the Gothic way of building; it would have been easy and understandable for each architect to have left his 'signature' in some identifiable change of style. At Amiens, which took twenty years less to build, there is an obvious change between the nave and the choir. At Reims the visitor would assume the whole building to have been the work of a single master mind. The expert will find minor variations in the profiles of the great piers, distinct discrepancies in the decoration of the capitals, subtle differences in the cut of the masonry. These, however, are not necessarily evidence of a change of architect. The picture which John James has created for Chartres of successive teams of workmen arriving, carrying out a campaign of building and moving on, perhaps to return a year or two later, must have been the pattern for all the other cathedrals. These minor changes in the detail of the design are more likely to denote a change of workmen than a change of architect.

This aspect of the building of Reims is the subject of the most important recent work on the Cathedral, an article in the *Bulletin Monumental* for 1979 by Jean-Pierre Ravaux entitled: *'Les campagnes de construction de la Cathedrale de Reims au XIIIe siècle'*. Francis Salet had put almost everything back in the crucible in an article in the same journal for 1967. Ravaux begins to recreate the picture.

Certain texts have survived which provide a skeleton history. In July 1221 we get our first glimpse of the *chantier*: the chapel of St James – the central and largest of the five apsidal chapels – is referred to in a charter issued by Archbishop Guillaume de Joinville as being available for worship. Since the easternmost chapel could only be reached by means of the ambulatory, there are good grounds for supposing that this was complete also.

As Louis VIII was crowned at Reims in 1223 and his son, St Louis, in 1226, we may make further deductions. The ambulatory and apsidal chapels could hardly have sufficed for so august an occasion; it is therefore reasonable to suppose that the old nave was still serviceable.

Somewhere about this time must be fitted in the drawings of

Villard de Honnecourt. In his album he includes two elevations, one interior, one exterior, of one of the apsidal chapels – which are surprisingly accurate – and one showing both elevations of a single bay of the choir, which is surprisingly inaccurate. The interior of the chapel shows a building not yet vaulted. Here Villard makes his only major mistake. He draws the colonnette that is to support the vault shaft beginning to branch out into three ribs. The actual colonnettes only support one rib. So Villard was drawing something which he did not see, presumably because it was not there.

If the building was really not yet vaulted when Villard made his drawings, then his visit to Reims must have been before the chapel was opened for use in 1221. This would mean that the other drawing, presumably of the same date, is clear evidence that at least one bay of the choir was already up to the clerestory windows. Villard specifies that he has drawn the façades 'com eles sunt' – 'as they are', but adds, 'in the same manner will be those of Cambrai'. It is probable that he was the architect of Cambrai and that his most inexplicable inexactitudes represent not what he saw at Reims but what he intended to do at Cambrai.

On the next page of his album, Villard gives an accurate plan of the complex section of one of the great piers of the crossing and a rather less accurate section of one of the piers of the nave. The implications are obvious. If this dating of Villard de Honnecourt's visit to Reims is correct – and it is that accepted by Reinhardt – it imposes the picture of the choir carried up to triforium level, with the ambulatory complete and the apsidal chapels ready for vaulting, with the crossing piers and at least one pier of the nave already planted so that their sections could be copied, all previous to the occupation of the eastern chapel of St James in July 1221.

The evidence for the completion of the choir, however, does not come until twenty years later. On 6 July 1240, Archbishop Henri de Braine died and was buried in front of the high altar, and the east window above it bears his name which indicates that he was the donor. Finally, on 7 September 1241, the Chapter took formal possession of their new choir. The *Annales de St Nicaise* make it quite clear: 'intravit capitulum Remense chorum suum novum'.

One of the reasons for the delay is also documented. In 1233 the population of Reims, unable to endure the arrogant pretensions of their pompous prelate, revolted against the Archbishop. A text in the archives specifies that the actual stones which had been dressed ready for use on the Cathedral were used as ammunition on the barricades. For two years the Canons were exiles from their own city. Very little building activity could have taken place in such circumstances.

Reims: Interior and Exterior Façade, by Villard de Honnecourt

Into this rather conjectural chronology, Ravaux has inserted the course of events suggested by the variations in the cut and profiles of the masonry itself. He has analysed twelve major campaigns of construction between 1210 and 1275 and he allots these campaigns to six different architects.

It is against this background of historical fact and learned speculation that must be set the tortuous problem of the labyrinth. Until the year 1779 there could be seen inlaid in the floor of the nave a marble miz-maze, as at Chartres and Amiens. At the four corners were brass plates on which were represented four *maîtres des ouvrages* and in the centre was a larger figure. Some have seen in this a fifth architect. But when the medieval artist made a figure larger than the others it was usually to emphasise his relative importance. The central figure was not dressed like the other four, but wore a long flowing robe. At Amiens it is known that the central figure was that of the founder Bishop, Everard de Fouilloy. In all probability the central figure at Reims was Aubry de Humbert.

Between the figures was traced a marble track whose intricate but symmetrical convolutions compressed the longest possible length into the neatest possible space. It was a favourite game for children to follow the circuitous passage from the entry to the maze to the octagonal opening in the centre and in so doing they distracted the Canons from their devotions. In 1779 the Chapter had the offending labyrinth removed.

Fortunately its passing was not unrecorded. In the sixteenth century an artist named Cellier had made a drawing of the labyrinth. One of the four architects is shown tracing the plan of the choir; the second holds a set square; the third is indicating something with his left hand; and the fourth is drawing a large circle with a pair of compasses.

In 1640 a certain Chanoine Pierre Cocquault wrote a description of the labyrinth, noting the inscriptions attached to the four corner figures. They give the names of four *maîtres des ouvrages*, the length of time that each held office and tantalizingly inadequate hints as to the portions of the edifice that each had accomplished. No guidance was offered as to the order in which they succeeded one another. Their names, reading anti-clockwise from the south-east corner were: Jean d'Orbais *'qui en commença la coiffe de l'église'* (the word 'coiffe' usually meant the choir); Jean Loup, *'qui commença les portaux'*; Gaucher de Reims, *'qui ouvra au vossures et portaux'* (the *voussoires* could be the architraves of the portal); Bernard de Soissons, *'qui fit cinq voutes et ouvra à l'O'* (he was the figure drawing the circle; it has been suggested that this represents the great rose window).

A century later two antiquarians attempted to decipher the

inscriptions, by now almost obliterated. Although they could read less than Cocquault was able to, they include words which he does not mention. This suggests that Cocquault had put the inscriptions into his own words. It is possible that when he says *'qui ouvra à l'O'*, he was merely describing the engraved figure.

Reinhardt puts the architects in the above order and Ravaux agrees with this, while assigning to each rather different periods of activity. They both agree that the credit for the whole magnificent design must go to Jean d'Orbais, the one depicted drawing the plan of the choir. Francis Salet remains agnostic but has no positive solution to propose. Let us call the first builder Jean d'Orbais.

Very little is known of him except what the stones of Reims will tell us. They tell us that he was a master builder of great experience and skill who was gifted also with a rare aesthetic sense and imagination. He clearly knew what was being done at Laon and Chartres and Soissons; he knew also, and may have been partly responsible for, the lovely and interesting Abbey Church of Orbais, some twenty kilometres south-west of Épernay on the edge of the Champagne country. He had the sort of mind that could conceive the broad lines of a grandiose conception and also the mechanical understanding that could introduce improvements into the system of abutement and counterpoise on which the Gothic style depended.

His grand design for Reims, which has been reconstructed by Viollet-le-Duc, was essentially a refinement and a logical development of the theme announced at Chartres. It was to have had a tall central spire flanked by four lower spires rising from the four angles of the crossing and two more spires at the west end. So weighty a superstructure demanded the most solid of supports. Jean d'Orbais managed to provide this sturdy solidity and at the same time to increase the amount of space open to the glazier.

Not only were his windows larger than those of Chartres and Soissons; he had at his disposal a new device. At Chartres the builders had contrived the grouping of two lancets beneath a rose within a single window embrasure; but the rose was treated as an aperture to be pierced in a slab of stone. Now at Reims there appears, perhaps for the first time, the fully developed method of tracery, in which the stone work is moulded to frame the apertures. At every tangent in the design the junction point is carved of a single stone. This assures the solidity of the framework while at the same time greatly reducing the amount of masonry within the opening of the window.

There is a similar window in the nave at Orbais. Reinhardt sees in this the prototype of Reims; Héliot dates the building at 1220 when the windows of Reims were already constructed. In either case it is possible that Jean d'Orbais was the author of this revolutionary invention. By using the new tracery in the ground floor as well as the clerestory he achieved a new element in the design which was immediately taken up at Amiens and Beauvais. This feature was specially noted by Villard de Honnecourt. Beneath his drawing of the traceried window he explains that he drew it 'because I liked it so much'. Not often in the history of Gothic architecture has such a truly spontaneous appreciation been recorded by anyone so qualified to give it.

Reims forms the stepping stone from Chartres to Amiens. The disposition of the nave façade is very similar to that of Chartres but more than ten feet taller. A typical development can be found in the treatment of the clerestory windows. At Chartres the placing of a huge rose above the coupled lancets dictated the retention of the rounded arch. At Reims the rose is cut down to a size which allows the arch formed by the wall ribs to be pointed like all the others. The windows are thus brought into line with the rest of the architecture. In the great arcade the builder has renounced the contrast, of which happy use was made at Chartres, between smooth cylindrical and crisp-cut polygonal shafts. At Reims all is smooth and cylindrical.

The interior façade of Reims is at its most successful in the apse, where a small but distinctive development was introduced. The central mullion or colonnette which divides the two arches of the clerestory is continued downward into the triforium, thus uniting triforium and clerestory into a single decorative unit.

The ground plan of Jean d'Orbais's Cathedral also had much that was clearly derivative from Chartres, though Ravaux has suggested that it was originally intended to have double aisles to the nave as at Notre-Dame and Bourges. Some of the features, however, reflect traditional and regional characteristics. The nave is long, the choir is short and the transepts project but a single bay beyond the nave aisles. The same accentuation of the nave could be found at St Rémi de Reims and at Laon as it was first constructed.

This shortening of the choir necessitated the positioning of the canons' stalls in the eastern half of the nave, which in turn enabled the High Altar to be placed at the focal point of the Church – the centre of the crossing. The crossing vault thus became its canopy and the apse the theatrical backdrop for the performance of the liturgy. A more impressive setting could hardly be imagined.

Unfortunately it has lost its two most distinctive features, the Bishop's throne and the High Altar. The Bishop's throne, in all probability that of St Rémi, was placed, according to ancient custom, between the central pillars of the apse. It was five feet tall and built of stone – 'sedes lapidea antiquissima'. During an interregnum,

Guillaume Marlot informs us, the Bishop's crozier was left to occupy the throne until it was taken up by the new incumbent of the See. This throne was destroyed, along with the High Altar, in 1744, when many of the medieval glories of Reims were swept away by a passion for 'good taste' translated into action by the unfortunate liberality of the Chanoine Godinot.

An inventory of 1470 gives a picture of the Altar in all its glory and claims that it was the gift of Bishop Hincmar towards the end of the ninth century. 'The front face,' writes Marlot, 'is of pure gold, six feet long and two and three quarter feet high. The Holy Virgin is there represented in the middle, holding her child; around them stand the four Evangelists with St Peter and St Paul. Above them is a crucifix surmounted by a chalcedony stone, much esteemed. The left hand side of the altar is also of pure gold; here are figures of St Nicaise, Ste Eutropie and St Florent, martyrs. The other side is only silver gilt, with figures of St Rémi, Clovis, Clotilde and several Bishops who assisted at the Baptism of the King. All these figures, executed in relief, are enriched with precious stones 'which gives a wonderful brilliance to the whole work.'

Around the altar stood six silver columns – presumably riddel posts – two of them surmounted by angels in silver gilt and the other four by praying figures. At the back of the altar stood a cross, two and a half feet high, bordered with precious stones, in which 'one of the notable parts of the true Cross is enshrined'. On major festivals a large silver gilt figure of the Virgin was also placed on the altar, ready to be carried out in the procession. It was alleged to contain several drops of her mother's milk.

The rest of the sanctuary appears to have been a real treasure house. In it were exhibited the heads of St Nicaise and Ste Eutropie *'d'argent vermeil doré, enrichie de plusieurs pierres précieuses et soutenues par des anges d'argent'**; the reliquary of St Rigobert, of gilded copper *'d'un ouvrage fort exquis'*†; the heads of St Marcel, Ste Barbe and Ste Anne (notwithstanding the claim of Chartres to possess the original) and an arm of St Andrew were all exposed in a blaze of jewellery and gold. A later inventory of 1518 adds considerably to their number.

Each king, at his coronation, contributed to the enrichment of the treasury. An Easter Sepulchre from Henri II; a golden sun, used as a Monstrance on Maundy Thursday, from Charles IX; a silver gilt ship from Henri III and the head of St Louis from Louis XIII. There were reminders that the choir was the scene of the deeply religious

---

* 'of silver gilt, enriched with many precious stones and upheld by silver angels.'
† 'of the most exquisite workmanship'.

rite of the *Sacre* – the anointing and crowning of the kings of France. For this ceremony the royal throne was placed on the top of the choir screen, situated about a third of the way down the nave, which an imposing flight of steps on either side enabled him to mount with dignity.

Whether or not the requirements of the coronation rite influenced the design of Jean d'Orbais, it is impossible to say. The rite had reached its full and final form in the *Ordre du Sacre* drawn up under Louis VII in 1179 for the crowning of his son, Philippe-Auguste. Jean d'Orbais must have known that, among other things, he was designing the theatre for this stately and symbolic ritual.

The status of Reims as the church of the coronation seems to have conferred an especial dignity upon its canons. There were seventy-four of them, not all of them priests. We know from the book of ceremonial, quoted by Cerf, a number of details from their way of life. In the Cathedral they were very sumptuously attired. In winter they wore heavy copes specified as being '*à queue trainante*'. This could be supplemented by an almuse of fur which was worn round the neck like a scarf. In summer this was replaced by a rochet and cape. On certain high days the Canons wore violet cassocks, a distinction usually associated with the episcopate. One of them was '*en semaine*' or as we would say 'in residence' each week. On the Sunday of his residence he was obliged by statute to shave his head and chin – '*faire sa couronne et son poil*'. With seventy-four of them, this system would only have involved each one in two weeks' residence every three years. Nevertheless they often felt obliged to be represented by a Vicar for that arduous week.

A number of other officials known as *coutre-clercs* and *coutres-laïques* performed the more menial tasks of servers and sacristans. Besides these were the *sonneurs*, two of whom always slept in the Cathedral and ate their meals behind the High Altar. Their principal role seems to have been that of the Vestal Virgin – to keep the candles burning before the Blessed Sacrament and the relics of the Saints. They also did the sweeping, cleaned up the wax dropped by the candles and rehung the tapestries after Advent and Lent.

It is not known what these tapestries were. They were not the famous hangings which now adorn the nave. These were the inspiration of Archbishop Robert de Lenoncourt, who ordered them in 1509. They were not finished until 1530 and it is not known where they were made. All sixteen of them follow the same general composition with a scene from the life of the Virgin in the centre '*à fond de fleurettes*'. The scenes depicted are virtually copies of a series of wood engravings dating from the late fifteenth century illustrating 'The Poor Man's Bible' and 'The Mirror of Redemption', both of which date from the reign of St Louis. Whether by chance or by design these tapestries of the sixteenth century reflect a theology contemporary with the building of the Cathedral.

What the artist has done is to take the woodcuts and make them live. He made them live for his contemporaries by putting them into the costume of the day. Where architectural framing is used, it is in the very latest fashion of the Renaissance. Even the Gothic gatehouse in the scene showing the encounter of Anne and Joachim at the Golden Gate has been brought up to date. Like the famous gatehouse of Gaillon, it has been Italianised by the application of arabesques and a running frieze of dancing cherubs.

The theology was largely concerned to illustrate the harmony between the New Testament and the Old. Thus each scene, usually enclosed within an architectural frame, is surrounded by smaller scenes which demonstrate how the eternal purposes of God had found in Mary their ultimate fulfilment.

Auguste Rodin took special note of these tapestries which brought a warmth and animation to the cold, uncoloured stone. The tonality is subdued; the keynote is a soft and silver grey – *'grie argent, rehaussé de bleu, de rouge; la tapisserie s'assortit à la pierre; elle a la couleur d'encens'.*

The tapestries contribute also to the sense of unity which the architecture of the nave creates. But in spite of this apparent uniformity, the stones give unmistakable evidence of a clear break between two campaigns of building. This can be seen most easily in the capitals of the great piers. On the last three columns towards the west the capitals are formed of a single band of floral carving which enfolds both the central drum and the four engaged colonnettes. In the other piers of the nave the capitals of the colonnettes are treated separately from those of the central drum.

This observation brings us to a consideration of the west end of the Cathedral. As early as 1230 we learn from the terms of a lease that two houses on the *parvis* west of the Cathedral were destined to demolition 'propter accrementum fabrice Remensis ecclesiae' – 'on account of the enlarging of the fabric of the church of Reims'. It was not, however, until 1252 that they were demolished. This gives us a date for the beginning of the new west front. According to Ravaux, who furnishes these details, this was the year in which Gaucher de Reims took over the direction of the building. Whoever it was pro-duced one of the great masterpieces of the Gothic style.

He had to inspire him the west fronts of Laon – completed by 1230; of Notre-Dame, 1250; and of Amiens, carried up to the base of the towers by 1236 – for it must be remembered that, whereas Amiens was started ten years later than Reims, it was built from west to east, while Reims was built from east to west. The west front of

Amiens is therefore the earlier of the two. The builder of Reims had also the important church of St Nicaise at hand which was being constructed at the time by the architect Hughes Libergier.

It was probably from the latter that the builder of the west front borrowed his most striking innovation – the replacement of the tympanum over each of the doorways by a rose window. It seems certain that there was a real change of plan here. The north face of the northernmost buttress provides the clue. The ornamental arch frames the remnant of a group of figures, representing the discovery of the true cross, which was clearly carved for the decoration of a tympanum. Moreover it has the same width, 2.90 metres, as that of the side doors on the west front. There can be little doubt that the original intention was to fill the tympanum of each portal with carvings, as in almost every other French cathedral of the time.

The decision to open the tympanum for a rose window set in its mitre-shaped embrasure caused a difficulty which we can see at once from the inside of the central doorway. The exterior arch of the tympanum springs from the top of the doorway, while the interior arch springs from a point level with the capitals of the nave arcade, which is considerably higher. The discrepancy between the exterior and the interior arches – made visible by the insertion of a window – is one of the very few inelegances of Reims.

This reasoning would suggest that the interior façade of the west front was already up to the height of the fourth tier of niches when the change was made. It is quite clear that there is a break in style at this level. The niches above the spring of the arch are noticeably shallower and the floral panels between each tier are treated in a different manner.

In the same way there is an obvious difference between the rose over the central doorway and the great rose which has pride of place in the west front. The rose of the tympanum is constructed after the manner of the earlier traceried windows, such as that at Mantes-la-Jolie. The design is composed of a ring of arches with their points towards the centre and their sides radiating out like the spokes of a wheel. The great rose, following the pattern of Notre-Dame, reverses this arrangement. The points of the arches are on the outer circumference. This has the effect of distributing the stonework more evenly and of creating panels of glass which are more or less the same size.

The glass of the great rose has a large proportion of red in it, and the westering sun sets the window aflame so that it becomes, in Painton Cowen's words, 'a consuming ball of fire evoking the end of time. The subject is the death of the Virgin, symbolising the end of the Church and the end of time'. Though much restored, the great rose is still a strikingly lovely window. The rose of the tympanum, presenting the symbols of the Litany of the Virgin, was made by Jacques Simon in 1938. It recaptures to a remarkable degree the spirit of medieval glass.

Seen as a whole, the west front affords an interesting comparison with its precursors. It has come a long way since Laon. For while Laon offers a powerful composition modelled in deep relief, Reims is all lightness and delicacy of touch. *'La Cathédrale de Laon,'* writes Emile Mâle, *'semble refléchir profondément aux choses d'en haut.'** It has something of the gravity which deep-set eyes can give to a face. But at Reims this solidity has given place to a slender, open-work frame. The mood is one of exaltation. The arches are more narrowly pointed; the angles of the gables more acute; everything conspires to lead the eye upwards. The façade is lighter in both senses of the word; less ponderous and less obscure. This lightness, however, is somewhat deceptive: the original top section of the central gable, now in the Palais du Tau, weighs twenty-four tons. Some of the statues of the west front have been removed to the Palais du Tau and replaced by facsimiles. They are well worth seeing, if only to get an idea of the enormous scale of these figures.

In the centre of the west front, above the great rose window, the façade is set back a little behind a balustrade forming what is known as the *Galerie du Gloria*. This title derives from the impressive ceremonial of the Triumphal Entry celebrated on Palm Sunday – dimanche des Rameaux. It took the form of a procession round the town in which all the parishes joined. In many places it was the custom for the choirboys to mount the city towers and sing from the battlements. It is not specified that this occurred at Reims, but when the procession reached the *parvis* before the west front of the Cathedral, the boys climbed up to the *Galerie du Gloria* to sing the Latin hymn which we translate as 'All glory, laud and honour'.

The antiquarian Adolphe Didron, writing in 1848, could remember taking part, as a boy, in this performance – 'this lovely ceremony which made, on every celebration of Palm Sunday, so profound an impression on the whole population. All that has been destroyed today,' he lamented; 'each year sees the loss of another piece of the liturgy of Reims'.

The *Galerie du Gloria* is in fact a narrow passageway in front of the central portion of the *Galerie des Rois*. The most striking difference between the west front of Reims and that of Amiens is that at Reims the *Galerie des Rois* is above the great rose and at Amiens it is below. This means that at Amiens the sculpture is concentrated in the lower half of the façade, whereas at Reims it is more evenly distributed. The

---

* 'The Cathedral of Laon seems to be engrossed in meditation on things above.'

replacement of the tympanum in each of the portals by a stained glass window had further reduced the concentration of carvings in the lower storey. The three portals, nevertheless, are still used as a major decorative theme.

The statuary of these three portals presents a confusion of styles and of iconography which might have proved insoluble had not Henry Deneux, who carried out the great restoration of the Cathedral after the First World War, discovered positioning marks on most of the figures. It is possible to assign these to their proper places, which in turn often makes their identification easier. Almost the whole tangle can be unravelled.

It is necessary, however, to begin this process by considering the two portals of the north transept. It does not take a very practised eye to detect that these two portals formed no part of the original design of the façade. A panel of wall has been built out beyond the face of the buttresses to accommodate them, and the left hand portal is clearly too wide for its position. These were, in fact, two of the portals that were planned for the west front by Jean d'Orbais. The figures belong in style to the same period as that of the angels on the buttress piers of the apse – in other words, about the year 1220. They are of the most exquisite workmanship.

The fact that there are only two portals to the north transept suggests that this ensemble of Jean d'Orbais's was never completed. Some of the statues for the third portal, however – which was to have been at the south end of the west front – were already carved. They represented the Annunciation and the Visitation. Since they fitted into the iconography of the new west front they were re-used in the central embrasure, where they form part of the group to the right of the door. The two scenes are so arranged that the two figures of the Virgin, one of the Annunciation and one of the Visitation, stand side by side. They could not be less alike. In the same group at Amiens the two Virgins are as it were identical twins. Here at Reims they represent the work of two strikingly different schools.

The Virgin of the Visitation and the figure of Elizabeth show unmistakable signs of influence from Roman Antiquity – or indeed from the source which itself inspired Roman art, the sculptures of Ancient Greece. Emile Mâle has drawn attention to the fact that during the fourth Crusade two Knights from Champagne – Geoffroi de Villehardouin and Guillaume de Champlitte – assisted in the conquest of the Peloponnese and that Otto de la Roche had become Duke of Athens in the early thirteenth century. It is an attractive theory that Grecian influence may have come direct to Reims.

With the fussy folds of her gathered garments, the 'Greek' Virgin of the Visitation offers a conspicuous contrast with the easy flow and simple lines of the almost priestly robes of her sister figure. These are in turn reflected in the group opposite, the Presentation in the Temple. The four figures of this scene, although in the wrong order, are clearly all in the same style as the Virgin of the Annunciation. They belong to the first school of the new west front begun in about 1250.

Supreme among these was the Queen of Sheba, the figure facing west between the central and the left embrasure. Just as Solomon – the Judge *par excellence* of the Old Testament – was regarded as prefiguring the person of Christ, the final Judge, so the Queen of Sheba, who had come from the ends of the world to hear the words of Solomon, was held to prefigure the Church. She stands at the entrance to the Cathedral, a perfect illustration of the dignity of simplicity. The folds of her long and ample dress flow in a gentle spiral, as if she had turned slightly to face the visitor in a gesture of welcome.

Here she stood until 1914 when, on 17 September, the Germans under General von Heeringen deliberately directed their artillery on the Cathedral. The north tower was under scaffolding at the time and the west end of the nave was filled with straw to provide a bedding for wounded soldiers, and on 19 September the whole Cathedral was ablaze. Among the many figures to suffer that of the Queen of Sheba was knocked from her dais and smashed on the pavement below. The fragments were piously put together again, but only the pre-war photographs enable us to see her in all her glory.

To the left of the Queen of Sheba, as one faces the façade, the north porch is devoted to a number of saints. Various theories have been advanced as to their identity, but the most convincing is that of Hans Reinhardt. It was often the custom to accord a place of honour on the west front to those saints who were venerated in the chapels of the Cathedral. It is known from early texts what were the dedications of the altars in the apsidal chapels. Their names can be fairly confidently assigned to the statues in the *Portail des Saints*.

The scalpless figure on the left hand side, next to the *Ange au Sourire*, thus becomes St Nicaise – the Bishop martyred at Reims in 407 when trying to obtain quarter from the barbarian invaders. Opposite him on the right is his sister Eutropie – who is seen in the north transept porch smacking the face of her brother's executioner – and the Deacon St Florent who lost his life on the same occasion. Beyond St Nicaise and his supporting angels should be Pope Calixte in his tall conical tiara (actually in the south embrasure) and Bishop Rémi, who baptised Clovis.

The muddle caused by the wrong positioning of the statues is nowhere more evident than in this north embrasure. Not only is

Calixte absent from his rightful place: the wrong Angel is standing on the left of St Nicaise. This Angel is, according to his positioning mark, the Angel of the Annunciation. If he were exchanged with the one at present occupying that place, St Nicaise would be flanked, as he was intended to be flanked, by two figures of the same date and style.

This style represents a new departure. The earlier schools, still under the influence of the Realists, were concerned to create, in Marcel Aubert's phrase, 'an idealised figure which represented a type rather than an individual.' The Realist believed that the generalisation 'Humanity' had a *real* substance which could therefore be portrayed. The Nominalist, regarding 'Humanity' as a mere *name*, found reality only in the individual.

These statues of the third school have an animation that is all their own; there is more movement in the stance, which communicates itself to the generous flow of their draperies; there is more expression to their faces, which imparts a lifelike quality to the whole figure. As Rodin said of the Virgin who stands between the central doors, *'c'est la vraie femme française, la femme de province, la plus belle plante de notre jardin'*.

The carvings of the west front are continued on the inner façade, which thus has a richness and a distinction peculiarly its own. It was achieved around the year 1265 probably under Gaucher de Reims and belongs to the third and last school connected with the Cathedral.

Seven tiers of niches, each separated from the one above by a panel of exquisitely carved foliage, fill the entire space from floor to triforium. The fifty figures contained in them include scenes from the life of the Virgin and of Jesus Christ. As usual they were accompanied by their precursors of the Old Testament. Isaiah, holding a model of a crib, predicts the Virgin Birth, while Moses with his ever-burning bush and Gideon with his untouched fleece proclaim the continuing virginity of the Mother of God. In the same way the person of Christ, in his priestly and eucharistic role, is prefigured by the scene of Melchisidek bringing out bread and wine to Abraham.

For many years this scene was called 'the Communion of the Knight' which indeed it resembles. One does not, without adjustment, picture Abraham as a Knight. But he was returning from a military foray when he encountered Melchisidek and the artist has not unreasonably assumed that he was armed. He therefore represented him in the armour of the thirteenth century. It would be like depicting him in battledress today.

This custom of representing scenes from the Bible in the modern dress of the time became more pronounced as the Middle Ages advanced and it survived into the Renaissance period. Instead of presenting the episodes of the Bible as remote and archaic, it made them contemporary and relevant. As Paul Wescher says of the miniatures of Jean Fouquet: 'they are like variations on a great theme: God in France; the ever present Christ and his Saints seen under a French sky, standing resolutely on French soil'.

The lowest tier of niches stands on a podium carved to represent the folds of a ceremonial drapery. It is probably right to associate this with the real draperies with which the Cathedral was decorated for the ceremony of the *Sacre*.

CHAPTER TWELVE

The Coronation of a French King

The special interest of Reims is that it was the Coronation Church –
the Westminster Abbey of France. With only very few exceptions, the
Kings of France were anointed and crowned here since Hughes
Capet in 987.

The iconography of the Cathedral made many references to this
specific role. Kings lined the gallery over the west front; kings, and
the archbishops who crowned them, looked down from the stained
glass windows of the clerestory. The statues round the west rose
reflect the theme of kingship – Saul anointed by Samuel, Solomon
crowned by Nathan. They tell also of the virtues expected of a king.
David killing Goliath represented Courage; Solomon giving the
mother her baby, Justice; Solomon building the temple, Piety. At the
summit God is seen blessing kings.

Above the rose the sculptures depict the Baptism of Clovis by St
Rémi, with the miracle of the Holy Oil – the Sainte Ampoulle, which
played so significant a part in the coronation rite. Thus the spectator
was reminded that France was first converted to the Christian Faith
in the person of her king. If the Cathedral was to be a book for those
who could not read, at least it was perfectly clear in this instance
what the message was.

The coronation rite, with its biblical precedent in the idea of the
Lord's Anointed, made the king the Lord's lieutenant in the land.
Voltaire, in his *Siècle de Louis XIV*, wrote that the French regarded
their King 'as a sort of Divinity'. The rite also symbolised the alliance
between the Crown and the Church – a coalition which had resulted
in the centralisation and unification of France at the expense of
feudalism. It was to this powerful sense of national unity that
Viollet-le-Duc attributed the motive force behind the Cathedrals'
Crusade.

All the great Gothic cathedrals built on Capetian territory thus
symbolise the marriage between the royal and the ecclesiastical
authority, but this is especially true of Reims, for it was here, in each
reign, that the solemnisation of that marriage was re-enacted.

The coronation of Louis XVI is in some ways the most obvious example to choice. The last to take place before the Revolution, it shows how the ancient forms and ceremonies had survived the Age of Enlightenment. In spite of Montesquieu's sarcasm on the subject, Louis XVI touched 2400 sufferers from scrofula, who were assembled in the belief that the formula: '*le Roi te touche, Dieu te guérisse*' would cleanse them from their malady. Fifty years later, when the same ceremony was performed for the last time by Charles X, an old man turned up at the hospital to give thanks for the healing touch of Louis XVI.

This particular coronation has also, of course, the poignant interest that we can see, with the perspective of history, the shadow of the guillotine across the path. As the comte de Ségur was to write; 'as for us, the gilded youth of France, we walked on a carpet of flowers which covered an abyss'.

But, above all, the coronation of Louis XVI can be reconstructed with great accuracy thanks to the books of the period. A large double folio full of engravings had been published after the crowning of Louis XV, showing every incident in the ceremony and every detail of the costumes. This collection was revised and re-issued under Louis XVI. To this can be added the eye witness account of that prince of memorialists, the duc de Croÿ. Few amateur chroniclers have brought more life to their accounts of their times than this sharp-eyed, appreciative nobleman brought to his observations of the Court of Versailles.

It was in early June 1775; the weather was fine and dry and everything possible had been done to improve the roads and to embellish the wayside, so that from Compiègne to Reims 'it was like one garden'. Posting horses had been concentrated in vast numbers along the route, to the great inconvenience of travellers in other parts of the country. At Soissons alone there were six hundred available.

During the early days of the month, colourful detachments of the Royal Household and the magnificent equipages of the aristocracy were to be seen converging upon the coronation city. The approaches to the town had been adorned with a succession of triumphal arches; everything seemed to smile at the prospect of the happy event. But at Fismes, where the King traditionally spent the last night before his state entry to Reims, the duc de Croÿ had been appalled at the price of bread. The contrast between the poverty of the people and the lavish extravagance of their guests might well have occasioned unfortunate demonstrations, such as had recently occurred in Picardy, but nothing untoward was recorded except for one man at the roadside who greeted the King by pointing to his open, empty mouth.

On his arrival at Reims, the Duke lost no time in going to inspect the Cathedral – *une des plus belles que j'aie vues et digne de l'honneur qu'elle a'.** The duc de Duras and the staff of the *Menus Plaisirs* had been busy with the construction of the royal tribune and the boxes for the spectators and with the decorations in general. The passage of the King from the Palais du Tau to the west porch was carpeted with fleurs de lys, lined with tapestry and entirely covered overhead. It culminated in the colonnade before the entrace, *'un morceau superbe qui réussit à perfection et qui, quoique d'un autre ton, faisait bien avec ce beau et ancien portail'.*†

As for the choir itself, where the ceremony was to take place, they had completely obscured the architecture of the Cathedral behind a decoration of Corinthian columns more like the Chapel – or indeed the Opera House – at Versailles. The Duke did not approve of it: 'it looked too theatrical, too much like a *salle de spectacle* inserted in the most superb nave of the Gothic church'. De Croÿ had the gift, rare among his contemporaries, of appreciating the taste of the thirteenth century and he found this gaudy finery *'un petit morceau de carton doré dans un grand et noble edifice'*. But he was delighted with the tapestries.

He next went to the Palace and inspected the regalia. The King was to offer a golden ciborium – *'un morceau superbe et d'un travail exquis'* – to the Treasury of the Cathedral. Richest of all was the King's crown, encrusted with the most beautiful gems and estimated at a value of sixteen million livres. It weighed only two pounds and the Duke was able to lift it with one hand. The coronets to be worn, the *couronnes d'honneur*, three with the strawberry leaves of a Duke and nine with the raised pearls of a Count, were also on exhibition. In the French ceremony only twelve peers had coronets; these were not put on at the moment of the King's crowning, as in England, but worn throughout the ceremony. These were the Six Lay Peers – the three Marshals of France, the Grand Maître, the Grand Chambellan and the Premier Gentilhomme de la Chambre du Roi. All except the first three Lay Peers wore the coronet of a Count irrespective of their personal rank and title.

The Twelve Peers of France, of whom six were lay and six ecclesiastical, were a body whose origins were supposed by romantic imagination to date back to Charlemagne. In fact their existence can only be traced to the reign of Robert I, and their number was only fixed under Philippe-Auguste. They were the Dukes of Normandy, Burgundy and Aquitaine; the Counts of Flanders, Champagne and

---

* 'one of the most beautiful things I have seen, and worthy of its honourable status'.
† 'a superb piece, which succeeds to perfection and which, although in a different style, went well with this fine old portal.'

Toulouse; the Archbishop of Reims, the Bishops of Langes and Laon, all of whom were also Dukes, and the Bishops of Beauvais, Noyon and Charlons, who were also Counts. Their proper function was to act as a High Court to arbitrate in disputes between the King and his Tenants-in-Chief. A notable example was the use of this court by Philippe-Auguste to try the English King John for the murder of his nephew Arthur. As Duke of Normandy, John could only be tried by his peers. They found him guilty and deprived him of his possessions. He was known thereafter as Jean-sans-Terre or John Lackland.

Each of the Twelve Peers had a ceremonial function at the coronation. All of them 'upheld' the crown while it was on the King's head. On one occasion, Menin informs us, at the coronation of Philippe V, the King's mother-in-law, Mahaut, comtesse d'Artois, 'assisted in the rank of Peer of France and bore up the crown with the other Peers, who murmured at it and maintained (but in vain) that their High Offices, any more than the Crown itself, could never belong to the Distaff'.

By 1775 they had long since lost any political or juridical importance 'Les Pairs de France,' wrote Victor Hugo, 'étaient plus hauts et moins puissants que le pairs d'Angleterre, tenant au rang plus qu'à l'autorité, et à la préséance plus qu'à la domination,' adding, with a certain sarcasm, 'il y avait entre eux et les lords la nuance qui sépare la vanité de l'orgeuil'.* As the territories from which their duchies or Counties were named became engulfed in the Kingdom of France, the Lay Peers became mere courtesy titles offered by the King, usually to members of his own family.

From his inspection of the regalia, the duc de Croÿ returned to the Cathedral for a closer look at the arrangements in the sanctuary. On the south side were the seats for the Bishops, Ministers and Lawyers; opposite them were the Marshals of France, the Six Lay Peers and the *Cordons Bleus*. There was just a bench – upholstered of course – for the *Cordons Bleus sans Fonction*, that is to say, the Knights of the St Esprit who had no special charges at Court. No individual places were reserved and the Duke made a mental note to arrive early in order to get the best seat. He then retired to his lodgings and spent the evening reading all that he could about the ceremony of the *Sacre*. We know that he read Menin's *Traité historique et chronologique du Sacre et Couronnement des Roys et Reines de France* which was published in 1723.

On Friday, 9 June, the King arrived at about five in the afternoon,

---

* 'The Peers of France were more exalted and less powerful than the Peers of England, valuing rank more than authority and precedence more than dominion . . . there existed between them and the *lords* the subtle distinction which separates pride vanity from pride.'

escorted by a detachment of the Household Cavalry. De Croÿ was in ecstasies: *'La beauté de ces équipages, le noble tapage des fanfares et timbales et de la grosse cloche annonça bien le maître'.** His coach, *'superbe, singulier et immense,'* was drawn by eight horses whose tall, white plumes distinguished them from those of the outriders.

The King was received by the Archbishop and his suffragans at the west porch and was conducted into the cool emptiness of the Cathedral, where a few prayers were said. The King then inspected the decorations and arrangements and complimented the duc de Duras on all that he had done. De Croÿ noted narrowly the King's deportment: *'il avait toujours son air de bonté, mais ennuyé de la représentation; et il aurait fallu, à tout cela, le grand air qu'y mettait Louis XIV'.*†

Trinity Sunday, the day appointed for the coronation, dawned as fine and warm as ever. De Croÿ went to the Cathedral at four o'clock and obtained the best seat at the end of his bench.

At 6.30 the Six Lay Peers of France made their entry – 'our six princes, representing the three ancient Dukedoms and the three ancient Counties of the Kingdom, in all the magnificence of their majestic robes, with their coronets on their heads'. The dukes were represented by the King's two brothers, the comte de Provence and the comte d'Artois, together with his second cousin the duc d'Orléans, and the Counts by the other Princes of the Blood, the duc de Chartres, the prince de Condé and the duc de Bourbon. *Monsieur*, the comte de Provence, later to be Louis XVIII, but never to be crowned, conducted himself with considerable dignity, but the young Artois, *'fait pour plaire aux dames'*, and later, as Charles X, to be the last King crowned at Reims, behaved with a careless irreverence which gave offence to many.

Having taken their places on the north side of the altar, opposite the Ecclesiastical Peers, they now formed a procession to go to the King's Bedroom and to escort him to the Cathedral. The Bishops of Beauvais and Laon came first to the King's door. Twice they knocked, and twice they received the answer; *'Le Roi dort'*. The third time they were admitted. The other robed and coroneted figures now took their places in the procession together with the Chancellor, who wore a scarlet mantle and a cloth of gold toque in place of a coronet. The other officials, such as the Maréchal de Contades, who carried the royal crown, were in Court dress, consisting of white silk stockings, trunk hose and a cloak reaching to the knees. They wore plumed hats on their heads.

---

* 'The beauty of these coaches and horses, the noble noise of the fanfares and kettledrums proclaimed the presence of the Master.'
† He still looked as kind as ever, but bored by State occasions; what was lacking in all this was the air of grandeur which Louis XIV would have brought to it.'

At 7.30 this august procession entered the Cathedral. The duc de Croÿ was deeply impressed and made note of all the details – the great ermine-lined mantles and the long cloth of gold surcoats created an effect 'which is all the more imposing for being never worn but on this day'. On reaching the altar the procession was confronted by the no less impressive robes of the Archbishop and his clergy 'which exhibited with the greatest possible brilliance the pomp of the Church'.

At last the King took his seat in an armchair under the great canopy in the centre of the crossing. *'Chacun est à sa place en silence'*.

The service began with the *Veni Creator*, sung by the King's musicians behind the altar. During their singing, the procession of the Sainte Ampoulle made its way up the nave, and, passing beneath the royal tribune, entered the sanctuary. The Holy Oil had been brought from the Abbey of St Rémi by the Prior. Four noblemen were given as hostages for its safe return. Four barons, whose lands carried with them this peculiar obligation, upheld the canopy, beneath which the Prior rode on a white horse.

The Sainte Ampoulle having been placed with great reverence upon the altar, the Archbishop now donned his vestments for the Mass and the service proper began.

First the King took his oath to preserve the Church in all its privileges, to protect his people and to maintain *'équité et miséricorde'* throughout the realm, ending with the words: 'I promise these things in the name of Jesus Christ to my Christian people subject to me'. The Bishops of Beauvais and Laon then asked the people if they accepted their King, to which they gave assent 'by a respectful silence'. The King then took another oath in Latin. The duc de Croÿ noted that Louis pronounced this oath in a firm, clear voice, *'appuyant sur les mots avec respect et attention, et comme s'il disait à chaque mot: "je m'engage à celà de bon coeur." '* *

A Te Deum was now sung, during which the King and the Archbishop prostrated themselves before the altar. Meanwhile the Abbot of St Denis placed the regalia upon the altar, which was then blessed by the Archbishop.

The King now approached the altar. The Premier Gentilhomme divested him of his cloth of silver surcoat. His scarlet camisole was made to open at the chest, between the shoulders, above each shoulder and at the crook of each arm – the points of the royal anatomy to which the holy oil had to be applied. The Grand Chambellan placed a pair of silk shoes, embroidered with fleurs de

---

* 'stressing the words with respect and attention and as if he said after each word: "I commit myself to that with all my heart." '

lys, upon the King's feet, and the comte de Provence, representing the duc de Bourgogne, attached the spurs, which he then took off again and returned to the altar. The Archbishop took the Sword of Charlemagne, which was named 'Joyeuse', from the altar, girded the King with it, ungirded him, drew the sword and gave it to the Connétable de France, who held it for the rest of the ceremony. As he gave it he said: 'Take this sword given to you with the blessing of God, by which in the strength of the Holy Spirit you may be able to resist and repel all the enemies of the Holy Church and defend the Kingdom committed to you'.

Now came the solemn moment after which the ceremony of the *Sacre* was named – the anointing with the Holy Oil. All good Frenchmen implicitly believed that this oil had been brought from Heaven by a dove for the baptism of Clovis. The Archbishop, using a little golden bodkin, took a drop from the Ampulla and mixed it with some oil on a golden patten, ready for the anointing of the King, who, as the rubrics of the service stated, *'seul entre tous les Roys de la terre resplendit de ce glorieux privilège qui est singulièrement cinct de l'Huile envoyée du Ciel'.** After the singing of a Litany, a tedious incantation in the course of which fifty-five Saints were invoked by name, the Archbishop proceeded to anoint the King on the head and in the six places where there was an opening in his camisole, while the choir sang the anthem *'le Prêtre Sadoc et le prophète Nathan oignirent Salomon Roy en Jérusalem, et venant joyeux dirent "Vive le Roy éternellement."* '†

The duc de Croÿ noted the significance of these actions: 'thus the King receives all the minor Orders of the Church, with the exception of the Priesthood'. There was thus an ecclesiastical significance in the royal robes with which the King was now vested by the Grand Chambellan – a blue dalmatic, such as a deacon wore, and over that the blue coronation robe covered with fleurs de lys and lined with ermine. It was made to hang so that the King's right hand was free and draped over his left arm 'like a priest's chasuble'. The ring was placed upon his finger, the sceptre in his right hand and the Hand of Justice in his left.

The moment for the coronation had come. The Chancellor, mounting the steps of the altar, turned to the congregation and said in a loud voice: *'Monsieur, qui représentez le duc de Bourgogne, présentez-vous à cet acte'.*†† One by one, as he named them, the twelve Peers of

* 'alone among all the Kings in the world enjoys the splendour of this glorious privilege, which is to be the only one to be annointed with the oil sent from Heaven'.
† 'Zadok the Priest, and Nathan the Prophet, annointed Solomon King in Jerusalem. And all the people rejoiced and said: "May the King live for ever." '
†† 'Monsieur, representing the Duke of Bergundy, come forward for this act'.

France took their places to either side of the King. Taking the crown of Charlemagne from the altar, the Archbishop held it over the head of the King and all the Peers reached out to "uphold" it while the prayers were read. *'Dieu d'éternité, duc des vertus, vainqueur de tous ennemis, bénis cettuy ton serviteur à toy inclinant son chef'.** Then the Archbishop placed the crown upon the King's head. 'This supreme moment,' noted de Croÿ, 'caused the greatest sensation possible.'

Louis was now conducted up the steps of the tribune and ceremonially seated upon the royal throne. The Archbishop, followed by the other Peers, now paid their homage; each, having made a profound reverence, had the honour of kissing the King, saying at the same time: *'Vive le Roi éternellement!'*

The completion of this ceremony was the signal for an outbreak of popular rejoicing. 'The doors were thrown open,' writes de Croÿ, 'the people poured into the church. Birds were released and all the trumpets announced with their blaring tones the presence of the Master – but what announced it even more were the hearts of the French. At this moment tears of joy ran down every cheek. The excitement was so great that an outburst of applause – something which has never happened before – accompanied the cries of "Vive le Roi!' and everyone was beside himself with emotion. I know that I have never experienced such enthusiasm: I was quite astonished to find myself in tears and to see everyone else the same. The Queen was so overcome with joy that her tears fell in torrents and she was obliged to produce her handkerchief. This only served to augment the general emotion.'

Marie-Antoinette was not herself crowned, but was seated in a superb tribune not unlike the royal box at an opera. For the King this must have been the greatest experience in his life. *'Le Roi parut bien sentir ce beau moment,'* continues de Croÿ, *'et nous vîmes enfin ce qu'on ne voit que là, notre Roi revêtu de tout l'éclat de la royauté, sur le vrai trône, coup d'oeil qu'on ne peut rendre, tant il fit d'effet.'*†

A little later, when once more master of himself, the Duke reflected: 'It must be admitted that this moment was sublime, but somewhat contrary to good order. It has never happened before – people clapping in church, and for so long and in so uncontrolled a manner'. Just as the decor of the Cathedral had reminded him of a *Salle de*

* 'God of Eternity, leader of all virtues and victor over all enemies, bless this thy servant who bends his head to Thee'.

† 'The King appeared very sensible of this great moment, and we saw at last, as one can only see on that occasion, our King decked in all the radiance of royalty on the true throne – a sight which cannot be conveyed, so deep was the impression which it made.'

Spectacle, so the behaviour of the people reminded him more of an audience than of a congregation.

After the Mass, the King exchanged the crown of Charlemagne for the lighter, modern one already described, and the procession formed up to conduct him back to the Palais du Tau for the banquet. 'The King, with this beautiful crown on his head, carrying the sceptre and all the ornaments, surrounded by these twelve men in their coronets and all their rich and majestic robes, made a really impressive exit.'

It was 11.30 in the morning when he regained his apartment. The ceremony had lasted four hours. It had been a tremendous burden on the old Archbishop. His Coadjutor was there ready to take over and everyone was expecting him to faint at any minute. But he had carried it all out himself, never putting a foot wrong.

It was not until five o'clock that the duc de Croÿ was able to take his own dinner, 'after which our only thought was to rest ourselves, but we all agreed that this ceremony had been even finer than we had expected.' Some had attended in the first place with a certain reluctance, but now that it was over, *'chacun convint qu'on aurait été bien fâché de n'y avoir pas été.'*

Thus began to reign of Louis XVI. It was to end in circumstances that are only too well known. On 21 January 1793, he went to the guillotine. On 7 October of that year a Conventional at Reims named Philippe Ruhl, after publicly deriding the Holy Oil 'which monks claimed to have been brought from the sky by a pigeon', smashed the Sainte Ampoulle against the base of the statue of Louis XV in the Place Royale. It must have seemed that the rite of the *Sacre* would never – indeed, *could* never – be re-enacted at Reims.

But in due course the Monarchy returned. That Louis XVIII intended to be crowned seems certain. He announced his intention in 1819 at the opening of the Chambre des Députés. Furthermore, the ceremony was destined to take place at Reims, for there exist in the Bibliothèque Nationale designs by the architect Percier for the decoration of the Cathedral for that event. It was a curious and ungainly attempt to adapt the *style Empire* to a crude and imperfectly understood Gothic.

The King's health did not permit. It was for his brother, Charles X, to revive the ceremony of the *Sacre*. On 22 December, 1824, Charles announced his intention to both Houses from his throne in the Louvre, of being crowned at Reims. "There, prostrate before the same altar at which Clovis received the Holy Oil, in the presence of the Judge of Nations and of Kings, I will renew my vow to maintain and enforce the laws of the State.'

The idea was to unite France in a reborn enthusiasm for the

legitimate Monarchy – *'renouer la chaine du temps'*. It was a hope forlorn in principle and foredoomed in practice. There were those who felt the Revolution was a page in the History of France which should be torn out; there were those who recognised that certain irreversible changes had occurred. There were those who feared the return of royal absolutism; there were those who were more afraid of the revival of clerical power. There were those who wanted the coronation to be in Paris; there were those who insisted on the tradition of Reims. And to these had come an unexpected reinforcement – the announcement that a miller named Hourelle had recovered some of the fragments of the Sainte Ampoulle and with them some drops of the Holy Oil. The central ceremony of the *Sacre* could be maintained with unbroken continuity.

The traditionalists won the day. Slowly and expensively the cumbersome paraphernalia of the *Ancien Régime* creaked and rumbled back into activity. Eighty vehicles were required merely for the transport of the *Musique de la Chapelle Royale*, not counting the three hundred white fiacres which brought a supplementary choir from Paris.

The city of Reims was in a state of chaos and excitement and prices were ludicrously inflated. The Duke of Northumberland, who represented the United Kingdom with great magnificence, paid three times the purchase price of a house for three days' rent. The officers of the *Menus Plaisirs* were busy obscuring the beauties of the west front of the Cathedral. Madame de Castellane was contemptuous: 'The King had not found the façade of this church, before which sixty-four kings had bowed their heads, sufficiently elegant. He had another made of painted wood – exactly like the little boxes in which we put our matches.' Chateaubriand was, if possible, more cutting, with his passing reference to the Cathedral 'decorated with coloured paper'.

Inside, the pure and simple architecture of the thirteenth century had been dressed up in a false and fussy imitation of the late Flamboyant Gothic. Victor Hugo found it *'d'assez bon goût . . . cette decoration annonce encore le progrès des idées romantiques'*.* The Duke of Northumberland was more critical. The interior, he found, 'presented few of those sober and solid graces to which an English eye is accustomed, but was covered with gilding and painting and rich hangings of crimson velvet and gold'. But he greatly admired 'the long and gorgeous vista beaming with innumerable lights towards the High Altar'.

* 'in good enough taste . . . this decoration proclaims once more the progress of Romantic thought.'

In contrast with the pseudo-Gothic decorations of the choir was the imposing Corinthian order of the triumphal arch over the pulpitum on which the royal throne was set. It stood beneath a circular canopy from which the ermine draperies hung in ample folds, like the elaborate mantling of some princely escutcheon.

The service followed the historic pattern, but in certain significant ways the old order was modified. It had an ecumenical aspect well in advance of its time. The Orthodox, Anglican and Protestant Churches were represented and in the procession there walked a Jew and a Muslim. The King's oath included an undertaking to govern *'conformément . . . à la Charte Constitutionelle'*. The King had only decided at the very last minute to include these words, which he pronounced, the Duke of Northumberland noted, 'with great energy'. It produced a sensation. The Prime Minister Villèle was unable to disguise the relief and satisfaction which he felt, but the reactionaries or 'ultras' were disgusted. 'That the Most Christian King,' writes Duvergier de Hauranne, 'the Eldest Son of the Church, should in the presence of God put his seal to an impious pact, make a profession of religious indifference and give the lie to beliefs which he has held all his life, that was cause for indignation to every honest man.'

As for the Charter, the baron de Méchin may speak for the 'ultras'. *'Ce spectacle me déplait et me choque, c'est beaucoup trop républicaine'*.* But perhaps anti-clericalism provided the platform for the sharpest criticism. The duc de la Rochefoucauld-Doudeauville observed maliciously that 'the Archbishop of Reims was far too intoxicated with his own glory and not enough with that of the King.'

In spite of the dissatisfaction of the reactionaries, the whole event was of a strongly reactionary nature. There was an implicit claim to Divine Right in the practice of touching for scrofula. Against the advice of an increasingly scientific world Charles insisted on maintaining this tradition. One hundred and twenty sufferers were touched, five of whom recovered.

On the following day there was an institution of Knights of the St Ésprit. 'The King was superbly dressed as Sovereign,' wrote the Duke of Northumberland, 'but I persuade myself that the Habits and Ensigns of the Garter with which he is so soon to be invested, will not suffer in comparison.'

To many spectators the coronation of Charles X, with all its pomp and all its magnificence, savoured of an attempt to keep alive institutions and traditions which had already outlived their usefulness. Maurice Renard compared the Monarchy to a corpse

* 'This spectacle is offensive and shocking to me, it is far too republican'.

'dressed up and galvanised; the Lily of France exhaled its final breath of perfume – *comme une fleur coupée et plongée dans un vase de Sèvres rempli d'eau bénite; superbe, elle était déjà morte.*'*

---

* 'like a cut flower thrust into a Sèvres vase filled with Holy Water; superb, it was already dead.'

CHAPTER THIRTEEN

Amiens

It would be tempting to claim for Amiens the first place among
Gothic buildings, but, as its great historian Georges Durand has
said: *'on n'établit pas de concours entre les chefs-d'oeuvres'*. Laon,
Notre-Dame, Chartres, Bourges, Reims – all have their unique
place, their proper claim to our appreciation. Nevertheless, in considering the perfection peculiar to Amiens we must agree with
Viollet-le-Duc that this is the Cathedral in which Gothic art came
nearest to realising its own ideal – *'l'église ogivale par excellence'*. This
was where the fully developed resources of the new style were all
available, the high point beyond which no progress was possible and
after which the development of the style begins its slow decline into
the vagaries of ornamental fashion.

A reason for this decline is proposed by François Cali. In the
rigorous logic of its construction and in the total harmony of its
proportions, Amiens improves upon Chartres. But Cali suggests that
in passing from Chartres to Amiens we have made an almost imperceptible transition from 'the love of God to the love of Wisdom –
which is order, number and harmony – which *can* be equated with
God but which need not be'. The very perfection of the architecture
can lead us from the worship of God to mere admiration of the
architect. *'Cathédrale de la raison, Amiens est autant une affirmation de
l'homme que de Dieu . . . cette grande, totale lumière écarte de lui toute crainte.'**

There is truth in what he says; the all pervading light may well
eliminate that fear of the Lord which is the beginning of wisdom; but
the difference between the two Cathedrals would be less apparent if
Amiens had retained its full array of stained glass or if the glass at
Chartres had not been darkened by oxidisation. In their original
forms, Chartres would have been lighter and Amiens darker than
either appears today. If Amiens has lost and Chartres has gained a
sense of the numinous which arises from the dimness of its
illumination, this is due more to the chance effects of history and time
than to any change in architectural ethos.

* 'Cathedral of Reason, Amiens is as much an assertion of Man as of God . . . this
strong and even illumination banishes any sense of awe.'

Nevertheless, Amiens stands at the apex of an ascent beyond which begins a decline. Obviously it owes its position in the development of the Gothic style to the exact moment at which it happened to be built, but one other circumstance contributes to its pre-eminene. It was completed in a relatively short time – some fifty years only – so that the general appearance of the whole building is controlled by the original conception of its creator. Only in decorative detail do the later parts differ from the earlier. Since it has lost most of its stained glass the building is more amply illuminated than most of its peers. We cannot help having our attention concentrated on the architecture in a way which is almost impossible at Chartres.

To enter Amiens Cathedral and to place oneself immediately inside the great west doors is to expose onself to one of the most overwhelming architectonic experiences which the builders of the Middle Ages ever prepared for us.

The first impact is that created by its immense size. Its noble vault is carried at 139 feet – fourteen higher than at Reims which held the previous record. We feel here what Joseph Addison meant when he said that cathedrals 'by opening the mind to vast conceptions, fit it better for the conception of the Deity'. But at Amiens this immensity is nowhere oppressive. This is because every part is properly proportioned to the whole, every detail drawn to scale. Sometimes this regard for proportion involves, because of the great altitude, the subtle use of optical illusion. Seen in elevation – that is to say from its own level – the triforium is out of proportion; the arches are tall and attenuated, the capitals unduly elongated and the bases so raised as to be almost on stilts. Seen from floor level, some seventy feet below, they appear just right.

The ornament is always drawn to scale. The decorations are more highly finished in the lower parts, where they may be viewed more narrowly, but become, in proportion to their distance from the eye, more bold and broadly treated. The tracery of the windows is simple and robust; the mouldings are simple and robust, creating a rich chiaroscuro of light and shade in carefully considered contrast to the plain surfaces.

In the façades of the nave the balance is nicely struck between the upright and the horizontal accents. The great band of richly sculptured foliage which underlines the triforium passes in front of the vertical shafts which carry the vault ribs. So does the simple taurus moulding that runs between the triforium and the clerestory, so that the uprights are divided at carefully calculated intervals, avoiding the dizzy verticality of Beauvais. This verticality is confined to the great piers of the crossing, where the clustered colonnettes rise without interruption to their capitals at the spring of the arch, there

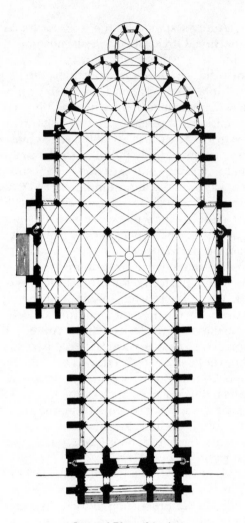

Ground Plan of Amiens

to fan out into the lierne and tierceron vaulting which distinguishes the central canopy.

In order to appreciate the excellence of the original design it is necessary to take note of an important and unhappy modification that resulted – as so often – from the desire to proliferate altars. The outward arches of the two nave aisles now open into chapels which are lit by windows filled with rather banal tracery. These outward arches should contain huge windows of a design still preserved in the inward angles of the nave and transepts. Here the containing arch is divided into two simple lancets surmounted by a large rose – a broad and masculine design which is in correct proportion to the surrounding architecture.

If, in our mind's eye, we can replace these windows into their original positions we can visualise the appearance of the bays of the nave as they were first built.

The band of floral carving beneath the triforium divides the façade into two halves, of which the lower is devoted to the great arcade. In the upper half, clerestory and triforium are treated as a decorative unit. The colonnette which divides the twin arches of the triforium is continued upward to become the central mullion of the clerestory window, thus drawing the two upper divisions into a single, all-embracing whole.

The balance of the composition is perfect. The heavy mouldings of the lower windows give place, in the upper ones, to a light and airy tracery, better suited to their more exalted situation.

The architect of this beautiful, majestic edifice was called Robert de Luzarches, the builder also of the Abbey Church of Port Royal. Because of the churches which already occupied the site, and the need to maintain Divine service in one of them until some portion of the Cathedral was ready for use, he took the unusual step of starting with the nave and progressing from west to east. It is probable that his original intention was to build the choir and apse in the same simple and robust design as the nave and transepts. In fact his successor, Thomas de Cormont, made certain alterations in the detail of the choir which proclaim their later date.

The nave was begun in 1220, the same year as Salisbury Cathedral; it is probable that it was completed by 1232. In April of that year Bishop Geoffroy d'Eu made a grant of land east of the Cathedral for the construction of a cloister and Chapter House. Everything implies that the first campaign of construction was sufficiently near completion to enable the builders to draw breath and to think of lesser things. With the nave ready for use, nothing could be more natural than for the Chapter to require its place of meeting. In the same year the church of St Firmin, which occupied more or less the site of the north transept, was pulled down and the Bishop granted its parishioners the right to worship 'in one side of the Cathedral'.

The limits of this first campaign of building can be accurately established by an inspection of the fabric. The band of sculptured foliage which runs right round the Cathedral below the triforium reveals an abrupt change of style as it enters the choir. In the nave and transepts its continuity is unbroken. The west façades of the transept reflect the same dispositions as the nave up to and including the clerestory windows, whereas in the east façades both triforium and clerestory clearly belong to the style of the choir. Obviously the vaults could not have been built until these east walls were completed.

We must therefore at this stage see the nave, in all its pristine purity of style, ending in the roofless transepts with, presumably, a provisional partition wall enclosing the western aisles of the transepts.

The second campaign followed almost immediately. Between 1236 and 1247 the east side of the transepts was built up and the great vault erected; at the same time the choir was carried up to triforium level together with its side aisles, ambulatory and apsidal chapels. The easternmost chapel must have been well advanced by 1245, when the Sainte-Chapelle in Paris was started. The Sainte-Chapelle is almost a copy of it, but with certain refinements which show that Amiens was the original.

In order to help to finance the building of the choir, the relics of St Honoré were taken in procession round the diocese in 1240 to stimulate the generosity of the faithful. There is an entry in the Cartulary of the Abbaye de Corbie for that year ordering that the relics should be received 'in an honourable and praiseworthy manner'. When Bishop Arnoult de la Pierre died in 1247 the building of the choir was sufficiently advanced for his body to be interred between the two easternmost pillars of the hemicycle.

The final phase of construction was started in about 1259 under the episcopate of Bernard d'Abbeville. The triforium, clerestory and high vaults of the choir all belong to this campaign. In 1269 the east window of the clerestory over the high altar was set up and an inscription in the glass records that it was the gift of Bishop Bernard. It is reasonable to conclude that this marks the completion of the main body of the Cathedral. It had taken forty-nine years to build.

Although in general architectural form and disposition the choir closely resembles the nave, there are nevertheless certain significant differences. By far the most important new departure is the glazing of the outer wall of the triforium, producing an effect of fenestration known as a *clairevoie*. These outer windows are set higher than the triforium arcade so as to allow the light to pass obliquely down into the choir. In order to obtain this extra lighting the roofs of the side aisles and apsidal chapels had to be devised on completely new principles.

A triforium is in origin the upright side of a right-angled triangle of which the hypotenuse is formed by a penthouse roof over the aisle. This sloping roof, which is used in the nave at Amiens, gives place in the choir to a series of flattened pyramidal roofs over each bay of the aisles and of taller pavilion roofs to the chapels, which stand far enough away from the triforium windows not to obstruct the light. A *clairevoie* of this sort had already been introduced both at Troyes and Le Mans and was adopted more or less simultaneously at Beauvais and at Tours.

There are certain other differences of style to be detected in the choir. The bays of the triforium are slightly lower so as to make room for the distinctive little gables which are set like eyebrows over each of the arcades. The tracery of the windows, too, is slightly more complex in form – subdividing into three narrow lancets surmounted by a trefoil instead of two surmounted by a rose – and the detail is more finicky and less easily appreciated from ground level.

This predilection for a more slender and openwork style of decoration was applied externally with nearly disastrous results. The flying buttresses of the choir, with their slim arches and elegant, fretted arcades proved inadequate to their task. In 1497 the first pillar on the north side of the choir began to give and had to be rebuilt – a delicate undertaking which was entrusted to the master mason, Pierre Tarisel. The task was difficult, not to say dangerous, and the workmen who had to execute it were at risk. On Sunday, 14 June, therefore, the statue of the Virgin Mary was taken in solemn procession round the Cathedral, followed by all the workmen carrying lighted candles. All had made their confessions and all had received Communion in the Mass which followed. It is not recorded whether this spiritual safety precaution proved efficacious or not. But the pillar was rebuilt.

The pillars next to this one soon had to be rebuilt also and the flying buttresses above them were strengthened by the addition of a supplementary arch beneath the existing one – a device which at once deprives the whole structure of its beauty. In their attempts to be too elegant, the builders of the choir caused their successors to introduce the only inelegant feature. In the whole, gigantic operation of building the Cathedral, this is the one false move that can be detected.

By 1269 the main hulk of the Cathedral had assumed its definitive shape. The west front had been carried up to the cornice above the rose window. The choir and apse were complete and in all essentials as we see them today. The transepts still lacked the upper storeys of their north and south façades – and presumably some provisional infilling had been contrived to keep the weather out. The nave was complete and still retained its robust alternation between the massive buttresses and the huge aisle windows which have already been described. On the south side this would have produced a powerful shadow projection as the oblique rays of the westering sun cast ever deeper pools of darkness in the recesses between the buttress piers.

It was not to last. The cult of the Virgin Mary had inspired the Cathedral as a whole: the cult of the lesser saints was to destroy its noble unity of style.

In 1292 Bishop Guillaume de Mâcon erected in the first bay of the south aisle, nearest the transept, a chapel dedicated to St Margaret. No doubt the dedication had as much to do with Marguerite de Provence, the wife of St Louis, as with any of the six Margarets who had found their way into the hagiography of the church. In the same year Drieu Malherbe, sometime Mayor of Amiens, bequeathed properties for the founding of a chapel to St Agnes, which answered that of St Margaret in the north aisle. In September 1297 King Louis IX was canonised and by 1302 there was a chapel built and consecrated to him next to that of St Agnes. Since Guillaume de Mâcon had been chaplain to Louis and had been one of the chosen emissaries sent to solicit his canonisation from Pope Nicholas IV, his desire to found a chapel here is understandable.

The next two chapels on either side were clearly built at the same time and dedicated to St Honoré and St Nicholas. The first three chapels on either side of the nave, starting from the crossing, are all very similar in style and each has a simple quadripartite vault. The remaining three on the south side and one more on the north were added in the early years of the fourteenth century. They are chiefly to be distinguished by their lierne and tierceron vaulting.

All these chapels were contrived within the spaces between the buttresses which have been extended to provide more ample accommodation. The original outline of the buttress can in most cases be seen on the side wall of the chapel. From within, the chapels do not seriously upset the dispositions of the nave. From without their effect is simply deplorable. In place of the deeply recessed bays, the outward façade presents a flat wall; in place of the strong and simple tracery of the original aisle windows, we have the flimsy fretwork of differing but always indifferent design.

The two westernmost chapels on the north side were the gift of Jean de la Grange, a most distinguished person who became Bishop of Amiens in 1373. A canon of Notre-Dame and recently elevated to the Deanery of Laon, he was a man who enjoyed the full confidence of Charles V. He only stayed for two years at Amiens, being made a Cardinal in 1375 and recalled to Avignon, but in these two years he achieved a considerable amount. He immediately completed the transformation of the nave by filling in the two remaining spaces with chapels dedicated to John the Baptist and John the Evangelist. An inscription in the window of the former gives to 'the Voice crying in the wilderness', the man who lived on locusts and wild honey, the strangely inappropriate title of "Monseigneur". It was, in fact, the normal style accorded to a saint.

These chapels are remarkable for their exquisite workmanship and for the Flamboyant design of the tracery, which here makes its first appearance at Amiens. But above all they are distinguished by the nine statues which ornament their façades. They rank with those of Pierrefonds and La Ferté Milon among the greatest works of French sculpture of the late fourteenth century. We may feel confident also, from the studied realism of their execution, that they offer us authentic portraits of the characters which they represent, in particular those of Cardinal la Grange himself together with Charles V and his two sons, the Dauphin (later Charles VI) and the duc d'Orléans, to both of whom la Grange had previously been tutor. It has been pointed out by Emil Mâle that this is a departure from the best traditions of the Middle Ages. In the thirteenth century no king or cardinal would have been represented on the same scale as the Virgin or St John. If they appeared at all, such figures would have been in miniature and prostrate at the feet of the Virgin or saint.

The building of these chapels was integrated with the erection of a supplementary buttress to the north tower – no doubt in consideration of the extra weight which would be added when the tower was completed.

The mention of the north tower brings us to a consideration of the west façade. Next to the interior of the nave, this is one of the greatest successes of Amiens Cathedral and, except for the upper storeys of the towers, it was almost certainly built according to the original design and intention of the architect, Robert de Luzarches. It rises like a great cliff face from the *parvis* before it and dominates the town. It has a noble symmetry, to which there are only the most insignificant exceptions, and a complexity proportionate to its size.

Its most original feature is in the shape of the towers which are oblong in plan, presenting their broad façades to the west and their narrow flanks to the north and south.

Inside this has the effect of eliminating the narthex which is the logical result of square towers as in Paris or Reims. Such a narthex requires a strengthening of the westernmost piers which upsets the unity of the nave. At Amiens there is nothing in the interior architecture to suggest the presence of the towers at all. The noble *ordonnance* of the grand arcade continues right up to the west façade. Outside, the towers are simply the logical coronation to the massive abutment of the nave and aisles provided by the whole west front. This thickness provides the depth required for the cavernous recesses of the three portals, enabling the architect to emphasise the central archway by setting its doors several feet further back than the two side entrances.

The great triple porch of the west front provides the focal point to the façade. It is clearly the work of a closely integrated team of sculptors all steeped in the same tradition and all working to a fully thought out master plan. It is not possible to distinguish the hand of one artist from another. As with the architecture, the style of the sculpture is one of a broad and noble simplicity – *'un art en pleine possession de lui-même,'* wrote Georges Durand, *'et qui ne produit son effet que par la beauté des grandes lignes.'** The folds of the long robes are simple, ample and natural, but never stylised and revealing an astonishing variety in their arrangement. Detail is reduced to a minimum and is all the more effective for its scarcity. In the central statue known as the *Beau Dieu* the exquisite, bejewelled binding of the book which he holds forms a most effective contrast with the majestic simplicity of the figure.

In some of the humbler figures this economy of detail is particularly impressive. Look at the figure of a deacon – in all probability St Domice – placed between two bishops on the right hand side of the left porch; observe how the drape of his heavy woollen garment is suggested with a few bold strokes of the chisel – and how the artist has enjoyed the flat surfaces of the hands and the folds in the sleeves of his dalmatic. His face is obviously a living portrait; there is in it a slightly perplexed naïvety which offers a telling contrast with the expression of shrewd authority in the bishop on his right.

The *Grand Portail* of Amiens derives the main theme of its iconography from the service of the dedication of a church – one of the most beautiful in medieval liturgy. It is a sermon in stone upon the text of Ephesians 2 verses 19–22: 'Ye are no more strangers and foreigners, but fellow citizens with the saints, and of the houshold of God; and are built upon the foundation of the Apostles and Prophets, Jesus Christ Himself being the chief corner stone; in whom all the building, fitly framed together, groweth unto a holy temple in the Lord; in whom ye are also builded together for an habitation of God through the spirit.'

Thus in the central archway, the *Porte du Sauveur*, the apostles and prophets are represented as pillars of the church, while the figures of the faithful complete the building.

Beneath the apostles, in a double row of quatrefoils, are little bass reliefs representing the virtues and vices. Since the time of Augustine these had been regarded as having the power to open or close the doors of Paradise. It is significant that the passage from Augustine

* 'An art in full possession of itself and which produces its effect simply by the beauty of the main lines.'

referred to comes from his sermon 'On the Dedication of a Church'.

The theme of the open and the closed door is taken up again by the placing of the Wise and the Foolish Virgins on the jambs to either side. It is not far to seek the connection between this thought and the Last Judgment which occupies the tympanum.

In the centre of all this carefully thought out symbolism, the figure of the *Beau Dieu* occupies the place of honour on the pier that divides the two doors. He is given a slightly awkward stance in order that his two feet may tread one upon a lion and another upon a dragon, beneath which, as if to emphasise the point, is carved an adder and a basilisk. The 'adder' – quite distinct from the viper – was a rather endearing little dragon that could be charmed by song. Its protective attitude was therefore to stand with one ear to the ground and the other stopped by its tail. According to Honorius of Autun it thus became 'the image of the sinner who closes his ears to the words of life'. The basilisk was the symbol of death. The *Beau Dieu* of Amiens tramples Sin and Death under his feet. In the niche below the *Beau Dieu* is the figure of a king – in all probability Solomon – with a rose and a lily in the narrow arches on either flank. The presence of Solomon is connected with the custom of using the front porch of a cathedral for certain judicial purposes. The porch at Léon in Spain – a Cathedral which obviously owes much to Amiens – bears the inscription *Locus Appellationis* – the Place of Appeal.

The right hand embrasure, or *Porte de la Mère Dieu*, as was by then traditional, was devoted to the life of the Virgin. The statues on the right represent the Annunciation, Visitation and the Presentation in the Temple; those on the left show the Three Kings, nearest the door, followed by Herod, Solomon and the Queen of Sheba.

The left hand portal follows a new fashion, shared notably with Bourges and Reims, of celebrating the local worthies of the Cathedral. Here at Amiens it is consecrated to St Firmin, the saint who evangelised Picardy and whose body, miraculously re-discovered, was the principal relic of the Cathedral. It is designed to reflect symmetrically the dispostions of the *Porte de la Mère Dieu*.

St Firmin himself occupies the place of honour against the central pier and gives his episcopal blessing to the scenes of daily life depicted in the quatrefoils which ornament the base of the whole composition.

The other statues are less easily identified, but the presence of one woman and one deacon suggests that these are the saints whose bodies were interred within the church. That would make the lady Ste Ulphe and the deacon St Domice. There were ten such relics, including St Firmin. This leaves only nine to fill the twelve places required by the symmetry of this porch with that of *la Mère Dieu*. The

Middle Ages, however, were seldom embarrassed by statistical accuracy of this sort. Indeed, in the archivolts of the *Porte du Sauveur*, the Elders of the Apocalypse number twenty instead of twenty-four for the simple reason that there was only room for twenty. In smaller churches it was not uncommon to find the number of the apostles reduced to eight if space were lacking for the whole array. We need not be too concerned that there are three unidentified saints in the *Porte St Firmin*.

The west front of Amiens with its three portals naturally suggests a comparison with that of Notre-Dame de Paris. It is customary to praise the latter as the perfect expression of Suger's 'Gateway of Heaven'. In its almost perfect symmetry and in the justice of its proportions, it is certainly one of the great successes of the style. It is, however, possible to criticise it on the grounds of an undue emphasis on horizontal lines. The *Galerie des Rois* forms a complete break between the lowest storey and those above. The balustrade which surmounts it obscures the lower portions of the coupled lancets on either side of the rose, making their appearance slightly squat.

At Amiens the architect had to mask a building thirty feet taller than Notre-Dame and he had room for a further arcade, which he inserted below the *Galerie des Rois*. He has always allowed his vertical elements to dominate. He has made the towers break forward from the central façade, and the perspective involved interrupts the horizontal lines. He has emphasised the great buttresses by crowning their first projection with tall, octagonal spires and where the *Galerie des Rois* passes in front of the buttresses, he has accentuated the niche containing the King with a tall gable, continuing and reflecting the upward movement of the spires.

Although the west rose formed part of the thirteenth-century design, the tracery was renewed in the Flamboyant period. The centre stone bears a coat of arms with three cocks – in all probability the escutcheon of Robert de Coquerel, a Canon of the Cathedral who died in 1521. The glass which this rose contains is already in the style of the Renaissance and suggests a date early in the sixteenth century.

In order to obtain a perfect square for this rose, the architect has been obliged to raise the cornice above it by about three feet. An oblique view of the façade will show how this is achieved. But owing to the fact that this part of the façade is recessed behind the level of the towers, this elevation of the cornice is counteracted by the perspective so that the spectator is quite unaware of the device.

On the internal face of the rose an enormous clock was installed, the figures being attached to the circular frame and a large hand, ten metres long, indicating the hour. It was removed in the nineteenth century by Viollet-le-Duc.

At the entrance to the south transept is another porch known from its central figure as the *Porte de la Vierge Dorée*. It does not need a very practised eye to detect that there are here two successive phases of work. The architecture, including the eight full-length statues, belongs to the earliest period of the building. It is almost identical to that of the west portal, except that the statues are slightly inferior and have a somewhat wooden appearance.

By contrast the figure of the Virgin, together with the scenes in the tympanum and the statuettes in the architraves, betray the lighter spirit of a later age. The exact similarity of the band of sculptured foliage above the heads of the twelve statues in the lintel with that which runs beneath the triforium in the choir, suggests a date somewhere between 1258 and 1269.

The tympanum tells the story of St Honoré. It starts at the bottom and reads from left to right. The first scene, in the lower left hand corner, illustrates his reluctance to accept the bishopric of Amiens; to the right he presides over the discovery of the bodies of St Fuscian, St Victoric and St Gentien. In the row above on the left is the Miraculous Mass of St Honoré, in which the hand of God, stretching out from a cloud, is seen consecrating the elements. To the right of this is the healing of two blind people, one of whom appears to have a canine guide. Above this is a procession of relics which is almost wholly a nineteenth-century reconstruction.

High above this portal is the lovely rose window enframed above a double *clairevoie* which can be dated at about the year 1400. The rose is circumscribed by an outer arc and in the space between is a particularly fine example of a 'wheel of fortune', with all the figures on the left climbing up and all those on the right falling down.

The north transept contains a rose which is rather larger than that of the south and considerably earlier in style; the tracery is not unlike that of the nave chapels built about the year 1300. The design of the rose is based on the five-pointed star, which is an unusual and very attractive feature. Unfortunately the huge area of glass involved was too unstable and the window began to bow outwards. This was remedied by the construction of two outer buttresses which are so slender and so skilfully tapered as to cause a minimum obstruction to the light. This window contains the most important survival of what was once a complete and perfect set of the most beautiful stained glass. In 1677 the windows in the nave clerestory were still all intact when they were described by du Cange. They were still there in 1755 when Dom Grenier was preparing his notes for a guide book on Picardy. 'All this glazing,' he wrote, 'although in colours, sheds on all sides an even light, without any suspicion of obscurity. The glass, apparently, is less thick than in other churches of the same date.'

In 1806 Rivoire describes these windows all in the present tense from which we may conclude that they were still *in situ*. But in 1815 Baron distinctly implies that they have disappeared. His description is based on du Cange and is in the imperfect throughout. In 1812 a considerable sum, nearly ten and a half thousand francs, was paid to one Dupetit, glassmaker of Paris, for the 'repair' of the clerestory windows. The accounts shed no light on the problem, but it seems likely that the removal of the old glass and its replacement by plain glass came within the term 'repairing'. Not only had the eighteenth century made plain glass fashionable, but it was held at that time that the colouring of medieval glass was a lost secret.

Such, at any rate, was the opinion of Le Vieil, who wrote his *'Traité Historique et Pratique de la Peinture sur Verre'* in 1774. At the time he was writing, he claims that there was one solitary practitioner of the art in France and that he was only employed for the occasional armorial blazon.

The reason that he gives for the dislike of his contemporaries for medieval glass were twofold; one practical and one moral. 'Better educated than our forefathers' – such was his ignorant and patronising claim – 'we know how to read and we have service books' – had he never seen any of that beautiful calligraphy which first attracted the opprobrious epithet of 'Gothic'? – 'but how can we use them in temples rendered obscure by so much painted glass?' His moral objection is less easy to understand. He accuses these old windows of being peopled 'with figures so ridiculous and even so indecent that we felt we could do no better, in order to conceal this ignorance and superstition, than to withdraw these pictures that are so filled with fables and so scandalous.' More reasonably, he complains that the windows were often in a pitiful condition. 'They had remained unrepaired for mere want of any glass painters to repair them,' he admitted; *'c'est un secret perdu'*.

The nineteenth century made various attempts to recover the damage done by the passage of time or the activity of vandals – first by patching up with pieces of medieval glass, then by matching as best they could with their own imitations. Most of the surviving windows have become incomprehensible jumbles. In the central chapel of the apse, however, there is one window – immediately to the left of the east window – which is virtually in its original condition, so far as human interference is concerned. But during the centuries a process of oxydisation has darkened the colours, notably the reds which are nearly black, and thus robbed it of that clear luminosity which Dom Grenier had noted was the essential characteristic of the glazing.

It is in the rose windows that we see the most complete survivals of the original ensemble. That of the north transept is as fine a specimen of early fourteenth-century glass as can be found in France. Its design consists of a central circle of a lovely royal blue, against which the five-pointed star stands out in scarlet. The petals which radiate from this circle are much lighter in tone, making an extensive use of colourless glass. In the outer ring of roundels the brilliant blue of the central core is again reflected.

In the south rose the angel figures in the principal compartments have survived from the original late fifteenth-century glazing, but the rest of the window is of relatively modern date. It is none the less extremely beautiful.

At the west end of the nave the rose retains its contemporary glass which is already in the style of the Renaissance.

Enough survives to demonstrate that in its pristine glory the Cathedral of Amiens was endowed with a set of windows entirely worthy of its architecture. Because of the enormous acreage of glass, and because of the paler, more translucent colours used, they would have provided sufficient illumination to show up the architecture in all its beauty and in all its grandeur, while eliminating the glare which, where plain glass is used, makes an appreciation of the surrounding stonework extremely difficult.

Thus in the early years of the sixteenth century the dream of Robert de Luzarches was finally and fully realised. Thanks to the complementary labours of the mason, the carver and the glazier, one of the loveliest buildings ever erected to the greater glory of God now stood complete in all its splendour.

Within this masterpiece of stone and glass the Chapter now proceeded to create a second, smaller masterpiece of wood. The choir stalls of Amiens rank among the great artistic wonders of the world. There must have been stalls of some sort from the moment that the choir was made available for divine service, but they were presumably of inferior quality, for the decision was made, in the early sixteenth century, to replace them with something more worthy of the building they were to adorn – and a more ambitious scheme could scarcely have been devised.

Fifty-five lower stalls for the chaplains are backed and overtopped by sixty upper stalls for the canons, raised on a high plinth and crowned with a Flamboyant canopy which soars into an airy pinnacle thirty feet high over each of the 'master' stalls at the four extremities of the enclosure. There is a uniformity created by the main architectural framework of the canopy, but a uniformity relieved and tempered by the seemingly endless variety of the decorations.

The enterprise was undertaken at a time when the last phase of the Gothic style was in full decline. But, either because of the exceptional qualities of the artists themselves, or because this complex, open-work elaboration is more suited to the wooden furnishings than to the stone fabric of a building, the stalls of Amiens offer an amazing combination of artistic excellence and technical skill – like a sudden shaft of unexpected light from a setting sun. The marvellous standard of the carvings is only equalled by the astonishing precision of the joinery – *'une oeuvre de menuiserie'*, as Georges Durand describes it, *'absolument prodigieuse'*. The joints, often cleverly concealed in the convex curve of some reverse moulding, are almost imperceptible, so impeccably are they cut and so perfectly have they held together throughout the centuries.

The ornamental sculpture can be divided into two main themes: a floral decoration which is closely related to the architectural forms, and a series of scenes from biblical and contemporary life to which the former provides the framework. This architectural framework is a fantasia on a Flamboyant theme. The curves and counter curves are seldom segments of an arc and therefore cannot have been described by aid of compasses, but are traced freehand – a freedom which liberates the design from the often brittle stiffness of the style. The shapes are supple and answerable to the artist's will. It is precisely this that has made possible the marriage between architectural structure and floral decoration which is the basis of the whole conception. Cusps and crockets curl in upon themselves and blossom out into the fronds and tendrils of the acanthus and the fern; trefoil arches merge imperceptibly into interlacing branches of rose and bramble; pinnacles shoot up into tender saplings and pendants hang in clustered knots of foliage. The sturdy oak seems to take on a score of different forms and substances. 'Under the carver's hand,' wrote Ruskin, 'it seems to cut like clay, to fold like silk, to grow like living branches, to leap like living flame.'

Only a prolonged and minute inspection can reveal the delicate and accurate depiction of the whole vegetable kingdom of Picardy, enlivened by the occasional intrusion of snails, mice, insects and reptiles – the normal inhabitants of such vegetation. But even this abundant source did not satisfy the artists, who have not hesitated to invent a flora of their own fancy.

Superimposed upon this background of architecture and decorative nature are the three thousand, six hundred and fifty human figures for which the stalls are chiefly famous. They add a new dimension of interest, pathos and humour to the whole gigantic composition. Apart from the incidental figures, the serious iconography of the stalls comprehends some four hundred subjects. There is the biblical theme – one covering the main events from the Creation to the Book of Job, while concentrating on the story of

Joseph, and the other illustrating the history of the Virgin from her Conception to her Coronation.

The Old Testament scenes occupy chiefly the misericords, which played a role of fundamental importance to the scheme. The very word 'stall' means a place where one stands, and the long periods of standing during the Offices were tedious to the clergy. The misericord, a projecting ledge on the under side of the seat, enabled the occupant of the stall to retain an upright posture while transferring some of his weight from his feet to his posterior.

The history of the Virgin is for the most part displayed in the panels at the ends of the stalls and on the passageways from the lower to the upper series. An illuminating insight into the mentality of the artist is afforded by the treatment of the Marriage at Cana on the ramp of the first gangway from the west on the north side. It shows the table spread for the nuptial feast, with a table cloth hanging in ample folds over the edge of the board. Beneath the cloth, and completely invisible to the spectator, the feet of those seated at the banquet are scrupulously carved.

Besides these two main themes there is a series of figures, mostly on the elbow rests, representing legends and fables and scenes from everyday life, for the most part wholly secular in character. It is typical of medieval religion that such subjects should be felt to have their place in the choir stalls of a cathedral. It is supremely here that the artist has shown himself the master of the facial expression. On a head smaller than a billiard ball he can render every nuance of human emotion that can be read in the smallest movement of the muscles of the eyes and mouth.

In the north-west angle, where two elbow rests meet at right angles, the artist has taken advantage of the juxtaposition of two figures occasioned by the junction to represent a woman making her confession to a priest. The expressions are delightful. There is a whole world of simple faith and obedient piety in the round forms and protruding upper lip of the face of the penitent: in deliberate contrast is the shrewd angularity of the confessor's. With a few deft strokes of the chisel the artist has managed to convey a mixture of personal asceticism, deep sympathies and a penetrating understanding of the ways of the world.

At stall 94, first from the left on the eastern half of the north side, is depicted *Le Ménage Brouillé* – a wife beating her husband. His expression is one of patient amusement. There was one day in the year – the Tuesday after Easter – when wives were allowed to beat their husbands, but his smile suggests that he is thinking that tomorrow, and for the following three hundred and sixty-three days, it will be his turn.

Sometimes the details can be related to local history. In the panel of the Massacre of the Innocents one of the soldiers is clearly a *lansquenet* or German foot soldier. Every detail of his uniform and equipment is accurately depicted. It is known that in 1513 a troop of lansquenets, under the command of the comte d'Aspremont, was billeted in Amiens, and there can be no doubt that one of them served the artist as a model.

The visitor to these stalls would do well to consider at some length the problem of conceiving so vast and intricate an ensemble and of translating this conception into terms of practical carpentry – the fitting together of hundreds of thousands of pieces of wood, some of them as much as eight and a half metres long.

It was an undertaking that did not daunt the Chapter. Four of their number, Jean Fabus, Pierre Vuaile, Jean Dumas and Jean Lenglaché, were nominated to supervise the operation. In 1508 they made a contract with Arnoul Boulin, *'maître menuisier à Amiens'*, to provide a hundred and twenty stalls with their canopies. A separate contract was made with Antoine Avernier, *'tailleur d'images à Amiens'*, for the seats and misericords. The principal craftsmen were therefore local men. Amiens was able to produce this masterpiece from her own resources.

They did not lose any time. The Grande Salle of the Bishop's Palace was made available as a workshop – perhaps because it was the only room in Amiens large enough for the purpose – and work began in July of the same year.

In the following year they seem to have decided that they had underrated the enormous extent of the task, and a further craftsman, also local, Alexandre Huet, *'menuisier à Amiens'*, was associated with Boulin in a further contract. Huet was to take over the south side of the choir while Boulin concentrated on the north side. During these first years Boulin and Huet made visits to Beauvais, Rouen and St Riquier to study the stalls there.

In October 1510 the Chapter paid the expenses of two monks from the Cordeliers at Abbeville, who were authorities on the subject of woodwork, to come over and give their advice. Finally in December 1516 another *'tailleur d'images'* was taken on, Jehan Trupin, who has secured his own immortality by appending his name to the figure of a woodcarver on the elbow rest below stall 85 – the last stall but one from the east on the north side. He has left his name also beneath stall 92 – the middle of the front row, on the eastern half of the north side: 'Jehan Trupin Dieu te pourvoie', (may God provide for you). History does not relate whether this was just a pious ejaculation or an oblique reference to the fact that he only received three sols a day – the same as an ordinary workman. The names of three woodworkers, described as *'serviteurs'* of Boulin's, appear in the accounts at three sols a day, but there is no means of assessing the total task force.

The stalls were finished on St John's Day, 1522 – fourteen years after they were first begun. Nine and a half thousand livres had been expended, of which fourteen hundred came from private donations, mostly by individual canons.

Less than a hundred years later the whole ensemble was nearly destroyed by fire when a caretaker, who slept in a cubby hole under the south-east master stall, forgot to put out his candle. The damage done must have been considerable, for the whole pinnacle had to be replaced. It can be seen at once that the pinnacle must have come from the same workshops, but is not in sequence with the rest of the stalls. According to the earliest authorities this was the processional canopy, known as a 'May', which was utilised to replace the damaged stall.

In 1642 the Bishop, François de Caumartin, wishing to insert an episcopal throne for himself, demanded the suppression of stalls 83 and 84. Ever since 1149 the Bishop of Amiens had held the post of Treasurer of the Cathedral and when in the choir sat in the Treasurer's stall. His demand for a more sumptuous throne was resisted by the Chapter who petitioned the King's Council to prevent this vandalisation of a series of stalls which they could proudly describe as *'les plus belles qu'il y ait dans le royaume'*. They might have gone one further and claimed that these stalls are the most beautiful in the world.

CHAPTER FOURTEEN

Tours

It sometimes happens that an individual is so attuned to his times that he can be said to represent in his person the spirit of the age in which he lived, so that in him can be seen both the ideals which inspired that age and also the failures for which it must be held accountable. Such a man was Saint Louis.

Son of Louis VIII and Blanche de Castille, he was the grandson of Philippe-Auguste and born in the same year as Bouvines. Bouvines, *'victoire créatrice'*, was, as the popular rejoicings which followed it proclaimed, a national as well as a dynastic event. *'Philippe-Auguste,'* writes the duc de Lévis-Mirepoix, *'du grand coup de Bouvines, avait enfoncé dans leur sol les racines de la France'.** It was a propitious year for the birth of an heir to the throne, and Louis seems to have been born to personify the spirit of his time and country. 'Saint Louis,' continues Lévis-Mirepoix, 'offers the most lifelike and the most fitting image of what the Middle Ages wanted to make of Man.'

He was religious in the best sense of the word and he was a great lover of the poor. His biographer Joinville records how a hundred and twenty poor men were fed daily at his table, the King sometimes serving them with his own hands. Wherever there was a monastery, or an *Hôtel Dieu* or a lepers' *Maladrerie* to be founded the royal almoners were ready with large sums. Aubin-Louis Millin, the revolutionary author of the *Receuil de Monuments* of 1792, complained that St Louis 'spent more on his monks than Louis XIV or Louis XV did on their mistresses'. The monks were, of course, somewhat more numerous.

But Louis' religion was not free from the taint of fanaticism and folly which also characterised the age. His attitude towards heretics, infidels and Jews would hardly be accepted as Christian today, and where the financing of a useless crusade or the purchase of a relic of doubtful authenticity was at stake, his prodigality knew no bounds; and it was his country's money that he was squandering.

When the Emperor Baudouin II of Constantinople offered to see an alleged Crown of Thorns, Louis paid the colossal price of 135,000

* 'Philippe-Auguste, with the master stroke of Bouvines, embedded the roots of France deep in their soil.'

livres. If we take into account that the whole cost of the building of the Sainte-Chapelle, which was designed to house this precious relic, only amounted to 40,000 livres, we begin to appreciate the sum involved. What was somehow typical of the medieval mind was that neither Saint Louis nor, so far as is known, anyone else appeared to be in the least bit troubled by the thought that the royal Abbey of St Denis already claimed to possess the Crown of Thorns.

Louis' disregard for authenticity cost France a fortune, but it left posterity the Sainte-Chapelle. 'It commands our admiration,' wrote Jean de Jandum in 1323, 'by the great strength of its construction and the indestructible solidity of the materials of which it is built. The subtle colours of its paintings, the costly gilding of its images, the pure translucence of its stained glass windows . . . have brought this house of prayer to such a pitch of beauty that on entering one could fancy oneself transported to Heaven and could well imagine one had been introduced into one of the most beautiful mansions of Paradise.'

It is certainly one of the most perfect achievements of the Gothic style and it is, in its architecture though not in its stained glass, virtually a copy of the triforium and clerestory of the Cathedral of Tours.

The connecting link between Tours and the Sainte-Chapelle is certainly St Louis. Tours had come into the hands of the Capetians in 1205, when John Lackland was judged to have forfeited his rights by the Council formed by the Twelve Peers of France. An attempt by John to recover Touraine was defeated by the Dauphin – the future Louis VIII – at La Roche-aux-Moines three weeks before Bouvines. The assumption of Tours within the royal domain was the signal for a remarkable campaign of ecclesiastical building. The choir of the great Basilica of St Martin de Tours, the Abbey Church of Marmoutiers and that of St Julien were all contemporary with the new Cathedral.

As ever, it was a fire that created the opportunity for a new building. In 1233 Archbishop Juhel de Mathefelon wrote to ask Maurice, Archbishop of Rouen, for permission to send *quêteurs* to his diocese. 'The glorious metropolitan Church of Tours,' he wrote, 'by an accident as unexpected as it was deplorable, has been at the same time ruined and overthrown in its most sacred place, the Sanctuary. It would be impossible to see anything so admirable and at the same time so pitiful.'

The sanctuary to which he referred was that started by Hildebert de Lavardin, who had shown considerable ability as an architect at Le Mans, where there is evidence that he took a creative part in the building, and who was Archbishop of Tours from 1125–1133. This was the church in which both Louis VIII and St Louis were installed as Canons shortly after their coronation. The newly acquired possession of Touraine was cherished by the King; Tours became, under St Louis, 'a second Paris'. In 1236, the year in which St Louis attained his majority and took over the government of France from his mother, the rebuilding of the choir was started.

We can get some idea of the progress of the *chantier* from the successive donations recorded. In 1238 a local Seigneur, Jean de Poillé, granted the Chapter permission to exploit the quarries of Charentilly, some ten kilometres to the north of Tours. The stones, '*dures comme l'acier*', provided a solid basis for the apse. In 1241 the King granted them the quarries at Cheillé, near Azay-le-Rideau. This was more tender stone, suitable for the work of the sculptor. A year later the Treasurer was obliged to provide a rope for the bell over the choir. In the first vault east of the crossing the hole can still be seen through which this rope passed. The detail confirms that the vaults were already up. In 1243 the King made a grant of trees in the Forêt de Chinon. This suggests that they were already beginning to think about the roof.

As at Chartres, the building of the new Cathedral was the occasion for an outburst of popular enthusiasm. A *Confrérie* was formed for the provision of voluntary labour. No one was admitted who had not first made his confession and renounced all hatred and vengeance. Stone and timbers were hauled as far as Langeais from whence they were conducted by barge in reverent silence up the Loire to Tours.

The new Cathedral was built upon the foundations of the old and, indeed, incorporated much of the original masonry. The scale of the building was thus dictated by the dimensions of its precursor. There is no attempt here to rival the immensity of Amiens or Beauvais. The dimensions are modest but the modesty has been turned to good effect by the builder. The smaller a building, the greater the need for attention to detail and it is precisely in such attentiveness that Viollet-le-Duc has identified the essential virtue of Tours.

'This charming edifice,' he writes, 'has been executed with a most particular carefulness. One cannot detect in any of its parts those negligences which are so common in our northern Cathedrals. At Tours one feels that everything has been thought out and carried out with deliberation. The choir is the work of a well-balanced mind, of one who is in full possession of his art and who only carries out what his available resources permit. One can assert that this gracious monument follows step by step the advances made in the art of the time.'

It is not possible to reach any conclusion as to who was the author of this distinguished building, neither can any certain attribution be

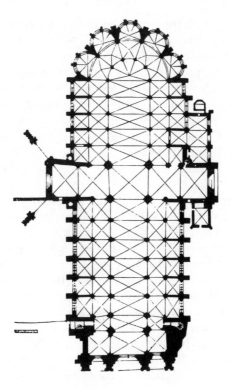

Ground Plan of Tours

made in respect of the Sainte-Chapelle. The name of Pierre de Montreuil has long been attached to the latter, but without any documentary evidence.

There is one feature, however, which puts Tours in the same group as the Sainte-Chapelle, the so-called Sainte-Chapelle of St Germer de Fly and the apsidal chapels of Amiens Cathedral: this is the form of the tracery in the east windows. The current formula was still the superimposition of a roundel above the arches of twin lancets, the whole inscribed in an outer lancet. But in this group of buildings there appears an arrangement of three trefoils in place of the roundel. Since the broader side windows are in every case true to the lancet and roundel formula, it would seem that the architect was not satisfied with the application of this to the much narrower lights of the apse, where the roundel has often the appearance of being just squeezed in. The architect of Tours wanted to divide his window into three narrow lights – an arrangement which virtually precludes roundels – and he had found an elegant solution to his problem with his three trefoils. It is just possible that the common factor of these tracery designs may link the three buildings with Amiens, where the architect is known to have been Thomas de Cormont.

But whoever the Master Mason was, he produced a building which has earned the praise and admiration of all who are capable of appreciating the architecture of the age. One of the earliest appreciations of Tours comes from an Italian, a Florentine named Florio, who wrote, in 1477, a long and eulogistic letter on the beauties of the Loire Valley. The Cathedral of St Gatien he describes as 'joyous and faultless and so well proportioned in all its parts that the mere sight of it, from within or without, turns sorrow into happiness and sadness into joy'.

The original intention was to build no more than a choir. That the architect did not foresee the building of a new nave answerable to his new choir is proved by the gross irregularities that he has accepted in order to accommodate his choir to the old nave. These show clearly on a ground plan. The north-east pier of the crossing is out of line with the main arcade of the choir; the first bays of the south choir aisles have been compressed in order to align them with the south aisles of the nave; the north transept opens through one broad archway into its choir aisles, whereas the south transept opens through two narrow arches. Since the nave and transepts were in fact rebuilt in the fourteenth century, one cannot help regretting the acceptance of these irregularities by the architect of the choir.

Apart from this he has produced a building which is so satisfying that it would be impossible to suggest any improvement. He was not trying to produce that overwhelming impression of verticality which may be observed at Beauvais. The triforium is not linked by a common mullion to the tracery of the clerestory; it forms an entity in itself, but its strongly horizontal accent is cut at regular intervals by the colonettes which carry the thrust of the vault ribs down to the capitals of the great arcade.

Another contrivance which adds to the general impression of spaciousness and light is that the spring of the vaulting arches is pitched high, and the vaults themselves describe an arc which is distinctly flat so that they obstruct as little as possible the clerestory windows of the hemicycle.

It is these litle touches which impart to the choir its own peculiar charm. One feels oneself to be in the presence of an artist who has given everything his careful consideration. *'Ce qui fait la beauté du choeur de St Gatien,'* writes the Abbé Boissonot, *'c'est que cela vit.'* The architecture is the expression of a living tradition. It contrasts with the rather uninspired formalism of the nave. 'The architects of the fourteenth and fifteenth centuries,' continues Boissonot, 'used all their ingenuity to harmonise the nave with the apse: nevertheless a great gulf is set between them . . . the choir is possessed of a soul; the other parts are not.'

The piers of the great arcade of the nave, with their meagre capitals and the shallow relief of the grouped colonnettes, which are meant to carry the eye upwards to the vault ribs with which they correspond, bear no comparison with the strong mouldings and deeply carved enrichments of the choir. One has only to compare the narrow, meaningless fluting of the western piers of the crossing with the bold statement of the vaulting system proclaimed by the eastern piers, to see what Boissonot means.

Only one major modification has been made to the original disposition of the choir. It was first built with double aisles to right and left, which gave the visitor the impressive sensation of walking among a forest of pillars. This was destroyed in the fourteenth century by the familiar need for a proliferation of chapels; but instead of filling in the spaces between the buttresses outside the periphery of the building, at Tours it was achieved by separating most of the bays of the outer aisles with partition walls.

There is one detail to be observed in the side aisles of the choir which was specially noted by Viollet-le-Duc. Above the capitals, at the spring of the architrave and vaulting arch, can be seen the sawn-off ends of wooden beams. This is the result of a constructional device whereby the whole system was locked together with a timber framework until the building was complete. Once complete, the operation of thrust and counter-thrust assured the stability of the whole and the wooden ties could be sawn off and removed.

In 1248 St Louis went on a Crusade and all work on the Cathedral was suspended. Eight years later he was back in Tours and it is probable that the great work of providing the new choir with a worthy set of stained glass windows was undertaken at this time. By 1260 some of them, bearing the heraldic devices of Louis and Blanche de Castille, were already in place and in 1267, on 12 May, the choir was ready for its solemn consecration.

The dates are significant; for whereas the choir at Tours had inspired the architecture of the Sainte-Chapelle, the Sainte-Chapelle was fully glazed by 1248, and in its turn inspired the stained glass windows of the choir at Tours. These improve considerably upon their originals. The windows of the Sainte-Chapelle – however glorious when seen as an ensemble – show signs of over-hasty expedition. As Viollet-le-Duc admits: 'we can detect many negligences: glass that was improperly fired; subject matter that has not been completed; a lack of carefulness about the details. They have only this point of resemblance with those of Tours – their overall effect is quite remarkable.'

At Tours, on the contrary, there is no lack of carefulness about the details. The Abbé Boissonot, who made an important study of the Cathedral and its glass in 1832, noted the precision with which each figure was drawn; 'their movements are full of energy and expression; the drape of their vestments is always graceful, the folds neat and close together'; everything is represented with due regard to its proper position and qualities; *'chaque objet est à sa place; chaque personnage est ce qu'il doit être'*. In order to achieve this in so small a compass the decor is reduced to what is indispensible: a tree will stand for a countryside, a gateway for a whole embattled town; two or three wavy lines will suffice for a river or even an ocean. Costume is always contemporary. Roman soldiers wear medieval armour and emperors the royal robes of France.

The fifteen windows of the clerestory are all authentic. The first light on the north side even retained its original leading until 1920. They offer some seven hundred square metres of coloured glass. Their survival is partly due to luck and partly to the fact that the Chapter had more respect for its heritage than was common in the eighteenth century. Attempts to have the windows replaced by clear glass were defeated and in 1771, after a freak hurricane had wrought havoc in the nave windows, the Chapter deputed two of its members, the Canons Jancourt and Frémont, to oversee a careful restoration of the glass.

The Abbé Bourassé, another authority on the subject, insists on the almost incredible state of preservation of these windows. 'They have survived six centuries,' (he was writing in 1849) 'braved the onslaught of twenty tempests, without the loss of a single medallion, a single group of figures. The archaeologian is certain of finding the original work. He has before his eyes the inspiration of the artist in its completeness without the slightest cloud to obscure his vision.' To stand at the entrance to the choir of Tours is to look straight back into the thirteenth century and to see both its architecture and its stained glass in their highest perfection.

By 1267 the choir and south transept were completed and the relics of St Maurice were translated to their new sanctuary. In 1320, when some sort of disaster occurred – probably that which necessitated the huge flying buttresses at the angles of the north transept – a Papal Bull referred to what we would call 'the Friends of Tours Cathedral' as 'la Confrérie de Monseigneur *Saint Gatien*'. St Gatien had been, according to tradition, the first Archbishop of Tours.

The change of patronage cannot have been lightly made. The Middle Ages took their hagiography with a seriousness which it would be difficult to recapture today. In his *Mirroir Historique*,

Vincent de Beauvais accords a few lines to the kings and emperors of the day before getting down to his real subject – the life histories of the saints and martyrs of the Church. The fall of the Roman Empire pales into insignificance before the Translation of the Relics of St Mexent; the Hermit St Die merits an ampler treatment than the Emperor Heraclius. The saint occupied a far more important place in the mind of the Middle Ages.

Probably named after a saint, the young man of the twelfth or thirteenth century, in choosing his profession, chose also his patron saint. If he were a stone dresser, he placed himself under the protection of St Thomas the Apostle; if he were a wool carder, under that of St Blaise; if he became a tanner, he was attached, by a somewhat macabre logic, to St Bartholomew, who was skinned alive. On the day appointed in the Calendar for his saint he enjoyed a holy day or holiday, probably attending Mass in the Cathedral and a dinner offered by his guild. The town in which he lived would have been under the patronage of another saint, and another day would be duly accorded to processions, mystery plays and general rejoicings.

The passing events of his life brought him temporarily under the auspices of another sacred name. Did he succumb to a fever? Ste Geneviève was invoked; was he bitten by a dog? St Hubert would protect him from rabies, but only if a metal key, blessed by the Saint, were heated red hot to affect a cauterisation. If he were a farmer, St Corneille would watch over his cattle, St Saturnin his sheep, St Antoine his pigs, and if necessary St Gall could be invoked to preserve his poultry. He would sow his barley on 23 April, the day of St Georges – which rhymes conveniently with *orge*; on 11 June he scythed his meadow for St Barnabé – which conveniently rhymes with *pré*. The saints, in fact, dictated the rhythm of his working year. There may well have been some heartburning over the change of patronage when the Cathédrale de St Maurice de Tours became the Cathédrale de St Gatien.

The subsequent history of Tours Cathedral is less distinguished. First the south transept was rebuilt and then the north, which in turn led to the reconstruction of the nave. Lastly the west front was carried up to its full height and finished with an appropriate flourish of Flamboyant decoration.

The south transept incorporates much of the twelfth-century work, one vestige of which may be seen on the east wall nearest the great pier of the crossing. It is a little colonnette, which shows the original proportions of the great arcade and triforium. Its capital is set obliquely to receive the transverse arch of the vaulting.

The north transept is an entirely new structure dating from about the year 1300. It is chiefly distinguished by its rose window, which shows a close similarity with the north rose of Notre-Dame. Exquisitely designed, it was badly built and had to receive extra support in the form of a stone mullion, which must be considered a blemish both from within and from without. At the same time the whole transept had to be shored up by two enormous flying buttresses which project obliquely from the corners.

The first two bays of the nave continue the architecture of the north transept. The rest of the nave was built in two stages: the great arcade, which follows closely the style of the first two bays, and the triforium and clerestory which clearly belong to the Flamboyant period. The silly little diamond-shaped panels above the apex of every arch in the great arcade were added in the eighteenth century, an age which saw fit to whitewash the whole Cathedral in an effort to 'correct the barbarism of the Gothic'.

The greatest success of the Flamboyant style at Tours is undoubtedly the west front. This campaign of construction may reflect the recovery of confidence occasioned by the career of Joan of Arc. Men usually show the extent of their confidence by the liberality of their contributions. Charles VII gave 2000 francs from the sale of wood in the Forêt de Chinon; Philippe de Koëtkis, who was Archbishop from 1427 to 1441, gave 400 *écus d'or*; the Chapter sold one of its forests; three Popes accorded indulgences to those who contributed to the fabric fund. Finally, one of the canons, Raoul Segaler, gave the princely sum of 1260 *écus d'or* 'for the library, the windows of the nave and the transept portals'.

According to one of the rare survivals of the building accounts, 1,328 livres represented the total annual expenditure on the Cathedral for the year 1466. Segaler, therefore, gave the price of three years' work.

The result was one of the triumphs of the French Flamboyant; a very fine and dignified achievement. The four great buttresses, which had constituted so conspicuous a feature of the west fronts in the earliest Gothic cathedrals, and which were so carefully disguised at Laon and Reims and Amiens, have now reappeared; but instead of standing out in the strong and simple lines of their forebears, which made no attempt to disguise their function, they are encased in a delicate and brittle screen of carving. But to appreciate this façade, the historical imagination must go behind the devastations of the Revolution. The tiers of empty niches, which alternate with the richly carved canopies above them, upset the balance of the composition. In the mind's eye, these niches must be peopled with the Saints and Martyrs of the Church who first inhabited them.

The construction of these towers continued into the sixteenth century. The cupola of the north tower was built in 1507 – well before the Renaissance fronts of Blois and Chambord, but already in Renaissance style. If the attribution made by Boissonot to Pierre de Valence is correct, the north cupola can be related to that earliest work of the French Renaissance, the Château de Gaillon. The completion of the cupola and the spiral staircase within it was marked by an inscription: 'In the year 1507 was made this noble and glorious edifice. This is the work of the Lord and it is marvellous in our sight.' Forty years later the south tower also was crowned with a cupola to match. The Cathedral may be regarded as having been finished.

At about the same time, the choir was enclosed by a magnificent screen of copper which was largely paid for by Archbishop Christophe de Brilhac. It was cast by *les fondeurs et canonniers du Roi* and set up in 1520. Unfortunately it fell victim to the outburst of Protestant iconoclasm following the Massacre of Vassy in March 1562. It was replaced a few years later by Simon de Maillé by another screen which, in turn, fell victim to the Revolution.

The Revolution, which did surprisingly little damage to the châteaux of the Loire, was all but fatal to the Cathedral of Tours. The statuary of the portals was smashed with painstaking thoroughness. In the choir they raised a 'mountain of earth' with an obelisk inscribed with the names of 'great men'. Never has such a miscellaneous short-list been compiled. The 'great men' were Marat, Socrates, Brutus, Cato, Jesus Christ, Rabelais and Voltaire! When the Cathedral was restored to its proper use, this earth was not removed, but spread over the floor of the choir and apse, raising the level by some thirty-two centimetres – enough to alter appreciably the original proportions.

This, however, must be set against the survival of the building itself in the face of the determination of the Prefect, Pommereul, to have it totally demolished. Failing in this egalitarian endeavour, he succeeded in depriving posterity of the magnificent basilica of St Martin de Tours.

The destruction of St Martin brought to the Cathedral its most important piece of monumental sculpture – the tomb of the two little sons of Charles VIII and Anne de Bretagne: Charles Orlando – 'young and hopeful Prince', who died at Amboise aged three years and three months, and his brother Charles who died at Le Plessis-lès-Tours having lived for only twenty-five days. They are both represented, however, as being almost the same age and large enough to wear the royal robes of a Dauphin of France.

There is a charming description of this monument in the account by Elizabeth Strutt of her six weeks on the Loire in 1833. 'I could not leave the Cathedral,' she wrote, 'without remarking the tomb of the two sons of Charles 8th and Anne of Britanny. The royal infants, lying tranquilly side by side, reminded me of Chauntrey's beautiful monument at Litchfield, of two children clasped in each other's arms; the first piece of sculpture that ever made me feel all that the breathing marble is capable of inspiring, under the chisel of a master hand. Angels kneel around the regal babes, and stories of Holy Truth and Classic Fable enrich every part of the monument; but it is the associations of innocence and peace with the tender ages of those to whom it was raised, and of sympathy for the grief which the royal parents were destined to feel, in common with the meanest of their subjects under similar bereavement, that gives the real interest to this famed production of the brothers Le Juste, who were natives of Tours.'

Neither the Abbé Boissonot nor Francis Salet accept this tradition which attributes the tomb to the brothers Le .Juste. Boissonot ascribes the whole ensemble to Michel Colombe, while Salet attributes the figures to Guillaume Regault, a pupil of Colombe's, and the lower carvings of the catafalque to Jerome Fiesole.

Elizabeth Strutt makes no comment on the architecture of the Cathedral, but she leaves us her impressions on the Archbishop. 'On Sunday I went to the Cathedral, and it being the feast of Pentecost, I had the pleasure of seeing the Archbishop officiate. I had previously heard that he was a most excellent character and bore his unexpected honours with a meekness which was the best evidence of their being well bestowed . . . His countenance was strikingly benevolent, at the same time dignified and humble; it seemed as if it expressed at once his Office and himself.' Such was the saintly Bishop Myriel in Victor Hugo's *Les Misérables*. If bishops of the Catholic Church had more often conformed to this standard of humility, the Church might have suffered less at the hands of Reformers and Revolutionaries.

CHAPTER FIFTEEN

Beauvais

It is not easy in these days, when the word 'bishop' conveys at worst an overworked ecclesiastical executive and at best a Reverend Father in God to a very small proportion of the population, to conceive of the importance of the bishop in medieval society. Often related to the King and always in close association with the royal Court, these were men of enormous wealth and corresponding power.

The Bishop of Beauvais was not just the spiritual leader of his diocese. He took his place at the apex of the feudal system as comte de Beauvais and vidame de Gerberoy – today acclaimed as the most beautiful village in the north of France, but then a *place forte* of some significance. The Bishop was thus the supreme civil authority with full powers of *'haute et basse justice'* and the right to mint his own money.

More surprisingly, the Bishop was often a man of war. The resounding victory of Bouvines in 1214 was largely due to the order of battle drawn up by the Bishop of Senlis and to the intrepid charge of Philippe de Dreux, Bishop of Beauvais, who clubbed the Earl of Salisbury off his horse.

François de Lasteyrie, in his *Histoire de la peinture sur verre*, described the figure of a Bishop of Beauvais – who, as one of the Twelve Peers of France, held the mantle of the King at the Coronation – dressed in cope and mitre as a bishop, beneath which he was 'armed at all pieces' as a count.

It took a man of this calibre to tackle the enormous task of raising a Gothic cathedral. It was fortunate that in 1225, when a disastrous fire had destroyed the newly-repaired Cathedral Church of Beauvais, the bishopric was in the hands of a man of action, Milon de Nanteuil. Appointed in 1217, he departed immediately on the fifth Crusade and was taken prisoner at Damietta. While awaiting his ransom, he distinguished himself by the conversion and baptism of some of his guards. Louis VIII died in his arms and it was he who crowned his young son, the future Saint Louis, with whom he was associated in the founding of the Abbaye de Royaumont.

Milon de Nanteuil addressed himself to the task of rebuilding his Cathedral with vigour and with vision. He engaged at once to give a tenth of his own revenue towards the fabric fund and persuaded not only the Dean and Chapter but also all the beneficed clergy in his diocese to do the same over a period of ten years. Any vacant living was held in suspension for one year so that its income could be diverted to this pious cause.

The Cathedral which he proposed to build was to outstrip all that had gone before. It was based on the design of Amiens, with some apparent borrowings from Bourges. The immense scaffolding of its flying buttresses, *'si délicats,'* claimed Godefroy Hermant, *'qu'on les voit souvent plier sous l'agitation des grands vents'*, was destined to uphold a quadripartite vault 157 feet above the floor. It was the highest ever built. In 1284 a portion of these vaults collapsed.

The technical reasons for this collapse have been exhaustively discussed by Stephen Murray. The point of weakness was the angle between the choir and the south transept.

The medieval builder had discovered that a vertical support could transfer some of its thrust obliquely if the stones were built out like a series of steps. This is known as a *porte-à-faux*. It is obviously a device which needs to be treated with extreme caution: if the overhang is too great, the stability of the building is undermined. As the result of the use of this system at Beauvais the intermediary piers of the flying buttresses were not directly above the columns in the side aisles which support them.

We may infer something of what were considered at the time to have been the weaknesses of the original building by the reinforcements which the architect of the reconstruction has provided.

First and most obviously it can be seen that he has inserted intermediary columns into the great arcade, dividing each of its arches into two. This largely destroyed the most original feature of the first architect's design which was concerned with the relation of the choir aisles to the choir. As at Bourges, the internal façade of the aisle is complete with three storeys – arcade, triforium and clerestory. When there were only three bays to the choir, the broad apertures of the great arcade opened up the perspective to the aisles which reflected in little the façades of the choir itself.

The insertion of intermediary columns, dividing each bay into two, largely obscured this. It also created an alternance of *pile forte – pile faible*, a disposition which almost dictates the use of sexpartite vaulting which looks archaic in a mid thirteenth-century building.

Whether these reinforcements were necessary or not is open to learned speculation. It was clearly thought to be necessary at the time, or the architect of the restoration would hardly have upset the noble *ordonnance* of the original choir. But in one obvious detail the

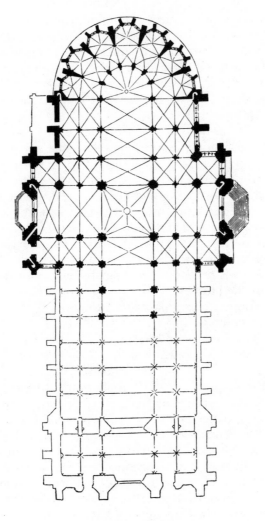

Ground Plan of Beauvais

anxiety of the builders about the *porte-à-faux* can be detected. On the south face of the choir, where it forms an angle with the transept, the ground floor window has been partially filled in. The outline of its containing arch is still apparent, but the new window is placed well to the right of the aperture so that the new masonry on the left can give more solid support to the buttress pier above. The slender colonnettes which mark the uprights of the new window carry the 'signature' of the new architect in the moulding of the base, which takes the form of two clearly defined rings a few inches apart.

The buttresses which had to be rebuilt can also be detected by a difference of style. They are the two piers in this corner, one projecting east from the transept and the other projecting south from the choir. The original buttresses are decorated with a blind arcading upheld by slender shafts which are just free-standing. The architect of the rebuilding has abandoned this system and decorated the surfaces of his piers with simple recessed panels.

An attentive scrutiny of this same angle between the choir and transept reveals another interesting fact. The new buttress which projects east from the transept is decorated on its south side with a tall fluting which bears no relation to the rest of the building. If we now enter the Cathedral by the south door, it will be seen that the first pier of the great arcade on the right is of the same massive dimensions as those which uphold the crossing. The same is true of the last pier on the right of the north door. This can only mean that these two piers were intended to carry a far greater weight than the more slender ones next to them. The obvious conclusion is that the architect intended to build two towers to north and south of the last bay of the choir. Towers flanking the transepts were planned for Chartres, Laon and Reims.

This theory is confirmed by a text in the Departmental Archives which has been carefully studied by Stephen Murray. It is headed *'Mémoire de ce qui reste à parfaire de l'église St Pierre de Beauvais'*. It is in a seventeenth-century hand which must represent a copy of a much older document, for the dimensions which it quotes can only refer to the choir and apse before any transepts were built, in other words to the time of the reconstruction following the collapse of the vaults.

It outlines a scheme for building two towers with tremendous buttresses to the west and for forming a western *portail* between them. The project must be regarded as an expedient for finishing off the choir without nave or transepts. It would have looked most peculiar.

If these towers, which are specified as containing belfries, were to have had the tall louvred openings customary in towers of the period, the fluting on the exterior buttress would become explicable as being the side of one of these openings. No doubt Martin Chambiges, when he undertook the building of the transepts, decided to dispense with these towers and incorporated the masonry already erected into his buttress pier.

But it must not be forgotten that the history of Beauvais Cathedral is not wholly concerned with collapse and rebuilding. It was an important centre of liturgy and worship, which often took the form of sacred drama.

The liturgies were written with an exquisite calligraphy, brilliantly illuminated and beautifully bound, so that the text itself

Beauvais: Section of Choir and Aisles

became a work of art. Such was the Missal of Roger de Champagne, of early eleventh-century date, which was bound between two boards of gilded copper. Breviaries, often of a similar standard of workmanship, were frequently mentioned in bequests to the Cathedral, that of Jean d'Auchy specifying that it was to be attached by a chain to his former stall.

Above all, Beauvais was celebrated for its music. Bornet, in his study of *Les enfants de choeur de la Cathédrale de Beauvais*, tells how Anne de Bretagne, Queen to Charles VIII and Louis XII, asked for a singing boy from here for the Chapel Royal in 1508. She was sent one called Janet, and two of the Canons were detailed to accompany him

199

to Blois. The poor boy was miserable and ran away in the following year.

There is an impressive epitaph to one of the musicians of Beauvais, Nicole des Celliers de Hesdin, who died in 1538. 'Atropos – alas the too cruel enemy of the sonorous Muse – if you think you have taken away the life of Hesdin, you deceive yourself. Hesdin, whose genius gave birth to so many melodies, lives and sings in a thousand voices. He lives on in the lives of his pupils whom he has begotten by his instruction in the art. His name, passed from mouth to mouth, will resound to all eternity.' Atropos was the third of the *Parcae* or Fates who cut with her scissors the thread of human life.

For the dramatisation of the liturgies, imaginative use was made of the almost celestial height of the Cathedral. At Matins on Christmas Day the clergy enacted the Adoration of the Shepherds. At the moment when the Heavens opened and the angelic chorus was heard, the high arches suddenly resounded to the joyous chant of Gloria in Excelsis. The choirboys – *septem pueri stantes in alto loco dicanti* – had been positioned aloft in the triforium.

At the Epiphany, a star, moved by some ingenious mechanism, was propelled eastwards beneath the vaults, guiding the Three Wise Men into the santuary. At Pentecost, during the singing of Veni Creator at Tierce, bits of flaming tow and fire-coloured wafers were showered from containers a hundred and fifty-seven feet above the heads of the congregation.

Most of the historic scenes of the Gospel story were presented in drama. At Easter three choirboys, dressed as the three Marys, mimed the discovery of the empty tomb and, turning to the assembled worshippers, proclaimed the Resurrection. On easter Monday it was the Supper at Emmaus which provided the theme, with the scene of Doubting Thomas to follow. The music, set to plainsong, has survived and is published by Gustave Desjardins.

As the Middle Ages drew to their close, the taste for these liturgical dramatisations declined. In 1481 the clergy were forbidden to carry their shepherds' crooks in the scene of the Adoration – possibly because they were thought to infringe thereby the prerogative of the episcopate. In 1529 the *Fête des Fous* was abolished *'propter ridiculosas insolentias quae fieri solent'* – 'on account of the ridiculous and unseemly things that are wont to be done'.

The fifteenth century had not been a propitious time for building. The country round Beauvais had been overrun during the Hundred Years War and the sentence was added to the Litany: *'A crudelitate Anglorum libera nos Domine'* – 'From the cruelty of the English, good Lord deliver us'. But towards the end of the century peace and prosperity returned and it was possible to contemplate the addition of a crossing and two transepts to Beauvais Cathedral. We learn of the decision from two pages of accounts which have survived because they were used in the binding of a book. On 19 August 1947, under the episcopate of Villiers de l'Isle Adam, *'bon ménager et grand bâtisseur'*,* it was decided to proceed with 'the construction of a new transept as a precaution against the ruin of the choir, which is in danger, because there is neither transept nor nave to support and sustain it.'

On 21 September 1499, soundings were made for the foundations. For twenty-three days they continued to dig and to pump water. The foundations were thirty-two feet deep and rested on firm ground. Martin Chambiges was summoned from Paris, where he was directing the building of the Pont Neuf, to design the new transepts and, on 21 May 1500, the foundation stone was laid in the course of a Mass celebrated by Villiers de l'Isle Adam, dressed in a white cope and mitre.

Under the supervision of Jean Vast – a local master mason from the village of Marrisel, near Beauvais – the masons, plumbers, carpenters and glaziers set up their lodges in the Place St Pierre, towards the Bishop's Palace, and a forge was installed for the ironsmiths. Under the cover of their 'lodges' the workmen could continue without interruption in adverse weather conditions.

The building operations went on for nearly half a century. In 1532 Martin Chambiges died, the Chapter entrusted the continuation of the work to his son Pierre and the original design was respected.

Work began on the north front, where the presence of ermines, daisies, capital F's and salamanders bear witness to the donations from Anne de Bretagne, Marguerite d'Angoulême and François I. On 28 October 1548, the completion of the south front was marked by the setting up of the statue of St Peter over the gable – and the Chapter voted one *écu d'or* for a *vin d'honneur* for the workmen.

To pay for this vast enterprise, the Bishop agreed to contribute 800 livres annually from his own resources. The Chapter offered the same sum and undertook to raise more. To this end Pope Leo X issued an indulgence to be published by the Cardinal de Châtillon, who became Bishop of Beauvais in 1535. It was posted on the door of every church in the diocese.

'Our Holy Father the Pope,' ran the text, 'duly informed of the sumptuous, tall and magnificent building of the choir of the Cathedral Church of Beauvais . . . and that the choir is without crossing or nave, by means of which it is in total ruin and tottering to its fall . . . and that the rebuilding, perfection and upkeep of the same

---

* 'a good manager and a great builder'.

cannot well be accomplished without the liberalities of all good people, our said Holy Father, moved by charity and devotion, has opened the incomparable treasure of the said Church militant . . . and has given the great pardons, mercies and indulgences of plenary remission which follow.' Confession had to be made on specified days before each of seven altars listed and an offering made to the fabric fund. Those who had sworn to make a pilgrimage to Jerusalem or Compostella could commute this for a donation. Permission to eat butter in Lent could also be purchased.

The offer of indulgences was only partly successful and appeal had to be made to the liberality of the King. The disaster of Pavia and the consequent imprisonment of François I at Madrid brought these subsidies to an end. The Chapter of Beauvais, possibly with an eye to future financial support, contributed handsomely towards the King's ransom, selling a silver cross and crown, two chalices and two golden bowls. It proved a wise investment. On his return to his Kingdom, François I duly renewed his subscription to Beauvais, giving a grant on the sale of salt. The beautiful transepts of Martin Chambiges were completed in every detail. These tall façades, with their stone facets almost obscured by the brittle encrustations of their finely chiselled ornament and their niches filled, according to Hermant, with '*une infinité de belles figures*', formed a worthy appendage to the thirteenth-century choir – a triumph of the late Flamboyant Gothic.

The huge windows offered the greatest possible opportunity to the glaziers, and at exactly the right time, for during the early sixteenth century Beauvais became the centre of a flourishing school of stained glasswork associated with the names of Engrand and Nicholas le Prince. According to Le Vieil, the eighteenth-century historian of stained glass, Nicholas le Prince – '*qui ne voulait donner que du parfait*' – sent his designs to the greatest painters of Italy and Germany for them to correct and improve, with the result that his compositions and colours were held to be '*de la dernière perfection*'. Cardinal de Janson, Bishop of Beauvais, 'never failed to conduct foreigners of distinction to St Etienne and to the other churches decorated by these beautiful windows.'

The south rose is the work of Nicholas le Prince and offers an iconography almost as complex as its own design. In the centre is God the Father, the typical Renaissance figure of an old man with a white beard. Around him, the inner six petals depict the six stages of Creation. The outer petals form a sort of Wheel of Fortune, showing on the right hand side the Fall of Man, starting with Adam and ending with the Tower of Babel, which signifies the inability of Man to reach God by his own unaided efforts. The left hand side, starting at the bottom, begins to reverse the process. The faith of Abraham strikes a new note of hope which mounts in a steady crescendo to the gift of the Manna in the Wilderness. The two topmost petals portray the Celestial Paradise, first lost and now regained.

The transepts, with their new glass, were a very glorious addition to the Cathedral, but there was still something unfulfilled in the spirit of the Church authorities – some *folie de grandeur* which was not satisfied with the creation and possession of the loftiest vault in Christendom. They wanted something even more spectacular.

On 21 March 1546, the momentous decision was made. The new transepts were to be crowned with a spire, and such a spire as the world had never seen. It was to be the tallest building in Europe. Competitive designs were invited from the masons and the carpenters, who each felt that such a construction was their own professional prerogative. It may be significant that the carpenter François Maréchal enjoyed the glorious title of *Archicharpentier*. In the end a compromise was reached; it was decided to build a lantern of stone surmounted by a steeple of wood, which was to be encased in lead.

On 6 April, masons were invited from the church of St Etienne de Beauvais to inspect the pillars of the crossing in order to establish that they were capable of sustaining this additional weight. Their report was favourable. Not content, the Chapter demanded further assurances; no one, apparently, warned them at this stage that, without the support of a nave, the westward pillars of the crossing were in perilous need of abutment. A year later all hesitations were laid to rest and in March 1557, two of the Canons went to St Leu d'Esserent, where the finest stone in France was quarried, to place their order.

It was not until 1563 that the spire began to rise above the already vertiginous height of the roof ridge. On 18 November 1566, the accounts record the payment of a *vin d'honneur* which always marked the completion of any particular feature. Two *écus d'or* were paid *'pour vin du charpentier Daily qui a confectionné la carcasse de la Pyramide'*. The *pyramide* meant the topmost section of the spire; it in no way resembled the mausoleums of the Kings of Egypt.

Later in the same month the ironsmith, Nicolas de Louvencourt, received fifty-five livres for the making and positioning of the cross which surmounted the spire. The wooden 'pyramid' was now clothed with lead, which was purchased at Rouen, and in June 1567, the glaziers were inserting their windows into the lantern. It is reasonable to suppose that by the end of that summer the *'nouvel oeuvre'* – as it is always called in the accounts – was finished in all its details.

It was the tallest building of its time. Denis Simon claimed that on a clear day one could distinguish the houses of Paris, a distance of nearly fifty miles, from the topmost windows of the spire at Beauvais. It rose 252 feet above roof level, making a total height of 461 feet from the ground.

It began as a square tower with a large window in each face and a slender pinnacle at each corner. Upon this was raised an octagonal stone lantern, almost entirely glazed and supported by a ring of free-standing buttress columns which helped to modify the transition from the square to the pyramid and from the larger to the smaller structure. This octagon was continued upward with the progressive diminutions of an extended telescope, culminating in the delicately tapered steeple so inaptly described in the accounts as the *pyramide*.

From inside, these progressive diminutions offered a kaleidoscopic perspective of stained glass, tapering towards its vanishing point, where the eye could just make out the painted and gilded vault ribs of the topmost steeple. On solemn feast days a lamp was hoisted into this cage of coloured glass so that it really became a lantern and was visible a great way off.

In spite of the previous soundings and precautions, the new spire began almost immediately to cause anxiety. In January 1571, the iron cross had to be removed from the top. Two of the King's masons, Gilles de Harlay and Nicolas Tiersault, came to inspect the four pillars of the crossing. All four were showing signs of movement; the two piers to the west, *'tirant au vide'*, had moved, one six and the other eleven inches.

The masons made a report urgently stressing the need for abutment from a nave, but suggesting temporary measures for immediate action. Nothing was done. On 17 April 1573, the Chapter was still 'taking advice'. It was too late. On 28 April, bits of stone began to fall from the vaulting and the tower above – *'un avis que Dieu donna par sa providence,'* wrote Godefroy Hermant, *'de se précautionner contre le péril dont on était menacé'.* *

30 April was Ascension Day and at seven in the morning 'the whole town of Beauvais, the clergy and all the Catholic people, were assembled most religiously in the Cathedral.' In the chapel of the Blessed Sacrament one priest, Simon Hotte, and his server, André Martine, were saying Mass. The procession of the relics was already passing out through the south doors and down the steps into the town when one of the masons, who had been sent to inspect the tower, gave a cry of alarm. The cracks were moving.

---

* 'an intimation which God in his providence gave that they should take precautions against the peril by which they were threatened.'

Suddenly the pillars on the side of the Episcopal Palace gave; the pillar on the right of the choir started to lean; all the weight was thrown upon the fourth pillar. It yielded in its turn. The spire, the bell tower with all its bells, the three tiers of the lantern and their vaults crashed towards the left, bringing down one of the piers of the choir and another pillar near the great clock, smashing the windows, the choir screen and the stalls. A 'torrent of stones' avalanched into the chapel of the Blessed Sacrament.

The collapse of a tall spire is attended by certain unexpected manifestations. The sudden compression of the air within the Cathedral was first experienced as a rushing mighty wind, *'un vent si impétueux qu'il en ferma les portes'.** The south doors slammed shut, pushing the bearers of the Reliquary of St Just out on to the *parvis*. If the catastrophe had occurred a moment or two earlier it would have killed thousands. As it was, even Simon Hotte escaped with only a broken arm. He received a pension of five livres tournois by way of compensation.

Louvet, who wrote within living memory of the disaster, records that the fall of 'this great mountain of stone' made so great a noise *'qu'elle faisait trembler la ville'*; the Cathedral itself disappeared in a cloud of dust that rose into the sky and hung like a pall over the stricken city. The inhabitants of Beauvais were so afflicted at the loss of their church that they could not control their grief – *'chacun avaient les larmes à l'oeil'*.

An immediate survey of the damage resulted in an estimate of 47,000 livres. It was beyond the resources of the diocese and in any case the disaster coincided with a scarcity of corn so severe that 'they were obliged to hold extraordinary meetings in the Bishop's Palace to discuss the means of providing for the poor'.

But still the jagged pinnacles of masonry remained, hovering dangerously over the site. No one dared to attempt their removal. Then in August the Chapter had the idea of offering the job to a criminal who was condemned to be hanged. He accepted. No sooner had he put his foot on the threatened masonry than it collapsed. A rope was hanging from the beams of the roof; he jumped for it, caught it and descended alive. As Godefroy Hermant wrote: *'la corde qui devait être le supplice de ce misérable, fut son salut'*.

The transepts, of course, had to be repaired, but the builders were by now totally discouraged. On 20 October 1574, it was decided to replace the great spire with a simple wooden belfry *'fort petit'*.

In 1604 a last effort was made to equip Beauvais with a nave and one bay was carried up, ready for vaulting. The vault became unsafe

---

* 'a wind so violent as to close the doors.'

and had to be taken down again. Perhaps it was too late; the techniques of the medieval builder were beginning to be a forgotten art. Two years later the last of Jean de Vast's masons, Martin Candelot, was laid to rest.

In 1630 Louvet wrote the epitaph of the history of Beauvais; 'The work when it was begun was the subject of astonishment for those who heard tell of it and even more to those who saw it; it was also the subject of despair to those who were never able to finish and to bring it to completion'.

They did themselves an injustice. The original apse remains intact – the tallest and one of the loveliest hemicycles ever built. The choir, despite the somewhat makeshift appearance conferred by the insertion of intermediary piers, is still a noble piece of architecture to which the beautiful transepts of Martin Chambiges form a worthy appendage. Even in its uncompleted state, St Pierre de Beauvais bears impressive witness to the utmost limits ever reached by the soaring ambitions of the Cathedrals' Crusade.

CHAPTER SIXTEEN

Goths and Vandals

Although Louvet, who wrote his *Histoire de la ville et cité de Beauvais* in 1613, seems to have appreciated the beauties of the Gothic cathedral his comments on the surviving portion of the older building, usually known as the *basse oeuvre*, reveal a surprising ignorance. He believed it to have been a 'pagan temple' and asserted that among the decorations of the west front were 'several idols whom the pagans worshipped'. The *basse oeuvre* is, in fact, a piece of tenth-century Christian architecture. This sort of ignorance was the first symptom of a movement of taste which led to an active contempt for medieval architecture which earned it the name 'Gothic' and was to do untold damage to the great achievements of the Cathedrals' Crusade. But those who most loudly stigmatised medieval architecture as 'Gothic' must themselves be charged with the more serious accusation of being Vandals.

One can distinguish three major forms of anti-Gothic vandalism: the iconoclasm of the Huguenots, the promotion of eighteenth-century 'good taste' and the destructions of the Revolution. To these must be added a fourth which was not intentionally anti-Gothic: the work of the restoring architect. As Prosper Mérimée wrote to Arcisse Caumont in 1834: *'les réparateurs sont peut-être aussi dangéreux que les destructeurs'*.

The Huguenot movement, starting as a well-earned protest against the abuses of Rome and the corruption of the clergy, became a quasi-political cause inflamed with Calvinistic self-righteousness. As with so many revolutions, it was the story of the Sorcerer's Apprentice: it is easier to unleash the powers of the Elements than to control them. The leaders of the Reformation were for the most part men of learning and the moderation which goes with learning. They may have inveighed against idolatry and therefore against idols. But the hordes of undisciplined and often unpaid 'soldiers' – more frequently enrolled in support of the political ambitions of the party leaders – went far beyond the intentions of the Reformers.

The attacks of the Huguenots which did the greatest damage to the cathedrals were mostly concentrated in the year 1562 and were reprisals for the massacre of Vassy. They usually only reached the more accessible and vulnerable members of a church – the ground floor windows and the projecting parts of statues. Only at Orléans did they do enough damage to cause the destruction of a Cathedral. The piers of the crossing were mined and the central tower brought crashing into the nave, after which the rest of the Cathedral was set on fire. When the Catholics regained possession they found nothing but *'des hautes montagnes de ruines'*.

The vandalism of the Huguenots was a direct expression of their hostility to the Catholic Church; some of the details have already been given in the foregoing chapters. The threat posed by the change of aesthetic outlook started by the Renaissance was of a new and more insidious nature.

In the sixteenth century the first attempts at Italianisation did not in any immediate way oust the Gothic. In many churches the Renaissance merely succeeded the Flamboyant as the Flamboyant had succeeded the Geometric. A church such as that of St Jacques-le-Majeur at Houdan, to the north-west of the Forêt de Rambouillet, still shows the medieval conception of a religious edifice, but the choir is executed in a classical idiom. In place of the clustered colonnettes and the floral fantasies of their capitals are now substituted columns in the Ionic order – but they support a medieval vault. The buttresses round the east end have also been translated into Renaissance terms – but the structural system remains true to the medieval formula. The builders of the Ile de France, in fact, showed remarkable skill in adapting the new style to the old method and in harmonising later additions to the earlier fabrics. For about a century Gothic and Renaissance enjoyed a peaceful coexistence.

The term 'Gothic' seems to have been first used by Lorenzo Valla in the middle of the fifteenth century, where he uses it to distinguish the uncial lettering of the medieval calligraphy from 'sweet Roman hand'. It is in this sense that Rabelais first introduced the word to France, but he extended its meaning by applying it to the Middle Ages in general. *'Le temps était encore ténébreux,'* says Gargantua to Pantagruel; *'et sentait la calamité des Goths'*.* In due course the word Gothic came to mean anything in bad taste.

In England, John Evelyn was one of the first to apply the term 'Gothic' to architecture, and always it is a term of abuse: 'a fantastical and licentious manner of building' – 'heavy, dark, melancholy, monkish piles' – 'slender and misquine pillars, or rather bundles of staves, and other incongruous props, to support incumbent weights and ponderous arched roofs without entablature' – 'other cut-work and crinkle-crankle'. It is often difficult to

* 'The times were still dark and savoured of the disaster of the Goths.'

know which phase of the Gothic was the least acceptable, but Evelyn is here being fairly comprehensive. His 'melancholy, monkish piles' suggest the Romanesque; his 'bundles of staves' the clustered columns of the High Gothic and his 'cut-work and crinkle-crankle' the delicate filigree of the Flamboyant style.

It was this latter which incurred the greatest contempt of the French critics. Fénelon, in his *Télémaque*, exclaims: '*On croit que tout va tomber . . . la pierre semble découpée comme du carton. Tout est à jour, tout est en l'air.*'* He never stopped to enquire whether such might not have been the deliberate and legitimate intention of the architects; the buildings failed by eighteenth-century standards, so they failed. Fénelon did, however, make certain distinctions. In his *Discours de Réception à l'Académie Française* he observed: '*Les ouvrages les plus hardis et les plus façonnés du Gothique ne sont pas les meilleurs*'.†

Other writers were more extreme in their opinion. Molière, writing in praise of the dome at Val-de-Grâce, contrasts its antique elegance with '*ces monstres odieux des siècles ignorants*'. La Bruyère boasts: 'We have entirely abandoned the Gothic order which was introduced by barbarians for palaces and temples; we have recalled the Doric, the Ionic and the Corinthian'. Boileau, in his *Art Poétique*, exults in the victory, Knowledge had triumphed over ignorance:

> *On chasse ces docteurs prêchant sans mission*
> *Et on voit renaître Hector, Andromaque et Ilion.*‡

The substitution is significant. After centuries of persecution and wars of religion, there were many who thought that a clear sky would look more like Heaven. The clouds of controversy were best dispersed by concentrating the attention upon more worldly objectives. Alexander Pope voiced this reaction in his famous lines:

> Know then thyself; presume not God to scan;
> The proper study of Mankind is Man.

The architecture of humanism naturally moved in the same direction. The style is contrasted with the Gothic by François Cali. 'It is subtle but prudent. The Cathedral is madly imprudent for those who do not know and do not want to know the reason of their imprudence: a confidence in the unity, in the goodness of Creation which comes with faith.'

---

* 'One feels that everything is going to fall down . . . the stone seems to be cut out like cardboard, everything is fretwork, everything is in confusion.'
† 'The works of Gothic Architecture which are the most daring and the most elaborate are not the best.'
‡ 'We dismiss these Doctors, speaking without authority, and we witness the revival of Hector, Andromache and Ilion.'

The confidence of the eighteenth century was in its own good taste. It was not a wholly arrogant assertion, for what was their taste but that of the Augustan age of Rome? And whence had Rome derived her inspiration but from the Greece of Plato and Praxiteles? But what these pious Palladians seemed to be totally unaware of was that Plato had also inspired the aesthetic theory of the so-called Gothic architects. When, in 1535, Francesco Giorgi drew up his memorandum for the church of St Francesco della Vigna, he wrote: 'This mysterious harmony is such that when Plato in the Timaeus wished to describe the wonderful consonancy of the parts and fabric of the world, he took this as the first foundation of his description, multiplying as far as necessary these same proportions . . . until he had included the whole world and each of its members and parts', he talks as if this were a new discovery. Rudolf Wittkower in his *Architectural Principles in the Age of Humanism* seems to be unaware of the theories of the Platonists of Chartres. The attitude of the seventeenth and eighteenth centuries to Gothic architecture is characterised by their total ignorance of it.

At its worst, the Age of Enlightenment was so sophisticated as to eschew Nature. Thomas Burnett, in his *Sacred Theory of the Earth*, had some hard things to say. It offered to his fastidious eyes 'the image or picture of a great Ruine, and has the true aspect of a world lying in its rubbish'. To save himself from the blasphemy of accusing his Maker of lack of taste, he attributes the degeneracy of Nature to the fatal impact of fallen Man, for whose sins Creation itself was subjected to Vanity. As a result it had become 'a broken and confused heap of bodies, placed in no order to one another, nor with any correspondency of parts'. If only Vanbrugh could have designed the mountains and London and Wise laid out the coastline! 'If the sea had been drawn round the earth in regular figures and borders, it might have been a great Beauty to our globe and we would reasonably have concluded it to have been a work of the first Creation.'

Like so many theorists, Burnett was not really true to his own principles, for elsewhere he wrote; 'There is nothing that I look upon with more pleasure than the wide sea and the Mountains of the earth. There is something august and stately in the Air of these things that inspires my mind with great thoughts and passions; we do naturally upon these occasions think of God'. Very much the same could be said of the great buildings of the Cathedrals' Crusade.

The contempt of the eighteenth century was not total. The *Dictionnaire Critique de la Langue Française* of 1787 gives under 'Gothic' – '*Ce mot se dit par mépris de tout ce qui est hors de mode*'. In particular it was used of medieval architecture, '*qui est le plus éloigné des proportions antiques, sans corrections de profil, ni de bon goût dans ses ornements* *chimériques'.** But the great architectural scholar and critic Blondel admitted that Gothic architecture, if 'corrected of its errors', was a style 'suitable for the decoration of our temples'.

It was to be corrected of its errors, however, in the most deplorable fashion, and, as the result of this doctrine, the great cathedrals and wealthier churches were now exposed to a new and deadly menace christened by Louis Réau *'le vandalisme embellisseur des Chanoines'.†* The campaign which was mounted during the eighteenth century to put these noble buildings *'au goût du jour'* was on a scale comparable only with that of the Cathedrals' Crusade itself.

One does not easily think of the eighteenth century as an age of prudery, but one of the first attacks made on the Cathedral of Amiens was the breaking of the figures of Adam and Eve which were revealed when the untidy 'lodges', which had always cluttered the foot of the Cathedral, were finally removed. They were broken because their nudity was found offensive. Louis Réau has listed other examples of this *'vandalisme pudibond'.‡*

This was not, however, the main battle field, or anywhere near it. If the seventeenth century witnessed the most uncompromising attacks upon the barbarisms of the Gothic style, these were for the most part confined to the remarks of critics and seldom translated into acts of demolition or disfigurement. The eighteenth century, more mild in its condemnation, was far more active in the removal of what it found offensive in medieval taste. It was those who came nearest to appreciating the Gothic who were the most ready to lay their hands upon the fabric.

Perhaps the most perceptive tribute to the architecture of the Middle Ages comes from the Abbé Laugier, who wrote his *Observations sur l'Architecture* in 1765. He found in the Gothic apse *'une distribution charmante, où l'oeil plonge délicieusement à travers plusieurs files de colonnes dans des chapelles en enfoncement'*. In the complexity of the perspectives he enjoyed *'un mélange, un mouvement, un tumulte de percées et de massifs, qui jouent, qui contrastent, et dont l'effet entier est ravissant'.§*

That reads well; but he goes on to say that all obstructions must be cleared out of the way so that this beauty may be enjoyed. The piers must be rounded into pillars and if necessary fluted or encased in

* 'This word is used contemptuously of anything that is out of fashion . . . which is the furthest removed from antique proportions, without correctness of profiles nor any good taste in its chimerical ornament.'
† 'the vandalism of "improvement" by the Canons'.
‡ 'the vandalism of prudery'.
§ 'a charming arrangement where the eye penetrates with delight through several rows of columns into recessed chapels . . . a mixture, a movement, a tumult of vistas and of masses, an interplay and a contrast of which the total effect is fascinating.'

211

marble; the capitals must be made *'plus correctes'* and the mouldings –
dismissed as *'barbares'* – must give way to new ones *'d'un bon choix'*.

It is exactly what the Canons did to the choir at Chartres. The
pillars, which have lost their capitals, have been rounded off and
marbled; the inside of the arches refaced and decoated with a series of
coffers and a suggestion of the Corinthian introduced in the half
capitals. It is simply deplorable – neither one thing nor the other. To
this the sculptor Bridan added the *gloire* behind the high altar and the
bas-reliefs behind the choir stalls. Emile Mâle has had the last word;
*'Quel abîme entre cette Vierge triomphante, dont la virtuosité enchanta les
chanoines, et la Vierge du portail septentrional qui s'incline si modestement
devant son Fils!'* *

A great deal of the clutter of Catholic devotion was removed *'pour
dégager les lignes'*. Again, there was often a real measure of appreciation behind this principle. The Sieur Nomis wrote in 1714 of Amiens:
'That which in my opinion diminishes considerably the beauty
of the nave is the prodigious quantity of pictures which they call
"voeux" which are attached to it. The Cathedral Church of Chartres
used to be the same. One used to see altars against all the pillars of
the nave. Since these altars have been demolished, the nave has
become very much more beautiful.'

It is possible to agree with all these sentiments, but behind this
apparent appreciation of the broad outlines of Gothic architecture
there was a real failure to recognise its unity. Laugier gives us the
recipe for the transformation of a Cathedral. 'Eliminate first of all
every obstacle that offends the eye. Destroy all the false ornaments
which block the vista . . . Let the choir be separated from the nave by
only an iron grille.'

The *jubé* or choir screen was the expression of an attitude to clergy
and laity which was by this time obsolete; it had effectively excluded
the laity from the place of worship. In 1791 the congregation of
Coutances petitioned for the removal of their *jubé* that it might *'laissez
libre la vue du prêtre qui prie pour lui'*.† This exclusion can hardly be
justified, but its architectural expression was often the finest
sculptural ensemble in the church. With the exception of Albi, all the
great cathedrals of France lost their *jubés*. In April 1763, the Canons
of Chartres, acting on the advice of their architect, Victor Louis,
agreed *'à l'utilité et à la nécessité d'une démolition'*. A letter from their
Bishop, dated, needless to say, from Versailles, conveyed to them his

---

* 'How great an abyss there is between this triumphant Virgin, whose virtuosity
bewitched the canons, and the Virgin of the north portal who bows so modestly
before her Son.'
† 'open up the view of the priest who prays for them.'

episcopal approval. Some of the finest carvings of the thirteenth century were destroyed.

It is only fair to the artists of the eighteenth century to state that, having wantonly destroyed some priceless piece of medieval art, they usually inserted work of the most excellent quality themselves. This is particularly true of the wrought-iron screens with which they so often surrounded the choirs. Rodin was a man who yielded to none in his admiration for Amiens – *'l'empire absolu de l'élégance sublime'*. He was none the less enthusiastic about the wrought iron: *'Les grilles d'Amiens font avec ce monument Gothique une parfaite harmonie. Comme toute les belles choses sont toujours d'accord entre elles!'* *

Having disposed of the choir screen, Laugier turns his critical eye on the stalls and the flooring. 'Let the stalls be without canopies; add to that a beautiful pavement of marble compartments and you will have a Gothic Cathedral decorated *de grand goût.'*

The mention of canopies makes one tremble for Amiens, and, sure enough, he goes on immediately to single them out for destruction. 'This building was disfigured by a horrible choir screen, by a grotesque and monstrous retable and by canopies to the stalls loaded with a mass of boorish baubles'. Laugier had obviously tried to get the offending canopies removed, but had found the canons resistant to his entreaties. 'Up till now it has not been possible to win over *messieurs les chanoines* to sacrifice these shapeless canopies; they hold to them from prejudice and from force of habit. It is true that the wood is cut out as if it were a work in wax. Nevertheless, if these canopies are not demolished, this beautiful choir will never be decorated in a becoming manner.' He ends inflamed with all the arrogance of his age: *'faut-il qu'un aveugle amour pour ces antiquailles lutte encore contre les principes du bon goût qui ordonnent leur destruction?'*

It is almost with a sense of relief that we turn from the improvements of the eighteenth century to the destructions of the Revolution!

Obviously the Revolution was potentially a greater threat to the cathedrals than that posed by the Huguenots, since in this case the hostility to the Catholic Church was backed by the government. Considering these circumstances, the damage done was surprisingly small.

The Revolutionaries were inspired by a real hatred. The Church was immensely rich and not often engaged in its proper business. The eighteenth century had not exactly been the Age of Faith. The marquise de la Tour du Pin, great niece of the Archbishop of Narbonne in whose household she was brought up, makes some

* 'the absolute dominion of sublime elegance . . . the wrought-iron screens of Amiens harmonise perfectly with this Gothic monument. How perfectly in tune with one another are all things of beauty.'

harsh criticisms. The Archbishop himself went seldom if ever to his diocese. He lived in Paris or his château near Compiègne 'on the pretext that the interests of his Province required imperatively his presence at Court, but in reality in order to live as a *grand seigneur* in Paris and as a courtier at Versailles'. It is hardly surprising, therefore, to learn that 'all the rules of religion were violated daily' in his household and that the little Henriette-Lucie was brought up under his roof subject to every influence that could 'spoil my character, pervert my heart, deprave me and destroy within me any notion of morality or religion'.

In 1783, Mercier noted in his *Tableau de Paris* that in fashionable Society one only went to church to avoid scandalising one's lacquais – *'et les lacquais savent qu'on n'y va que pour eux!'* Vespers was politely known as 'the Beggars' Opera'.

In the middle of the century d'Argenson had noted: 'The hatred of the clergy is pushed to the utmost limits. They hardly dare to show themselves in the streets'. There is something naturally distasteful to man about a rich and hypocritical clergy. As soon as the Revolution started, a hornets' nest was released about their ears. In the anticlerical publication *Le Père Duchesne*, bishops were lampooned as 'mitred bipeds' and their priests as 'the scourge of the human race'.

By a decree of 13 February 1790, the monastic orders were abolished. Their churches thereby became redundant, and having lost their *raison d'être*, were extremely vulnerable. It became a civic virtue to have assisted in their demolition. The marquis de Travannet, on trial for his life before the *Comité de Salut Publique*, advanced the plea that he had destroyed the Abbey Church of Royaumont 'which was built by one of our former tyrants to whom superstition had given the name of Saint Louis'.

Most of the abbey churches disappeared: none of the cathedrals did. There were many proposals put forward for their sale or demolition, but not one of them was put into execution. An attempt to offer the Cathedral of Reims for sale was countered by the Minister of the Interior in 1799, who asked the Minister of Finance *'à suspendre la vente de la Cathédral de Reims dont le portail est un chef d'oeuvre d'architecture Gothique'*. Perhaps this was the first time that the word 'Gothic' was used in an unpejorative sense. It was a rare moment of appreciation in a century of repudiation.

More often it was the sculptures which attracted the fury of the Revolutionaries. At Laon the destruction was ordered of *'toutes les effigies du çi-devant Christ dans les trois jours'*. Even the angels had become *çi-devant* before the revolutionary tribunal of Laon.

The position of church buildings in such a climate of opinion was perilous indeed, but with a curious but fortunate inversion of priorities the Revolution left Versailles and the great cathedrals largely intact while going to very great lengths to obliterate the most insignificant reminders of royalty and religion. It took the trouble to rename Rocroi – which had no etymological connection with the word 'king' – *Roc-Libre*, while St Sulpice de Favières – the loveliest village church in France – became *Favières-Défanatisé* – an alteration which only a fanatic could have suggested. Children of the more educated classes were likely to acquire forenames such as Epaminondas or Astyanax rather than names with any Christian origin or overtones. The less educated contented themselves with such rustic nomenclature as Ecrevisse, Aubergine or Concombre. The same process of purification was applied to packs of cards, where it was feared that the Kings and Queens might 'recall to players the spectre of despotism and inequality of conditions'. But Versailles and the cathedrals remained standing. The revolutionary mind was apparently more ready to strain at gnats than to swallow camels.

Nevertheless the threat to ecclesiastical buildings was real. By a curious return of fortune the very principles invoked by St Bernard against luxury in building were now professed by atheist and republican lips. St Bernard had deprecated towers and steeples for the Cistercians as 'contrary to the modesty of the Order'. Now they were regarded as an insult to the 'equality' of the buildings below. Fortunately for posterity the taking down of a spire in the middle of a city is a difficult and costly undertaking. It was not often achieved. Nevertheless the *flèche* over the crossing of Notre-Dame de Paris was removed *'comme contraire à l'égalité'*.

It is surprising that the towers and spires of the great cathedrals were not destroyed by the Revolution for what they were. No one in his right mind could seriously maintain that they were an offence against the 'equality' of buildings. There is no such thing. But a regime opposed to Christianity might well see fit to remove these landmarks so rightly described by Jean Bony as *'destinés à signaler à tous la présence de Dieu et à l'inscrire energiquement dans le paysage'*.* One has only to mount the north ascent to Laon to see how these towers dominate not only the town but the countryside for miles around. It would be difficult to deny that they had, *'dans la hardiesse de leur silhouette, quelquechose de publicitaire'*. This must have been recognised at the time, but the opinion of the *enragés* did not prevail.

There was one legacy of the Revolution which has been in many ways nefarious to the cathedrals of France; ownership by the State. Having weathered centuries of buffeting by the elements – which

* 'intended to indicate to all the presence of God and to register it vigorously upon the countryside.'

included some quite exceptional hailstorms and hurricanes; having survived, not without serious mutilations, the attacks of the Huguenots; having lost many of their Gothic glories to the unfortunate combination of wealth and 'good taste' of the eighteenth century; having passed not unscathed through the degradations of the Revolution, the cathedrals of France had to face in the nineteenth century a new enemy who was the more dangerous for not being hostile – the restoring architect.

That most of the buildings were by then in grievous need of repair is not disputed, but the distinction between reparation and restoration was not always clearly understood or carefully observed. The first attempts were mostly deplorable.

It was only to be expected. After two and a half centuries of contempt and neglect, the Gothic was a lost art. The first architects to try their hand at reconstruction had everything to learn. Not all had the modesty of Félix Duban who declined to take on the repair of St Denis saying 'the task is beyond my abilities'; they perpetrated monstrosities.

One of their first critics was the comte de Montalembert. Essentially he was a statesman anxious to found a political party 'Catholique avant tout'. But he included within his crusading zeal the great cathedrals of the Age of Faith. 'Ce sont des symboles de ce qu'il y a de plus vivace dans mon âme, de plus auguste dans mes espérances'.* This new vandalism of the architects was not in his eyes just brutality and stupidity – it was sacrilege. 'C'est un art à mes yeux Catholique avant tout'.† He set out, pen in hand, to preserve not only a religious but a national heritage. He was one of the first to appreciate the value of conservation: 'long memories make great peoples'. In an impassioned speech in the House of Peers on 16 July 1847, he attacked the 'methodical and premeditated vandalism' of the architects.

In 1837 the spire of St Denis had been struck by lightning and was simply removed on the sole authority of the architect Debret. At Rouen they had actually imposed a hideous spire of cast iron – 'cette effroyable flèche en fonte qui écrase cette Cathédrale si belle, et lézarde déjà la partie central du transept'.‡ The cast-iron spire was the work of the architect Alavoine, who made the presumptuous claim that 'the artists of the Middle Ages would have preferred cast iron to stone if

---

* 'They are the symbols of all that is most deeply rooted in my soul, all that is most venerable in my expectations.'
† 'It is an art, to my eyes, Catholic above all'.
‡ 'this hideous spire of cast iron which overweighs this Cathedral, which is so beautiful, and is already causing cracks in the central part of the transept.'

the technical means had reached the same perfection then that it has today'. Flaubert was more accurate, in his *Madame Bovary*, when he describes the spire as 'the dream of a delirious tinker'.

Montalembert's speech was lavishly spiced with wit. There are frequent mentions of '*hilarité*' in the verbatim account published in the *Moniteur Universel*. In a more serious vein, Montalembert reminded the Ministre des Cultes that he had under his care the finest buildings in the world: 'For I claim that there is nothing more beautiful in the universe than the Cathedrals of Reims, Amiens, Bourges, Chartres and Paris'. He asked the Minister if he had at his command men of sufficient calibre for the task – 'men well practised and most proficient in this science which is so delicate and so important'.

Montalembert was supported throughout his speech by frequent '*sourires d'affirmation*' from another important personality, the vicomte Victor Hugo. '*Je me félicite,*' he said, '*d'avoir dans ma pénible tâche l'appui de l'homme qui a le plus fait parmi nous pour régénérer l'étude et le respecte de nos antiquités nationales*'.*

Victor Hugo, in his *Notre-Dame de Paris*, made his own attack upon the architects: 'This magnificent art, it has been killed by the Academicians. To the centuries, to the revolutions, whose devastations are at least accomplished with impartiality and on a grand scale, there has been added a swarm of architects from school – authorised, sworn in and signed up – whose degradations are accomplished with discernment and the choicest of bad taste.' This was to him the most unkind cut of all – '*le coup de pied de l'âne au lion mourant*'.

But the oratory of Montalembert and the passionate prose of Victor Hugo needed to be translated into action. It was in another man of letters, Prosper Mérimée, that they found the man of action necessary for the undertaking. 'If Victor Hugo had not written *Notre-Dame de Paris* and if Prosper Mérimée had not stimulated the formation of the Commission des Monuments Historiques,' wrote Augustin Filon, 'all our ancient monuments would have been pulled down in order that buildings like the Madeleine and the Bourse could be put up.'

In particular Mérimée must have the credit for saving Laon. On 20 July 1846, he made a personal visit which led to the dismissal of the architect Van Cleemputte and the appointment of Boëswillwald. So began the great work of restoration which saved that marvellous

* 'I congratulate myself on having, in my arduous task, the support of the man who has done most of all of us to regenerate the study of, and respect for, our nation's antiquities.'

building for posterity, even if it did replace the fractured sculpture of the portals with some extremely indifferent pastiche.

Mérimée also contributed to the growing corpus of medieval scholarship, but by far the greatest work in this respect was that of Eugène Viollet-le-Duc. His *Dictionnaire Raisonné de l'Architecture Française du XIe au XVIe Siècle* is a truly monumental achievement and a rich source from which architectural historians still draw. But Viollet-le-Duc was a practising architect as well, and to him Mérimée entrusted some of the most important restorations of the age – notably Vézelay, Notre-Dame and St Denis. He began with the right intentions, professing that 'a restoration is perhaps more dangerous to a monument than the ravages of the centuries and the fury of the populace'. But as he advanced in age and self-confidence he succumbed to the temptations of the purist and began to hanker for the reconstruction of a building 'as it was'. There was only a short step from here to a reconstruction 'as it should have been'.

It is probable that Viollet-le-Duc was influenced by his great friend the naturalist Cuvier, who claimed to be able to reconstruct a dinosaur from a single vertebra. If that could be done, might not a medieval building be reconstituted from the remaining fragments? Paul Gout, his most eulogistic biographer, claimed that 'some of his restorations were the equivalents of original creations'. He meant it as a compliment, but it could be taken as the opposite. Viollet-le-Duc has come in for some very adverse criticism.

The danger of purism, as Louis Réau so rightly says, is that 'it does away with the continuing contribution of the centuries, that is to say the *life* of the monuments. If so many churches in France exhibit a painful nakedness and if the former furniture, which gave the feeling that they were inhabitated, has been replaced by pious rubbish, it is the doctrinaire purism of Viollet-le-Duc that is to blame.'

This question of the life of a cathedral is all-important. The danger of the State architect maintaining the State-owned cathedral is that the building may be divorced from its life. Ambroise Ledru, Canon of Le Mans and the great authority on the architecture of the Cathedral, made in 1927 a bitter complaint against an architect whom he tactfully calls Monsieur X.

'In this monument, built by the clergy in times past with the money of the clergy, he regards himself as absolute master, settling matters out of hand, restoring, destroying as it pleases him, all under the protection of the Beaux Arts, without listening to the least suggestion of those who, knowing the history of the building, do not share his opinion. The State – and he pronounces the word with the heavy emphasis of the pedagogue – is the owner of the monument, he says, and I represent the State so I am the owner.'

The particular crime of Monsieur X was to have removed the little pinnacles from the buttress piers round the apse and replaced them with copies of the larger pinnacles on the side buttresses. 'The inspired constructor on the choir,' writes Ledru, 'had appreciated that the thrust on these buttresses was less than that on the six lateral piers, and that it was open to crown them with lighter pinnacles'. One of the little details that showed the complete mastery of the builder of Le Mans was pointlessly obliterated by the arrogance of an architect who was probably anti-clerical and too proud to listen to an art-historian who was a priest.

The insensitivity of the restorers moved Auguste Rodin to some of his most impassioned outbursts. 'Look at those climbing crockets that have forgotten how to climb,' he exclaimed at Reims; 'heavy restoration – the balance has been upset.' He gave his solemn warning: *'Je vous supplie, au nom de nos ancêtres et dans l'intérêt de nos enfants, ne cassez, ne restaurez plus'.** This was written in 1914, a few months before the German shells began to fall on Reims.

The restoration of Reims, which had been reduced almost to total ruin, reflects nothing but credit upon another restoring architect, Henri Deneux. One little detail reveals the loving care with which he approached his sacred task. When the roof was burnt off, the lead naturally melted and much of it flowed into the conical cavities above the great vaults. Deneux recovered more than 400 tons of medieval lead *'riche en argent et d'une beauté de couleur que n'offre jamais le plomb moderne'.†* Refusing also the modern process of lamination, he studied the old and long-forgotten method of pouring moulten lead onto sand – a task which he carried out in the courtyard of the Palais du Tau. Together with the sculptor Rémi Havot and the glazier Jacques Simon, Henri Deneux restored to civilisation one of the masterpieces of all time.

A sympathetic restoration needs more than an understanding of the medieval methods of construction and decoration: it needs a full appraisal of the style. As Emile Mâle so wisely said, 'In order to have the right to judge the artists of the Middle Ages we must begin by understanding what it was that they were trying to do'. Their great achievements were never essays in the Gothic style: they were the expression of the faith of a deeply religious age.

But a great cathedral cannot be built by faith alone. That might produce the painful mediocrity of Lourdes. To create a Laon, a Bourges, an Amiens – that needs an architect in whom faith is

---

* 'I beseech you, in the name of our ancestors and in the interests of our children, do not destroy, do not restore any more.'
† 'rich in silver and of a beautiful colour which modern lead never offers.'

married to genius. This genius must soar within the limits circumscribed by his profession. The architect can never be a dreamer; he has to operate within a certain range of possibilities and these are determined by the techniques available to him, although he may himself contribute to the evolution of those techniques. He has to conceive in terms of structure, as all men have to think in terms of words. As Jean Bony expresses it: '*il ne conçoit que dans le concret de sa technique*'.* He is by virtue of this fact involved in a movement – '*solidaire de tout l'effort qui s'est fait avant lui et de toutes les recherches de ses contemporaines*'.† As such he must be a technician. But as an artist he uses his technique to make men free of his own vision, a vision in which he perceives a certain kinship between mind and matter which goes beyond the boundaries of knowledge. '*C'est pourquoi l'art est si facilement en accord avec la pensée religieuse,*' concludes Bony; '*pourquoi le plupart des Églises voient en lui une sorte de premier médiateur*'.

The artist's work is not only one of homage to God, not just a hymn to the Creation, but a gift to men, whereby they may find enrichment – an invitation to regard the world in a certain light already penetrated with a spiritual dimension.

Such were the men who created the cathedrals, who took their part in that great campaign that was to cover France in glory, to affirm her in her vocation and to ennoble her cities with the greatest buildings that the world has ever known.

* 'He can only form his ideas within the actual, material limits of his technique.'
† 'bound up with all the endeavour which has been made before his time and with all the researches of his contemporaries.'

Glossary

Abacus   A slab forming the crowning member of a capital.

Abside   French for apse.

Abutment   Solid masonry which resists the lateral pressure of an arch.

Ambulatory   The semicircular aisle of an apse.

Apse   The semicircular east end of a church or end of chapel.

Apsidal Chapel   A small chapel projecting from the apse.

Arcade   A range of arches supported on piers or columns.

Architrave   The moulded frame round a door or window.

Bay   A compartment carrying a canopy of vault.

Bourdon   A great bell.

Buttress   A pier of masonry built against a wall to resist the lateral pressure of an arch.

Capital   The crowning feature of a column or pilaster.

Chantier   French for a site where building is in progress.

Choir   The area of a church used by clergy and choir for services.

Ciborium   Originally a canopy over the altar, later used of the canopy of a vault.

Clairevoie   Openwork – often applied to a glazed triforium.

Clerestory   The topmost windows lighting nave, choir or transepts.

Colonnette   A small column.

Corbel   A block of stone projecting from the wall to support some structure.

Cross-ribbed vault   A vault with four, six or (exceptionally) eight transverse ribs.

Cul-de-Four   Literally 'backside of an oven'; the shape formed by a half dome.

Dormer   A window projecting from a sloping roof.

Embrasure   The bevelled recess of a door or window.

Façade   The face or elevation of a building. Of churches it often means the internal elevation of the nave and choir.

Flying Buttress   An arch springing from a detached pier to abut a high arch.

Jubé   A solid stone screen separating the nave from the choir.

Keystone   The central stone of a semicircular arch or vault.

Lancet   A simple window aperture with a pointed arch.

Lantern   A glazed spire or cupola.

Lierne   A short rib joining the tierceron to the main rib.

Narthex   A vestibule at the west end of a church separate from the nave.

Nave   The central vessel of a church west of the choir.

Oculus   A small, round window.

Pier   A mass of masonry which supports an arch.

Pilaster   A pillar engaged in a wall.

Pile Forte – Pile Faible   The alternation between massive and slender piers or columns that goes with sexpartite vaulting.

Ploughshare Vault   A twist which occurs in the vault web when the wall rib is raised in order to increase the size of the clerestory windows.

Porte-à-Faux   Overhang.

Porte Cochère   Projecting porch beneath which a vehicle can draw up.

Portal   Important doorway usually decorated with sculptures.

Portico   Colonnade forming an entrance or vestibule.

Quadripartite Vault   A vault divided into four compartments by two intersecting transverse ribs.

Quatrefoil   A panel, usually circular, divided by cusps into four nearly circular openings.

Retable   A carved or painted panel above and behind the altar.

Rose Window   A large circular window filled with tracery.

Roundel   A small circular compartment in a traceried window.

Sexpartite Vault   A vault divided into six compartments by the intersection of two transverse ribs and a cross rib.

Spandrel   A triangular shaped area to either side of an arch.

Tierceron   An extra vault rib springing from the capital of the pier.

Transept   The arm of a cruciform church projecting at right angles to the nave and choir.

Transverse rib   A vaulting rib which forms the diagonal of the area vaulted.

Tribune   A vaulted gallery forming a first storey over an aisle.

Triforium   The triangular space above the aisle or tribune of which the sloping roof forms the hypotenuse.

Tympanum   The space enclosed between the lintel and the arch of a doorway.

Vaulting arch   Any arch which supports a vault.

Wall Rib   A vault rib which enframes the arch of the clerestory.

Bibliography

CHAPTER ONE
Suger of Saint-Denis

Otto von Simson, *The Gothic Cathedral*, 1956.
P. du Colombier, *Les Chantiers des Cathédrales*, 1954.
S. Crosby, *L'Abbaye royale de Saint-Denis*, 1953.
E. Panofsky, *Gothic Architecture and Scholasticism*, 1951.
A. Lecoy de la Marche, *Oeuvres Complètes de Suger*, 1867.
E. Viollet-le-Duc, *Dictionnaire Raissonné de l'Architecture française du XI au XVI siècle*, 1854–66.
Roger Lloyd, *Peter Abelard, Orthodox Rebel*, 1947.
H. Pirenne, *Les Villes et Institutions Urbaines*, 1939.
P. Claudel, *Conversations dans le Loir et Cher*, 1948.
F. Clément, *La Drame Liturgique*. In *Annales Archéologiques*, Vol. VIII, 1848.

CHAPTER TWO
Sens

E. Chartraire, *La Cathédrale de Sens*, 1930.
L. Bégule, *La Cathédrale de Sens*, 1929.
F. Salet, *La Cathédrale de Sens et sa place dans l'histoire de l'architecture mediévale*. In *Académie des Inscriptions et Belles Lettres*, 1955.
T. Tarbé, *Recherches sur la Ville de Sens*, 1888.
O. von Simson, *The Gothic Cathedral*, 1956.
J.C. Morison, *The Life and Times of St Bernard*, 1868.
G. Leff, *Medieval Thought from Augustine to Ockham*, 1958.
C. Hadfield, *On the History of the rebuilding of the choir of Canterbury Cathedral*. In *Associated Architectural Societies' Reports and Papers*, 1877.
M. Vachon, *Une Famille Parisienne de Maître-Maçons aux 15e, 16e et 17e siècles. Les Chambiges*, 1907.
J. Bony, *French Influences on the Origins of English Gothic Architecture*. In *Journal of the Warburg and Courtauld Institutes*, 1949.

CHAPTER THREE
Chartres (I)

E. Mâle, *Notre-Dame de Chartres*, 1948.

O. von Simson, *The Gothic Cathedral*, 1956.

E. Lefèvre-Pontalis, *Les Façades successives de la Cathédrale de Chartres au XIe et XIIe Siècles*. In *Congrès Archéologique*, 1901.

Abbé Bulteau, *Description de la Cathédrale de Chartres*, 1850.

M. Aubert, *Le Portail Royal et la Façade Occidentale de la Cathédrale de Chartres*. In *Bulletin Monumental*, 1941.

Y. Delaporte et E. Houvet, *Les Vitraux de la Cathédrale de Chartres*, 1926.

CHAPTER FOUR
Senlis

M. Aubert, *Monographie de la Cathédrale de Senlis*, 1910.

E. Müller, *Monographie des rues, places et monuments de Senlis*, 1880.

E. Müller, *Senlis et ses environs*, 1896.

M. Menier, *Le Chapitre de la Cathédrale de Senlis de 1139–1516*, Typescript, 1944.

M. Vachon, *Une Famille Parisienne de Maîtres-Maçons, aux 15ᵉ, 16ᵉ er17ᵉ siècles*, 1907

J. Vanuxem, *Le Portail de Senlis*, In *Bulletin Monumental*, 1945.

H. Pirenne, *Les villes et institutions urbaines*, 1939.

J. Vaultier, *Description de Senlis*, 1834.

E. Mâle, *Le portail de Senlis et son influence*. In *Revue de l'art ancien et moderne*, T. XXIX.

CHAPTER FIVE
Laon

L. Broche, *La Cathédrale de Laon*, 1926.

A. Bouxin, *La Cathédrale Notre-Dame de Laon*, 1902.

S. Martinet, *Montloon*, 1972.

J. Marion, *Essai Historique et Archaeologique sur l'Eglise Cathédrale de Notre-Dame de Laon*, 1846.

M. Melleville, *Histoire de Laon*, 1846.

A. de Florival and E. Midoux, *Les Vitraux de la Cathédrale de Laon*, 1882.

P. Héliot, *Le Chevet de la Cathédrale de Laon*. In *Gazette des Beaux Arts*, April 1972.

E. Mâle, *L'Art Religieux du 13e Siècle en France*, 1902.

G. Dumas, *L'Etat de la Cathédrale de Laon vers 1850*, In *Mémoires de la Fédération des Sociétés d'Archeologie de l'Aisne*, 1964.

CHAPTER SIX
Notre-Dame de Paris

M. Aubert, *Notre-Dame de Paris*, 1920.

M. Aubert, *Notre-Dame de Paris: Architecture et Sculpture*, 1928.

J. du Breuil, *Le Théâtre des Antiquités de Paris*, 1639.

F.L. Chartier, *L'Ancien Chapitre de Notre-Dame de Paris et sa Maîtrise*, 1897.

V. Mortet, *Maurice de Sully. Extrait des Mémoires de la Société de l'histoire de Paris et de l'Ile de France*, 1889.

M. Lefèvre-Pontalis, *L'Origine des Arcs Boutants*. In *Congrès Archéologique de France*, 1919.

A. Erlande-Brandenburg and D. Kimpel, *La Statuaire de Notre-Dame de Paris avant les destructions révolutionnaires*. In *Bulletin Monumental*, 1978.

J. Bony, *Essai sur la spiritualité de deux Cathédrales: Notre-Dame de Paris et St Etienne de Bourges*, 1943.

CHAPTER SEVEN
Chartres (2)

E. Mâle, *Notre-Dame de Chartres*, 1948.

O. von Simson, *The Gothic Cathedral*, 1951.

L'Abbé Bulteau, *Description de la Cathédrale de Chartres*, 1850.

Y. Delaporte & E. Houvet, *Les Vitraux de la Cathédrale de Chartres*, 1926.

J. Villette, *Les Vitraux de Chartres*, 1979.

J. James, *Chartres. Les Constructeurs*, 1977.

V. Mortet, *L'expertise de la Cathédrale de Chartres en 1316*. In *Congrès Archeologique*, 1900.

V. Sablon, *Histoire de l'auguste et vénérable Eglise de Chartres*, 1671.

CHAPTER EIGHT
Bourges

R. Branner, *La Cathédrale de Bourges et sa place dans l'architecture gothique*, 1962.

J. Bony, *Essai sur la spiritualité de deux Cathédrales: Notre-Dame de Paris et St Etienne de Bourges*, 1943.

L. Gonse, *L'Art Gothique*, 1890.

R. Mark, *The Structural Analysis of Gothic Cathedrals*. In *Scientific American*, November 1872.

N. de Nicolay, *Description du Berry et du Diocèse de Bourges au XVIe Siècle*, 1865.

J. Rouvelon, *Description Historique et Monumentale de l'église patriarchale, primatiale et metropolitaine de Bourges*, 1824.

Baron de Girardot, *Les Artistes de la Ville et de la Cathédrale de Bourges*, 1861.

Baron de Girardot, *Histoire du Chapitre de St Etienne de Bourges*, 1853.

Chanoine Rousseau, *L'Ancien Chapitre St Etienne de Bourges*, 1955. Typescript in the Bibliothèque Municipale de Bourges.

A. Boinet, *Les Sculptures de la Cathédrale de Bourges*. In *Revue de l'Art Chrétien*, 1912.

A. de Champeaux et P. Gauchery, *Les Travaux d'Art éxécutés pour Jean de France, duc de Berry*, 1894.

F. Quiévreux, *Les Vitraux du 13e siècle de l'abside de la Cathédrale de Bourges*. In *Bulletin Monumental*, 1943.

L. Grodecki, *A stained glass atelier of the 13th century*. In *Journal of the Warburg and Courtauld Institutes*, 1948.

S. Clément et A. Guitard, *Vitraux de Bourges*, 1900.

CHAPTER NINE
Le Mans

A. Ledru, *La Cathédrale du Mans*, 1923.

F. Salet, *La Cathédrale du Mans*. In *Congrès Archéologique de France*, 1961.

Louis Gonse, *Art Gothique*, 1890.

H. de Berranger, *Le Choeur de la Cathédrale du Mans*. In *La Province du Maine*. 2me Série, T. 34, 1954.

P. Vérité, *Le tracé du choeur de la Cathédrale du Mans*. In *Bulletin Monumental*, 1908.

L. Grodecki, *Les Vitraux de la Cathédrale du Mans*. In *Congrès Archéologique de France*, 1961.

A. Bouton, *Le Chantier de la Cathédrale du Mans*. In *La Province du Maine*. 2me Série, T. 35, 1955.

Chanoine Pioger, *Les Orgues de la Cathédrale du Mans*. In *La Vie Mancelle*, September 1960.

Paul Claudel, *Conversations dans le Loir et Cher*, 1948.

F. Salet, *St Loup de Naud*. In *Bulletin Monumental*, 1933.

CHAPTER TEN
Coutances

E.-A. Pigeon, *Histoire de la Cathédrale de Coutances*, 1876.

P. Colmet Daage, *La Cathédrale de Coutances*, 1933.

A. Mussat, *La Cathédrale Notre-Dame de Coutances*. In *Congrès Archéologique de France*, 1966.

E. Lefèvre-Pontalis, *Coutances*. In *Congrès Archéologique de France*, 1909.

J. Toussaint, *Le Jubé de la Cathédrale de Coutances*. In *Revue du Département de la Manche*, 1969.

L'Abbé Lecanu, *Histoire du Diocèse de Coutances*, 1977.

E. Lefèvre-Pontalis, *St Etienne de Caen*. In *Congrès Archéologique de France*, 1966.
L. Bouyer, *Architecture et Liturgie*, 1967.
Y. Froidevaux, *Coutances; Cathédrale, s.d.*

CHAPTER ELEVEN
Reims

H. Reinhardt, *La Cathédrale de Reims*, 1963.
F. Salet, *Chronologie de la Cathédrale de Reims*. In *Bulletin Monumental*, 1967.
J.-P. Ravaux, *Les Campagnes de Construction de la Cathédrale de Reims au XIIIe Siècle*. In *Bulletin Monumental*, 1979.
H. Deneux, *Des Modifications apportées à la Cathédrale de Reims au cours de sa construction du XIIIe au XVe siècle*. In *Bulletin Monumental*, 1948.
C. Cerf, *Histoire et Description de Notre-Dame de Reims*, 1861.
G. Marlot, *Histoire de la Ville, Cité et Université de Reims*, 1843.
R. Branner, *Jean d'Orbais and the Cathedral of Reims*. In *The Art Bulletin*, 1961.
M. Guy, *Tapisseries de Reims*, 1973.

CHAPTER TWELVE
The Coronation of a French King

Vicomte de Grouchy, *Journal inédit du Duc de Croÿ*, 1906.
J. Goy, *Le Sacre des Rois de France*, s.d.
M. Menin, *An Historical and Chronological Treatise of the Anointing and Coronation of the Kings and Queens of France from Clovis to the present King. Faithfully done from the original French*, 1723.
Marquis de Ségur, *Au Couchant de la Monarchie*. In *Revue des Deux Mondes*, 1909.
J.-P. Garnier, *Charles X. Le Roi – Le Proscrit*, 1967.
Duke of Northumberland, *Letter to the Hon: George Canning, May 30th 1825.* MSS at Alnwick Castle.

CHAPTER THIRTEEN
Amiens

G. Durand, *Monographie de la Cathédrale d'Amiens*, 1903.
Vicomte Calonne D'Avesne, *Histoire de la Ville d'Amiens*, 1899.
L. Jourdain & T. Duval, *Amiens. Les Stalles et les Clôtures du Choeur*. In *Mémoires de la Société des Antiquaires de Picardie*, 1867.
G. de Tourtier & G. Prache, *Les stalles de la Cathédrale d'Amiens*, 1979.

CHAPTER FOURTEEN
Tours

H. Boissonot, *Histoire et Description de la Cathédrale de Tours*, 1920.
H. Boissonot, *Les Verrières de l'Eglise de Tours*, 1932.
F. Salet, *La Cathédrale de Tours*, 1949.
J.-J. Bourassé, *Verrières du Choeur de l'Eglise métropolitaine de Tours*, 1849.
G.M. Cury, *L'Eglise de Tours au 13e Siècle*. In *Histoire religieuse de Touraine*, 1962.
Duc de Lévis-Mirepoix, *St Louis, Roi de France*, 1970.
L. Grodecki, *La Sainte-Chapelle*, 1975.
E. Strutt, *Six weeks on the Loire with a peep into La Vendée*, 1833.

CHAPTER FIFTEEN
Beauvais

G. Desjardins, *Histoire de la Cathédrale de Beauvais*, 1865.
D. Simon, *Supplément à l'Histoire du Beauvaisis*, 1704.
P. Louvet, *Histoire et Antiquités du Diocèse de Beauvais*, 1635.
Abbé Delettre, *Histoire du Diocèse de Beauvais*, 1843.
A. Bornet, *Les Enfants du Choeur de la Cathédrale de Beauvais aux XIV, XV et XVI Siècles*, 1930.
V. Leblond, *La Cathédrale de Beauvais*, 1926.
M. Vachon, *Une Famille Parisienne de Maîtres-Maçons les Chambiges*, 1907.
M. Wolfe and R. Mark, *The collapse of the vaults of Beauvais Cathedral in 1284*. In *Speculum*, July 1976.
S. Murray, *The Collapse of 1284 at Beauvais Cathedral*. In *The Thirteenth Century, Acta*, Vol. III, 1976.
S. Murray, *An Expertise at Beauvais Cathedral*. In *Journal of the British Archaeological Association*, Vol. CXXX, 1977.
G. Hermant, *Histoire Ecclésiastique er Civile de Beauvais*. MSS in Beauvais Municipal Library.

CHAPTER SIXTEEN
Goths and Vandals

L. Réau, *Histoire du Vandalisme Les Monuments Détruits de l'art français*, 1959.
E. de Beer, *Gothic: origin and diffusion of the term; the idea of style in architecture*. In *Journal of the Warburg and Courtauld Institutes*, 1948.
Corblet, *L'Architecture du moyen age jugée par les écrivains des deux derniers siècles*. In *Revue de l'art Chrétien*, 1859.
M. Foisset, *Le Comte de Montalembert*, 1877.
A. Filon, *Mérimée*, 1898.
P. Gout, *Viollet-le-Duc. Sa Vie, son oeuvre, sa doctrine*, 1914.
A. Ledru, *Un Petit Drame Archéologique*, 1927.

P. du Colombier, *Les Chantiers des Cathédrales*, 1953.

A. Rodin, *Les Cathédrales de France*, 1921.

J. Gimpel, *Les Bâtisseurs des Cathédrales*, 1958.

G. Duby, *Le Temps des Cathédrales*, 1976.

F. Cali, *L'Ordre Ogival*, 1963.

L. Bouyer, *Architecture et Liturgie*, 1967.

E. de Coussemaker, *Drames Liturgiques du Moyen Age*, 1860.

M. Lassus, *Facsimile of the sketchbook of Villard de Honnecourt*, 1859.

E. Mâle, *L'Art religieux du XIIIe Siècle en France*, 1902.

E. Panowsky, *Gothic architecture and Scholasticism*, 1951.

W. Swaan, *The Gothic Cathedral*, 1968.

J. Fitchen, *The Construction of Gothic Cathedrals*, 1961.

P. Cowen, *Rose Windows*, 1979.

G. Poisson, *Moyen Age en Île de France*, 1965.

Index

(A medieval name, such as William of Sens, will be found listed under 'William'. A modern name such as Victor Hugo will be found listed under 'Hugo'.)